"A horror story, well-researched and very well told, which will make you rethink your ideas on desirable old villas and tightly packed terraced suburbs."

—*Evening Post* (Auckland)

"Hanson's book sifts through the ashes and comes up with some intriguing theories."

—*Daily Mail*

T0266105

ANOTHER PROSPECT OF THE SAYD C

1 Temple Church.   4 S. Benet   7 S. Martins by Ludgate   10 S. Nicholas   13 S. Foster   16 S. Mary Alde
2 S. Dunstans West   5 S. Andrew in Wardrop   8 S. Andrew in Holborne   11 Christchurch   14 S. John Zachary   17 S. Thomas Ap
3 S. Brides   6 S. Peters in Thamstreet   9 S. Pulchree   12 S. Augustines   15 S. Martins in Thamestret   18 Bow Ch

dral of S. Paul

THE RIVER

S. Laurence	22. Alhallowes y° great	25. S. Mary Wolnoth	28. S. Christopher	31. S. Michael, Cornhill	34. S. Denis
S. Mary Buttolf lane	23. S. Stevens Colmanstret	26. S. Lerence Poultney	29. S. Bartholomew	32. Alhallowes	35. S. Magnus
	24. S. Margaret	27. S. Stevens in Walbroke	30. S. Edmunds	33. S. Peters in Cornhill	36. S. Andrew Huba

THAMES

The...

The Tower

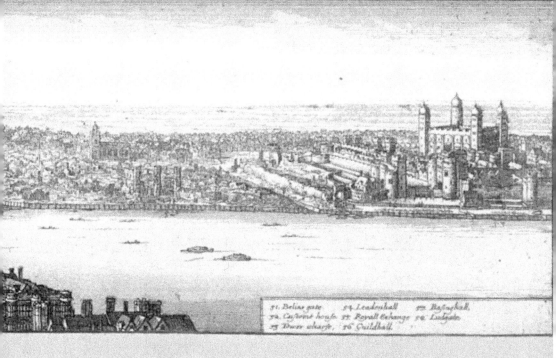

51. *Belins gate*	54. *Leadenhall*	57. *Bafinghall*
52. *Cuftome houfe*	55. *Royall Exchange*	58. *Ludgate*
53. *Tower wharfe*	56. *Guildhall*	

The Great Fire of London

Also by Neil Hanson
The Custom of the Sea
Goldfinder (*with Keith Jessop*)

The Great Fire
of London

IN THAT APOCALYPTIC YEAR, 1666

NEIL HANSON

John Wiley & Sons, Inc.

For general information about our other products and services, please contact our Customer Care Department within the United States at (800) 762-2974, outside the United States at (317) 572-3993 or fax (317) 572-4002.

Wiley also publishes its books in a variety of electronic formats. Some content that appears in print may not be available in electronic books.

Library of Congress Cataloging-in-Publication Data:

Hanson, Neil.
The Great Fire of London : in that apocalyptic year, 1666 / Neil Hanson.
p. cm.
Includes bibliographical references and index.
ISBN 0-471-21822-7 (acid-free paper)
1. Great Fire, London, England, 1666. 2. London (England)—History—17th century.
I. Title.

DA681 .H32 2002
942.1'2066—dc21
2002071329

Printed in the United States of America

10 9 8 7 6 5 4 3 2 1

For Lynn, Jack, and Drew

The Great Fire as foreseen by Will Lilly in Hieroglyphicks.

Contents

	Glossary	ix
	Acknowledgments	xiii
	Preface	xvii
1	Repent or Burn	1
2	The Hellish Design	25
3	The Lodge of All Combustibles	43
4	A Lake of Fire	59
5	A Hideous Storm	75
6	Outlandish Men	97
7	A Sign of Wrath	107
8	The Fires of Hell	119
9	Clamor and Peril	143
10	Firestorm	149
11	A Dismal Desert	161
12	The Fatal Contrivance	179
13	The Duke of Exeter's Daughter	201
14	The Triple Tree	215
15	The Wastelands	227
16	Dust to Dust	241
	Notes	251
	Bibliography	265
	Illustration Credits	285
	Index	287

Glossary

Ballers	*Ruffians, hoods, rakes, who roamed the streets in gangs*
Basset	*A card game*
Bavins	*Brushwood*
Bearers	*Carriers of the dead to the plague pits*
Bellman	*Watchman patrolling the city streets calling the hour*
Bridge	*London Bridge*
Buboes	*Inflamed glandular swellings, proof positive of the plague*
Chaldron	*Volumetric measure for coals, approximately equal to thirty-six bushels*
Close-stool	*Lavatory*
Coney burrow	*Haunt of prostitutes*
Cookshop	*Shop selling food where the customer's own meat could also be cooked*
Dancers of the ropes	*Tightrope walkers*
French pox	*Syphilis*
Gallant	*Man of fashion*
Garnish	*Bribe paid by prisoners to jailers*
Grenado	*Grenade*
Halberd	*Combined spear and battle-ax*
Herbs	*Salad greens*

Horse-gin	*Engine or mill driven by horsepower*
House of office	*Lavatory*
Jetty	*Projecting upper story of house*
Kennel	*Gutter*
Kitchen stuff	*Grease*
Lanthorn	*Lamp—a hollowed cow-horn, enclosing a candle*
Laystall	*Heap of refuse*
Liberties	*Areas controlled by the city though outside its walls*
Lighter	*Flat-bottomed boat*
Links	*Torches*
Linksman	*Torch bearer*
Mercer	*Dealer in fabrics*
Mountebank	*Quack physician*
Ordinary	*a. Eating house*
	b. Chaplain
Pattens	*Iron platforms worn under the shoes to raise the wearer's clothes above the mud and filth of the streets*
Pay-table	*Table in a tavern where on Saturdays merchants and tradesmen settled their debts and paid their employees*
Penthouse	*Lean-to*
Pestiferous	*Infested with plague*
Plague tokens	*Buboes or blisters*
Prentice	*Apprentice*
Quill	*Elm water pipe*
Rag Fair	*Market for secondhand clothes*
Raker	*Street cleaner*
Ratbane	*Rat poison*
Rookery	*Tenement slum*
Roots	*Vegetables*
Rue	*Evergreen shrub with bitter, pungent leaves*
Scantling	*Timber beam of small cross-section*
Scavenger	*Street cleaner*
Searchers	*Women who examined the bodies of the dead for signs of plague*
Small beer	*Weak beer drunk instead of water*
Stew	*Brothel*

Stink-pot	*Metal bowl or temporary hearth containing burning pitch, brimstone, or strong herbs*
Swill	*Contents of chamber pots*
Treadwheel	*Treadmill*
Triple-tree	*Triangular gallows at Tyburn*
Wainscoting	*Wooden paneling on lower part of wall*
Walloon	*Belgian*
Wherry	*Shallow rowing boat*
Wormwood	*Bitter herb*
Zeodary	*Type of ginger*

Acknowledgments

SO MANY PEOPLE HAVE HELPED ME IN MY RESEARCH THAT I cannot thank them all individually, but I must single out Richard Brabbs and Ian Purcell at the West Yorkshire Fire Service Fire Investigations Unit; Glenn Elkington, Crematorium Technician at Nab Wood Crematorium, Shipley, Yorkshire; Rachel Hill of the West Yorkshire Police; Peter Metcalf; Dr. Gustav Milne of the Institute of Archaeology; and Andrew Muckley of Redcar and Cleveland Psychological Services. My sincere thanks to them and to a number of other expert individuals who gave unsparingly of their time and knowledge, but who preferred to remain anonymous. I have drawn heavily on their expertise, but any errors are mine alone.

I am grateful also to the staff at the Guildhall Library, the British Library at St. Pancras, the Public Record Office at Kew, the Corporation of London Record Office, the London Metropolitan Archive, the Museum of London, the Historic Manuscripts Commission, and the International Genealogical Index.

Outside London, the Bodleian Library in Oxford, the British Library's Document Supply Centre at Wetherby, the Berkshire Archaeological Society, and the Cornwall, East Sussex, and Kent Record Offices have also been very helpful; and I'm grateful to the many other record offices and local archaeological and historical societies throughout Britain and Ireland that responded to my request for unpublished information, diaries, or correspondence about the Great Fire.

Acknowledgments

My thanks also to Mark Lucas, Kim Witherspoon, and David Forrer, to all the team at John Wiley, in particular Gerry Helferich, Stephen S. Power, and Michael Thompson, and to Paul Brown, whose chance remark set me on this journey.

My greatest debt, however, is to Lynn. Without her wisdom, help, and support, none of my books would ever be written.

Now nettles are growing, owls are screeching, thieves
and cut-throats are lurking. A sad face there is now
in the ruinous part of London: and terrible hath the
voice of the Lord been, which hath been crying, yea
roaring in the City, by these dreadful judgements of
the Plague and Fire, which he hath brought upon us.

Thomas Vincent,
God's Terrible Voice in the City, 1667

Preface

THE GREAT FIRE OF LONDON IS ONE OF THOSE CATACLYSMIC events that has burned its way into the consciousness of mankind. Everyone has heard of it and knows something about it, yet for all the wealth of contemporary accounts of the fire, and the detailed historical research that has been carried out down the centuries, much about the Great Fire remains misunderstood and many of the most intriguing questions remain unanswered.

The fire and the era in which it occurred have interested me for years, and the more I read, the more intrigued I became. When I began researching the subject I soon discovered that, although one man was hanged for the crime of starting the fire, he was almost the least plausible among a score of suspects. These included the baker, Thomas Farriner, on whose premises the fire began, foreign agents, religious fanatics, political factions, the Duke of York, and even King Charles II himself.

Over the course of a year I read, I think, every book on the subject and every relevant document of the period. Confronted by this tangled and often contradictory mass of evidence, half-truth, hearsay, and conjecture, I have been forced to accept that, barring the discovery of some long-lost deathbed confession, there can be no definitive answer to the question, who caused the fire of London? I've formed my own suspicions, but all I can do is to lay out the evidence, including some intriguing new possibilities, and then leave it to the reader to reach his or her own conclusion.

In the course of my research, I found other things that struck me as almost equally curious. In previous books on the fire, no one ever took the trouble to discover the fate of the baker, for example, and almost every writer accepted the scarcely credible claim that only a handful of people had actually died in the inferno that swept London.

In analyzing this claim I learned much from accounts of other urban fire disasters, including the destruction of Moscow in 1570, the great fire in Chicago in 1871, and such twentieth-century infernos as the bombings of London, Hamburg, and Dresden, and the fire in King's Cross Underground station. My wider research took me to criminal lawyers, police officers, and psychologists, who gave me valuable insights into the mental states and behavior patterns of those who witness disastrous events like great fires, those who ignite them, and those who confess—not always truthfully—to having done so. I also visited arson investigators, fire stations, forensic laboratories, and crematoriums. What I learned there helped me to discover the reasons the official death toll was so vastly different from the terrible reality.

The Great Fire did not just claim lives and destroy buildings, goods, and possessions. It also obliterated at a stroke virtually every trace of a medieval city that had been six centuries in the making. A few books and parchments were saved, a handful of buildings escaped the holocaust unscathed, but much of what we might have learned of the intimate details of medieval London was lost forever. Like the burning of the library at Alexandria, the fire of London stole from us an irreplaceable store of human knowledge.

I have used Thomas Farriner's wanderings as a device to help reveal something of the flavor of London in that long-vanished era, and I've tried to convey the sights, sounds, and smells of the city, and the human stories of those caught up in "the greatest fire that ever happened upon the earth."

Where possible, I have let the contemporary accounts speak for themselves. All text and spellings have been rendered into modern English— "doth" has been converted to "does" and "hath" to "has," for example. I have also unified the often inconsistent spellings of proper names, and as a help to the reader, I have given names to one or two minor, previously anonymous characters such as Thomas Farriner's servants.

No other liberties have been taken with the contemporary texts, and no dialogue has been invented. Everything in quotation marks is a direct quote from a document of the period, and numbered notes at the back of the book identify the sources.

The Great Fire of London erupted almost three and a half centuries ago, but it retains its power to shock and to terrify even to this day. In our world of metal, glass, and concrete, it is hard for us to picture the firestorm that devoured that ancient wooden city; but if modern materials, building techniques, fire prevention laws, and fire-fighting methods have made a cataclysm like the Great Fire less likely in some ways (except in wartime), the development of skyscrapers and the introduction of new, highly toxic and combustible materials like plastics, gasoline, and aluminum have heightened the dangers of urban fires still more. Whether we live in a village, a town, or a city, the fear still haunts us today. It is urban man's most terrifying nightmare: the city in flames.

Chapter 1

Repent or Burn

Saturday, September 1, 1666

A Bell Man

This glorious and ancient city . . . which commands the proud ocean to the
Indies and reaches the farthest antipodes.
John Evelyn, **Diary**

A S THE RIM OF THE SUN APPEARED ABOVE THE EASTERN HORI-
zon, darkness began seeping from the city like the ebbing of a black
flood tide. Driven before the light, it poured from the roofs, eaves, and gutters, and flowed down the steep streets and lanes, spilling across the
wharves to lose itself in the dark depths of the river.

Almost deserted at dawn, the sleeping city came to life and the river
and the streets began to fill with traffic. As the sun burned down, the easterly breeze raised a fog of dust in the streets, and smoke rose from ten thousand chimneys, dulling the blue of the sky.

Thomas Farriner stood in the doorway of his bakehouse, drinking a
mug of small beer to slake his thirst. His close-shaven scalp itched beneath
the coarse hair of his wig, and sweat trickled down his face. He angled his
gaze upward to the tiny patch of sky visible overhead. There was no trace
of cloud, no sign of relief from the heat.

He pulled on his coat and walked out along the passage, leaving his apprentices still with many hours of labor ahead of them. The war with the Dutch continued, and seven thousand pounds' weight of ship's biscuit was being shipped every week from the naval yards at Deptford, Chatham, and Woolwich. Thomas Farriner's ovens had not been cold in over a year.

As he reached the end of the passage, he heard the bell of St. Margaret's begin to toll. He would have recognized it anywhere, its peal as distinctive to him as the voices of his children among the noise of the city streets. The sound swelled at once, echoed by the bells of St. Magnus at the foot of the hill, St. George in Botolph Lane, St. Michael in Crooked Lane, and St. Leonard in Eastcheap, spreading out across the city, tolling from every church tower, with the great baritone peal of St. Paul's rising above them all.

Thomas paused at the entrance to his narrow shop. Although the business of the King's baker was to provide ship's biscuit for the Fleet, he also baked a few loaves to sell: brown bread for the poor, stamped with an "H" for housewife's bread, and the more expensive white, wheaten bread for the rich, stamped with a "W." He also supplied St. Margaret's Church, receiving an annual payment of four pounds "To Mr. Farriner, for bread."[1]

An apprentice was sweeping the street frontage clear of dust and dirt while another set out the bread on a trestle. Thomas took an armful of the brown loaves and carried them up the lane and through the churchyard to the vestry of St. Margaret's to await distribution to the poor and needy of the parish.

He then walked around the side of the church and climbed the low bank to the graveyard, the drought-burned grass crumbling to dust beneath his feet. The ground was rough and uneven, hollowed by collapsing graves. There were few memorials to the plague dead—too many of the living had followed close upon the heels of those who went before—but here and there graves were marked by stones or wooden crosses hung with funeral garlands, "wooden hoops dressed with artificial flowers of paper, silk or dyed horn . . . gilded or painted empty shells of blown eggs . . . together with long slips of colored paper or ribbons."[2]

Close under the wall at the northern end of the yard, there was a stone still hung with a fading garland of silk flowers. Thomas knelt before the grave, brushed the dust from it with the back of his hand, and adjusted the garland. Hanging from it was an empty hourglass and a yellowing parchment, cut into the shape of a pair of gloves. The sun had faded the ink, but the inscription was still legible: *Elizabeth Farriner 1630–1665*. No further burials had occurred here since then; no space remained in the little church-yard filled with plague dead.

Plague was "always smoldering" in London, but the Great Plague of 1665—the Poor's Plague, as it was also known—was the most terrible epidemic since the Black Death three centuries before. It began in May 1665, in Westminster, where "the mansions of nobles and courtiers rubbed shoulders with blind alleys, sheds and penthouses, springing up around, behind and against them."[3] At first "it appeared to be only in the outskirts of the town, and in the most obscure alleys, amongst the poorest people; yet the ancient men, who well remembered in what manner the last great plague (which had been near forty years before) first broke out, and the progress it afterwards made, foretold a terrible summer and many of them removed their families out of the city."[4]

The plague spread first to St. Giles in the Fields, site of "the worst slums and rookeries in all London." There it reached epidemic proportions and then spilled into the city itself. Almost without exception, it was most virulent in the poorest parishes, among the crowded tenements, cellars, and shacks in "close and blind alleys," where "if one die infected, it is more dangerous than in any house."[5]

It reached its height in September 1665, when thousands were dying each week. "Never did so many husbands and wives die together; never did so many parents carry their children with them to the grave, and go together into the same house under earth, who had lived together in the same house upon it."[6] "Death was the sure midwife to all children and infants passed immediately from the womb to the grave . . . it was not uncommon to see an inheritance pass successively to three or four heirs in as many days."[7]

The dead-carts were too few for the work of moving the bodies. They lumbered past still more bodies left lying in the streets, and the corpses were stacked like logs outside the city walls for days on end. "The number of sextons was not sufficient to bury the dead; the bells seemed hoarse with their continual tolling until at last they quite ceased."[8]

The epidemic peaked with that last outburst of terrible violence, however, and by the end of September it had begun a slow decline. In November the soldiers quartered in tents in Hyde Park—where even in that relatively sanitary environment one third had perished of the plague—returned to the city, and by December the tradesmen, merchants, and gentry were crowding back "as thick as they fled."

On January 20 the justices were ordered to see that "all bedding and other goods in the several infected houses were well aired, the rooms all new whited and the churchyards covered with earth two feet thick."[9]

Emboldened, the King and his court returned on February 1, and the news that His Majesty was back in Whitehall encouraged other, even fainter hearts. "Before the end of March the streets were as full, the Exchange as much crowded, the people in all places as numerous as they had ever been."[10]

The plague continued to spread outward beyond the city and raged throughout the country during the following year; but though Londoners continued to die of it—almost two thousand perished between January and September 1666—the losses were trifling compared to the previous year, and for the most part the citizens now chose to close their eyes and their minds to the threat that hung over them.

"The houses which before were full of the dead were now again inhabited by the living, the shops which had been most part of the year shut up were again opened and the people again cheerfully went about their wonted affairs. . . . They had the courage to marry again and betake to the means of repairing the past mortality . . . so that although the contagion had carried off . . . about one hundred thousand, after a few months their loss was hardly discernible."[11]

A fresh influx of country people to the city filled the places of those lost to the plague, and Londoners resumed their lives, many with an even greater appetite for the pleasures and indulgences that a great city could offer. Thomas had little taste for such revels. His wife, Elizabeth, had been among the plague dead, and by the blackest of ironies, the son he had sent out of plague-ravaged London to find refuge with relatives in Norfolk was now trapped there as the pestilence swept across East Anglia like a forest fire. England's second city, Norwich, was in its grip, and none could enter or leave without a certificate of health. Helpless once more, Thomas could only wait and pray.

As he thought about his son, memories flooded him of the boy, now almost a man. Every morning, before the rest of the household was astir, young Tom would pad down the stairs in his stockinged feet to watch his father at work in the bakery. Thomas would pretend not to have seen him, but without looking, he would toss over his shoulder a piece of bread still hot from the oven. The boy would leap and catch it, then sit to eat it on the brick floor, warmed by the heat of the ovens. He would look up and smile at his

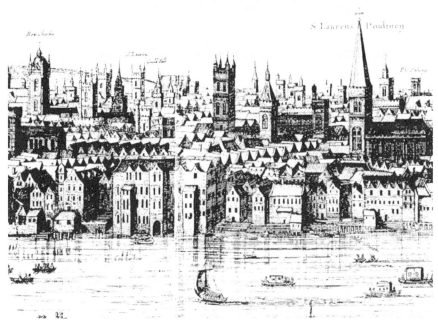

View of the city from Southwark.

father, his face lit by the dancing flames as the apprentices fed more wood into the fire. That look and that smile tugged at Thomas's heart like no other.

He remained kneeling for some time, his lips moving silently in what might have been a prayer or a whispered conversation. At last he hauled himself to his feet, using a gravestone for support. He stood, head bowed, for another minute, then turned and walked slowly away.

His servant, Teagh, sat in a cart awaiting him at the bottom of the lane. Thomas climbed up alongside him, and Teagh flicked the reins. Neither spoke as they made their slow way through the crowds thronging Thames Street and onto the bridge approach, past cart drivers and coach drivers leading their horses up and down to "warm their legs" before attempting the steep ascent of Fish Street Hill.

The bridge was the only river crossing in London—the King had already twice refused applications to build another bridge, and a petition to allow two ferries was still being considered three years after it had been submitted—and, as every day, it was blocked by the weight of people seeking to cross. The cart slowed to a halt almost at once. As they waited, Thomas glanced around him.

The surface of the river was black with craft, "like a floating forest from Blackwall to London Bridge."[12] A convoy of colliers from Newcastle escorted upriver by a man-of-war, grain and timber ships, merchantmen, fishing smacks, oyster- and eel-boats, coasters, and dung-boats jostled for space at the wharves and stairs, while watermen were everywhere ferrying passengers and goods around the city. Three thousand of them plied their trade on the river in an "infinite number of wherries, tide-boats, tilt-boats, barges, hoys."[13]

Thomas could see the tide lapping at the black, forbidding entrances to the water gates of the Tower, beneath walls bristling with cannon. The White Tower rose ninety feet above them. Built in Caen stone and mortar "tempered with the blood of beasts" as a symbol of the Norman conquest six hundred years before, for all its crumbling walls, it remained the symbol of English might and power.

Warships and tenders were crowding Tower Wharf. Stevedores and dock laborers, sweat-soaked and cursing, struggled under the weight of barrels of gunpowder and cannonballs, chain- and grapeshot. They manhandled them down the ramp from the armory to the quay where, guarded by soldiers armed with muskets and halberds, the stores were roped together and hauled aboard the waiting ships, each load swinging perilously, black against the sky, before disappearing belowdecks.

The noise was deafening. To the squeal of ropes through blocks, the crash of iron on stone and wood, the shouted orders of officers and the curses of their men, was added the bone-chilling roar of the lions in the King's Menagerie deep within the Tower.

Slaughterhouses and food stores for the navy sprawled around Tower Hill, and the sides of the filthy ditch surrounding the Tower were lined with offal. Beyond the ditch, great merchantmen and East Indiamen lined the wharf at the Custom House. Farther upstream, the narrow, rotting quays of Billingsgate were busy with fishermen hurrying to unload the day's catch. The ships clustered four and five deep around the wharves as corves and baskets of glittering silver fish were passed from hand to hand across the decks of the other vessels to reach the quayside.

As well as fish, fresh and salt, and shellfish, holds were being emptied of oranges, lemons, onions, potatoes, and other fruits and roots, and sacks of wheat, rye, and other grain. Billingsgate was also the port for Gravesend, where many ships from overseas disembarked their passengers, and the easternmost end of the quay was lined with passenger boats and wherries. Toward the western end, groups of dealers and merchants haggled with the captains of colliers, for the wharf was also the common exchange of the Newcastle coal trade.

Surrounding the main wharves were scores of lesser quays and boat-stairs, with little more than a rough flight of steps and a beam, rope, and pulley projecting over the river. All were crowded with coasters, merchant-men, and smaller craft. Porters ran to and fro across the shoreline between the wharves and boat-stairs, laden with bales and boxes, their bare feet sinking into the brown Thames mud. Men and boys dodged around them, mudlarks scouring the shore for driftwood, lost cargo, pieces of sea coal, or valuables exposed by the currents.

Thomas looked away as the cart lurched forward, but it took them a full forty minutes to cross to the south bank, picking a way among the crowds clustered around the shops and stalls and the press of people and carts heading into the city from the south.

They stopped at the granary at the Bridgehouse close by the southern end of the bridge, and leaving Teagh to tether the horse and load the cart, Thomas pushed his way through the crowd around the door of the Mer-maid tavern. The miller was at his customary table, his face and fleshy hands still dusty with flour. A ledger stood open beside him, and as he caught sight of Thomas, he called for drink to be brought, then set down his tankard and picked up his quill. Thomas settled his account, then drank deep of the proffered wine, feeling a warming glow coursing through him. He sat with the miller awhile, exchanging news of the war, then drained his tankard and bade him farewell.

Teagh was still loading the flour for the next week's baking, and Thomas helped him with the last few sacks, lifting them with his powerful forearms and swinging them up onto the cart as if they weighed nothing at all, though the work left him puce-faced and sweating.

The laden cart joined the queue of coaches, carts, and horse and foot traffic thronging the entrance to the bridge. Thomas walked alongside the cart. As he stepped onto the causeway, he could feel through the soles of his feet the low, bass rumble of the mill wheels turning in the arches beneath them.

They inched their way forward, carried on a tide of jostling humanity beneath the stone keep of Bridge Gate. Few among the crowd raised their eyes to the score of dark shapes outlined against the sky above the battlements, like a copse of bare winter trees. The heads of traitors were impaled on spikes there as a final humiliation and a warning to others. The ravens from the Tower pecked out the eyes and stripped the flesh from the skulls, which stayed there for years, and sometimes decades, swinging in the wind like creaking gates until they finally rotted and fell.

Among them were the skulls of Thomas Venner and thirteen other Fifth Monarchy Men, whose belief that the death of King Charles II would herald the coming of King Jesus and the reign of Christ upon earth had led to a feeble armed rebellion. Alongside their heads were those of several of the regicides who had signed the death warrant of Charles I.

The sunlight reflecting from the myriad leaded panes of the first great house upon the bridge forced Thomas to shade his eyes. The heat was baking, and he was glad of the temporary respite as the roadway, in cool shadow, passed beneath the house. As they emerged beyond it, they came to a halt.

A hackney driver and a coachman had come to blows near the middle of the bridge. Neither would give way, and as they attempted to force past each other their wheels had become interlocked. The frightened horses reared and kicked as the men lashed at each other with their whips, cheered on by their partisans among the crowd.

Thomas tried to control his mounting irritation, but as the minutes passed with no sign of an end to the impasse, he left Teagh to ensure the safe delivery of the sacks of flour and retraced his steps, pushing his way through the crowd. He hailed a lighter at the boat-stairs just upstream of the bridge, and was at once surrounded by a crowd of watermen, all clamoring for his custom.

He chose one and climbed in, and the boatman leaned on his oars and sent the craft scudding out from the bank. The air was hazed with smoke and dust, and even out on the river there was no respite from the heat. The boatman threaded a course through the multitude of skiffs, lighters, and wherries plying the river, keeping well clear of the dangerous currents around the bridge. The massive stone piers sunk deep into the riverbed were set in starlings—pontoons banded with iron and timber—breaking the force of the water and channeling it between the narrow arches.

They so restricted the flow that as the tide ebbed and flowed, the water level was a man's height greater on the upstream or downstream side, and water seethed through the arches in torrents so ferocious that few boats dared to shoot them. During the ebb in particular, the water gushing through every arch formed "so many cataracts pouring down with a tremendous roar and whirling around on the lower side in foaming eddies . . . the navigation through the bridge is so dangerous that scarcely a week passes without the loss of lives in these artificial straits."[14] For two hours at the height of each tide, it was impossible for any craft, large or small, to navigate the arches.

The slowing of the river flow also caused it to freeze from bank to bank during hard winters, and "frost fairs" were held on ice "so thick as to bear not only streets of booths in which they roasted meat, and divers shops of wares quite as in a town, but coaches, carts and horses."[15]

Thomas raised his gaze. Just beyond the lesser gate at the northern end of the bridge stood the crenellated walls of St. Magnus the Martyr, like a line of fortifications guarding the city. Beyond the church was a jumbled mass of interlocking planes clothing the twin hills on which London was built, reaching from the waterfront to the shadows at the foot of the city walls. Wavering lines of deep shadow, black as ink on parchment, marked the lines of streets, lanes, alleys, and courts threading between timber-framed buildings as gnarled and twisted as old oaks.

Palaces, churches, mansions, and guildhalls rubbed shoulders with warehouses, workshops, tenements, and slums. Around some of the great houses were gardens marked by the canopies of plane tree, ash, elm, walnut, pear, and mulberry, but crowding around and above them were rooftops and chimney stacks, casements and gables, bell towers and turrets, spouts and jetties, all groping upward toward the light like the branches of some petrified forest. High above them, kites soared on the thermals, their forked tails fluttering like pennants in the updraft of air as they scanned the streets and open spaces for carrion.

Earthenware roof tiles glowed red in the afternoon sun, above walls of gray-yellow or burnt-orange brick, some straight-coursed, some herringboned in Tudor fashion with contrasting bands of a deep bloodred. There were facades of peeling stucco bounded by bands of weathered oak studding, and mean houses weatherboarded with deal planks crudely daubed with pitch. Flags and pennants cracked and rippled in the stiff easterly breeze, and the sun glinted from the gilded signs lining every street.

Above the huddled roofs rose the spires and towers of a hundred and more churches. St. Mary le Bow, St. Dunstan in the East, and St. Lawrence Pountney soared high above their fellows, but were still dwarfed by the bulk of St. Paul's slumbering on Ludgate Hill, its vast leaden roof, almost six hundred feet in length and white with age, shimmering in the heat haze. Even without the spire toppled by lightning a century before, the great cathedral commanded the heights above the city, outlined against the reddening sky beneath the ever-present pall of smoke.

There were slum suburbs immediately outside the walls to the east and west of the city, but save for the great houses lining the Strand toward Westminster and ribbons of building alongside the roads outside the city gates, particularly those toward Clerkenwell and Spitalfields, London was surrounded by open common, meadow, and pasture stretching away to the distant villages of Islington, Highgate, and Hampstead on the hills north of the city.

Speeded by the last pulse of the high tide, Thomas was rowed upstream past wharves piled high with coal, wood, hay, and straw, and stacked bales and barrels. Finished cloth drying in the sun hung the whole height of one building, suspended from the windows of a weaver's garret.

Thomas watched with idle interest the bustle of the wharves and quays as the lighter slid past the Steelyard, the Vintry, and the waterfront landmarks, the Three Cranes and Baynard's Castle. The water was brown and stinking, laden with filth and sediment, of which "human excrement is the least offensive part.... All the drugs, minerals and poisons used in mechanics and manufacture, enriched with putrefying carcasses of beasts and men, all mixed with the scourings of the wash-tubs, kennels and common sewers. This is the agreeable potation extolled by the Londoners as the finest water in the universe."[16]

The boat left the Thames at the bleak walls of the Bridewell and nosed its way up the Fleet Ditch. Nothing larger than the small craft could have navigated the river, reduced to little more than a stream by the drought and the filth and rubbish littering its banks and encroaching on the channel.

They passed under Fleet Bridge. It was fenced with iron pikes and there were "lanthorns of stones"[17] at intervals where lights were placed on winter evenings. The dank smell of rotting wood from long-abandoned wharves and boat-stairs filled the air as the boatman rowed farther upstream, past ranks of crumbling tenements, shanties, and hovels, and privies erected on the mud banks to discharge their contents into the Fleet. They stood cheek by jowl with the smoke-belching stacks of dyers and brewers—who sometimes shared the same lead vats—vinegar makers, sugar refiners, iron smelters, cloth bleachers, soap boilers and salt boilers, the stinking yards of glue makers, skinners, tanners, fat renderers and tallow chandlers, and the scalding houses of butchers.

A group of mortar makers stopped their work for a moment to watch the lighter pass. Their skin and clothes were dusted with quicklime and their hands were so scarred by burns they looked frostbitten. Above them on the slope, a solitary broken-down nag circled endlessly around a horse-gin, driving some rumbling piece of machinery in the ruinous building next to it.

Hair and gobbets of rotting flesh and fat flensed from cowhides littered the banks of the ditch, along with dead dogs, rubbish of all sorts, and offal carried down Fleet Lane and dumped by the butchers from the Newgate Shambles. But worse even than these was the stench from the tanners' curing pits dug into the banks of the Fleet, where the raw hides were cured in a solution largely composed of dog turds and urine.

Among all this filth, lumbering black-bristled pigs rooted and foraged, fighting over the choicest scraps, as clouds of flies filled the air, dense as the pall of smoke above them. If Milton's vision of the infernal regions could have been realized anywhere on earth, here in the Fleet Ditch, that "abominable sink of public nastiness" within sight, sound, and smell of Newgate, was the place.

Thomas paid off the lighter at the boat-stairs, stepped gingerly across the cracked, sunbaked mud, and made his way up Fleet Lane. He settled his account with his lard supplier in a filthy tavern at the bottom of Seacoal Lane, the air heavy with the tannin reek of oak chips from another nearby tannery, and then, sweating and blowing from the climb, he paused at the top of the hill, resting his hands on his paunch as he gathered his breath.

Ahead of him stood Newgate, a single semicircular arch with iron gates and a portcullis, flanked by squat, unequal stone towers. The grit-gray pigeons that roosted on its battlements looked as "rough and grimy" as the massive stone walls. The terrible stench from the jail, where an open sewer ran through the middle of the prison, had assailed him long before he reached the top of the hill. Even among the thousand noxious stenches of "this stinking city, the filthiest of the world,"[18] Newgate's foul odor stood out.

Thomas saw a countrywoman, identifiable by her red cloak and the flowers in her hair, squatting in the dust at the side of the road. He bought a nosegay from her before moving any closer to Newgate and held it against his face as he edged past the queue of carts lining the road outside the gate, funneling through one by one as they paid the toll.

Carts carrying beer, coal, and wood, and "very filthy ones employed solely for clearing the streets and carrying manure," vied for passage with wagons, coaches, and sedan chairs flanked by liveried servants and African slave boys. Horsemen, droves of animals en route to the shambles, and a jostling mass of humanity also made what way they could. The congestion at Newgate and the other city gates and on the bridge often led to delays extending to hours.

Few of the crowd pushing through the gate even noticed the skeletal hands, the color of dust, extended from a barred opening at ground level in the thick stone wall of the prison. Croaking voices, lost in the noise of the rumbling carts and tramping feet, begged for alms.

All prisoners were required to pay for their "chamber and bed" and supply their own food and drink. Without money they were doomed, subsisting only on whatever they could beg or steal from their fellows, or "on the rats and mice they have catched." Some parishes even employed people to beg on the streets on behalf of those rotting in the jails.

With money a prisoner could buy additional food or drunken oblivion, or bribe his way up the hierarchy of the jail. The Keeper of Newgate was notorious for his corruption, presiding over "the only nursery of rogues, prostitutes, pick-pockets and thieves in the world."[19]

At the top of the prison was the Master's Side, where those with money or influence with the Keeper could dine on food from the cookshops, drink wine and brandy, and sleep on their own bed linen. Below that was the Press Yard, where prisoners of note were held. The rest were confined in the rat-ridden, subterranean dungeons of the Common Side, rife with jail fever—typhus, spread by the lice prevalent in the filthy prison—where only one in four condemned men survived long enough to make the journey to the scaffold.

Thomas hurried away from the jail along Newgate Street. Directly ahead, sprawling across the roadway, were the stalls of the Shambles. Here, as at the other city markets, the market bell rang six days a week, at sunrise in winter or six in the morning in summer. Housewives and servants had priority for the first two hours, haggling over the pick of the fresh-killed meat, before the hawkers, shopkeepers, and tradesmen moved in.

The air was heavy with the thick, sweet smell of blood. Butchers and their apprentices shouted their wares amid a bedlam of noise, their blue

A water seller.

sleeves and leather aprons soaked with gore. Beasts penned in small yards behind Newgate or tethered to the stalls were lowing, grunting, and bleating as they awaited their end. There was the thump of axes and cleavers on wood, the scrape of steel on bone, the wet slap of meat and entrails, and the buzz of hordes of flies, crawling over every surface.

Kites, tame as caged birds, stalked among the stalls, picking at the tripes and offal dumped underneath, apparently oblivious to the tide of humanity swirling around them. Haggard old women and scrawny children, their limbs twisted and wasted by rickets, also picked over the refuse for scraps of food. At night they took what rest they could lying under the deserted market stalls, or huddled in doorways and graveyards.

Scores of cheapjacks, hawkers, and peddlers moved through the crowds, carrying their goods in their arms, on their backs, or on their heads. Milkmaids and water sellers carried buckets hanging from shoulder yokes, and pairs of draymen had barrels suspended from poles carried between them.

The street cries for the different goods and trades had such a distinct timbre and rhythm that it was possible to distinguish them by the sound alone: the bellman's voice, high, clear and pure, against "the hollow charnel voice of a metal man," the falling cadences of the cry of "oysters" against the rising note of "nuts."

Some were buying, shouting for kitchen stuff—grease sold to tallow chandlers for soap and candles—and cunny skins, rabbit skins bought from scullery maids. Most were selling: fine writing ink, costers, small coals, wands and rods for scourging children, white St. Thomas's onions, salt, rock samphire, hot oatcakes, hot pudding-pies, oranges, pippins, codlings, mussels, oysters, eels, Poor Jack—dried hake—candles and lanterns, bed mats, pins, brooms, straw, tinderboxes, and singing birds.

Some sought only information on lost horses or lost wenches. Others cried for scraps for poor prisoners to eat, while beggars shouted for alms for themselves, rattling the wooden clack dishes in which they collected their money. Some had covered themselves in blood and mud to seem more pitiable, or mortified themselves or their children, scarifying the skin, or piercing it with nails and pins.[20]

Match sellers offered card matches and spunks—spills of wood or paper coated with wax or tallow and tipped with sulfur—that they had labored far into the night to make. They were almost all women, widows, abandoned wives, unmarried mothers, cripples, and the old, and were the poorest and most numerous of the street vendors. Only kennel rakers, rag-pickers, and beggars ranked lower in the hierarchy of the streets. They barely made a living, and many were forced to cadge slops to survive.

Pickpockets and whores looked for marks among the crowds listening to the balladeers and broadside sellers, or watching the vaulters, tumblers, and dancers of the ropes. A performing monkey dressed in clothes mimicking the fashions of the Court drew an audience of the gullible to the quack medicines of a mountebank.

In this "rattling, rowling and rumbling age," the uproar of a thousand voices clamored to be heard above bumping wheels and neighing horses, the creaking of harness and the jingle of bells clearing a way for the horses, the shouts of carters fighting to find a path through the crowded market, the curses of hackney drivers arguing and brawling with coachmen and footmen, and the clatter of the pattens—raised wood or iron platforms— that women wore under their shoes in a vain attempt to keep their skirts clear of the rivers of urine, dung, blood, and filth running over the cobbles and filling the kennels.

Twelve months before, the plague-racked city had been as silent as the grave, so quiet that the sound of the river rushing through the arches of the bridge on the flood tide had echoed through the empty streets. Now the life of London was once more in full, deafening spate.

Thomas called at a tavern in Queen's Head Alley to settle another account and then, with time still to spare, walked down across Paternoster Row, where the chandlers' shops filled the air with "the nauseous stink of tallow." A chimney sweep pushed past him, dragging his climbing boy behind him. Sweeps bought boys from orphanages, parish beadles, or destitute or drink-sodden parents. They fetched twenty to thirty shillings; the smaller the boy, the higher the price. This one looked no more than eight or nine. He was black-faced and hollow-eyed, and his skin was so rimed with soot that the only visible features were his eyes and mouth. His hands, elbows, and feet were hideously scarred and covered in weeping sores beneath the crust of soot.

At the bottom of the street Thomas came to one of the seven entrances to St. Paul's churchyard, the largest open space in the whole of the city. From a distance, the cathedral looked like some great, gray monolith, but close to, the facade was cracked and crumbling where the sulfurous vapors of sea-coal smoke, "that hellish and dismal cloud . . . corroding the very iron bars and the hardest stones,"[21] had eaten into its fabric.

Thomas walked the length of the nave among the strolling crowds, past the stone pillars plastered with notices of servants for hire, pausing from time to time to listen to the hucksters and scan the crude stalls full of tracts and cheap mementos. Around him—the city in microcosm—were "the knight, the gull, the gallant, the upstart, the gentleman, the clown, the captain, the apple squire, the lawyer, the usurer, the citizen, the bankrupt, the scholar, the beggar, the doctor, the idiot, the ruffian, the cheater, the puritan, the cut-throat, the highmen, the lowmen, the true man and the thief. Of all trades and professions, some, of all countries, some."[22] The shuffling feet and murmuring voices, echoed and distorted by the stone vaulting, created a sound "like that of bees, a strange humming or buzz."[23]

Thomas sat for a while in one of the pews, watching the dust motes swirling in the light filtering through the great rose window in the east wall and enjoying the coolness offered by the flagstones and thick walls. When he rose, he pressed his forehead against the cold surface of one of the massive stone pillars, then stepped out again into the furnace heat of the day. The wind was strengthening, soughing through the rooftops, but it blew from the east, a dry, dust-laden wind that brought no prospect of relief from the drought.

As he joined the hordes thronging Cheapside by the little church of St. Michael le Querne that half blocked the road, he heard cries and shouts. The crowds parted and a naked figure burst through and ran toward him, unkempt and wild-eyed. Thomas felt a momentary pang of fear; any man in such disarray brought an instant reminder of the plague still smoldering within the city.

Then he saw the brazier of burning coals upon the man's head, and heard his cry: "Oh the great and dreadful God. Repent or burn! Repent or burn!" His smoke-blackened face was streaked with white where the sweat trickling down his forehead had washed it clean. The onlookers jeered, "some rude people did abuse him," and a few children threw stones and refuse after him.

As the man ran past him, eyes fixed on eternity, Thomas smelled the stench of singeing hair. He stared after him until he disappeared from sight, his hoarse, reedy voice still endlessly repeating, "Repent or burn! Repent or burn!"

Thomas turned and walked on. Hannah was waiting, as arranged, by the conduit in Cheapside. His other daughter, Mary, had married earlier that year and moved out of Pudding Lane, but Hannah still lived with her father, caring for him. She was in profile to him, looking down toward Stocks Market, and did not see him at first. Although he saw her every day, for a moment the play of sunlight and shade about her features gave her such a strong resemblance to her mother that it caught at his heart.

He stood watching her, his brow furrowed. She was one of the fortunate few who had contracted the plague and recovered, but the disease had left its mark heavy upon her. Where once she had been stout of frame and temperament, she now seemed more frail, a lesser person in every way. Still a year shy of twenty, she moved with the slow, uncertain gait of a much older woman, and even her voice now had a faintly querulous timbre.

Sensing his scrutiny, Hannah turned her head and caught sight of him. At once he forced a smile onto his face. He walked toward her, stooped, and kissed her brow. She leaned heavily on his arm as he steered her through the crowds in Cheapside and Cornhill.

Some shops displayed their goods on a counter open to the street, bringing them in behind closed shutters at night. Others had opaque glass windows, luring the customers into the lavish painted and gilded interiors, with elaborately carved wainscoting hung with looking glasses and lit by candles in silver holders and wall sconces.

The young women tending the counters complemented their surroundings, hired as much for their beauty as for their ability. Thomas watched with a mixture of envy and disapproval as they flattered and flirted with passing gentlemen, using all manner of coquetry to entice them inside to buy.

The apprentices of mercers, silkmen, and lacemen hawking for trade for their masters spread shimmering bolts of laces, silks, and fine fabrics before Hannah. Despite her father's promptings, she bought nothing save a piece of fur to trim her coat against the coming winter.

Thomas and Hannah ate at an ordinary in Eastcheap: mutton, fowl, woodcock, and a venison pasty, served with bread and small beer. Edible roots and herbs were plentiful, but few regarded them as a primary part of their diet. The well-to-do ate meat as the main and sometimes the only constituent of their meals. The poor made do with bread, cheese, and the cheaper cuts of meat: offal, tripe, trotters, and hogs' puddings.

Thomas wiped the blade of his knife and returned it to his pocket; like all the other customers, he and Hannah ate with their own knives and spoons. Then they parted, Hannah to market and home, Thomas, as was his unvarying custom each Saturday afternoon, to a pay-table in the King's Head tavern.

For the next hour he drank and talked with the customers who came to settle debts with him, and paid out some of the money to his carter and firewood seller. Saturday, the end of the working week, was the day of receipts and payments, when all citizens paid wages and settled accounts. The markets, inns, taverns, and whorehouses stayed open well into the night to accommodate those with money to spend, "and too often in alehouses, the Poor's pockets then stored with money, are overflowing mostly that way."[24] By Sunday morning, many would again be penniless.

At four o'clock Thomas closed his ledger and drained his tankard. He walked down Thames Street and took another glass while paying his brewer and wine merchant, then set off to try to collect one final, substantial debt at the Naval Office.

At Billingsgate he had to thread his way through carts laden with barrels of oysters, and run the gauntlet of the fishwives outside Walton's tavern on Smart's Quay. The pipe-smoking, foul-tongued old soaks wore reeking quilted petticoats and balanced baskets of fish or buckets of live eels on their heads.

Near Wiggin's Quay he had to jump back into the shelter of the wall as a laden dung-cart, lurching and swaying over the ruts, spilled a stream of ordure from its brimming barrels. It splashed onto the cobbles, splattering his boots.

He walked up the hill away from the waterfront. Even from a distance he heard shouts, and as he turned into Seething Lane he saw a group of women at the door of the Naval Office, clamoring for their men's pay. They were held back by a watchman and a clerk whose wig had been knocked askew.

Thomas had some sympathy for the women; their husbands were sailors, and like the King's baker, they had not been paid by the navy in several months. The Crown's financial problems were well known. Parliament was regularly summoned and as regularly prorogued without voting the substantial additions to the Civil List that the King sought, but few blamed the Members of Parliament for this; His Majesty's willful extravagance, gaming, and whoring were the subject of common gossip and scurrilous broadsheets. The wave of euphoria that had greeted his triumphal restoration to the throne had long since been dissipated, and the King was now much reviled in London. The shouts of the women showed that they held the Crown, not Parliament, to be the cause of their financial misery.

The commotion brought to the door a bewigged, full-featured figure in a coat decorated with gold brocade. His fleshy lips pursed at the sight of the mob besieging the office, and he opened his mouth as if to speak, but then thought better of it and retreated inside without a word.

As Thomas hesitated, afraid to push his way through the crowd lest he be mistaken for an official of the Navy Office and rough-handled by the mob, he saw the man emerge from an alley at the side of the building. Unrecognized, he skirted the fringes of the crowd, looking neither to right nor to left, and strode away down the hill toward the waterfront.

Thomas called after him, raising his voice to be heard above the hubbub, but the Clerk of the Acts gave no sign of having heard him and if anything quickened his pace. Thomas pursued him across Tower Street and down Beer Lane, but his quarry still reached Galley Quay fifty yards ahead of him. By the time Thomas emerged from the foot of the lane, sweating and struggling for breath, Mr. Pepys had stepped into a waiting lighter and was being carried away upriver.

Cursing, Thomas retraced his steps, and walked back along Thames Street. His spirits lifted as he slowed his pace and strolled along, surrounded by the bustle and clamor of one of the great commercial arteries of the city. This narrow street encompassed in its length all the goods and produce of England and the known world: lead from Yorkshire; sea coal from Newcastle; iron and steel from Sweden; salt, raisins, and olive oil from the Mediterranean; wine and brandy from France, Spain, and the Canary Islands; pitch, tar, resin, and turpentine from the Baltic; Venetian glass; Chinese porcelain; furs from Newfoundland; gold and silver, coffee and chocolate from the New World; leaf tobacco from Virginia; tea from India; saltpeter, silks, and spices from the East.

Even as darkness approached, carts and barrows were everywhere, and men hurried to and from the quays completing the task of unloading the cargoes brought upstream on the high tide. The noise of iron-shod wheels, horses' hooves, and the shouts and cries of men, as constant as the ebb and flow of the tide, echoed from the high wooden walls of the warehouses lining the street. Every day they swallowed the flood of goods covering the quays and fed them out through the warren of streets and lanes into every corner of the city.

The hierarchy of streets, lanes, yards, and alleys mirrored the descending social status of the resident artisans, tradesmen, and craftsmen. Streets had light and air, and there was passing trade for the shop frontages. There was less in the lanes and almost none at all in the yards and alleys, where leather and textile workers, builders and carriers, and others not dependent on selling direct to the public were almost exclusively to be found.

Thomas paused in the shadow of Thurkettle's Warehouse and looked up Pudding Lane, past his house "not ten doors from Thames Street." It ran straight, aligned north-south, for almost half its length, then took a gentle curve from right to left around the houses flanking the rear of the churchyard, before feeding into Little Eastcheap a few yards east of Fish Street Hill.

Once it had been called Red Rose Lane, after the sign that still hung at the top on the right-hand side. Since the time of Richard II butchers had been permitted to use the lane to "cart offal, etc, to the Thames at ebb tide," and "from emptied tripes" it was renamed Pudding Lane. The puddings—intestines—"with other filth of beasts are voided down that way to their dung boats on the Thames."[25] The butchers of Eastcheap still had their "scalding houses for hogs" in the yards between Little Eastcheap and the northern end of Pudding Lane, and among Thomas's other neighbors were fish merchants, basket makers, wood turners, and ships' chandlers.

A water seller was laboring up the lane, and a stooped old woman led an ass from door to door. Asses' milk, pulled straight into the customer's own jug, was much favored for young children and the sick. A few people still hurried from shop to shop, even as the apprentices were sweeping the day's dust and rubbish into the street.

A cart stood outside the ships' chandler just below Thomas's bakery. The acrid smell of pitch filled the air as a succession of stoutly hooped tar barrels was unloaded and lowered into the cellar. The cart almost blocked the lane; the woman leading the ass barely had room to squeeze past it.

Always a lesser thoroughfare, the lane had been further narrowed over the years by the stealthy, inexorable advance of the shop and house frontages. Benches and trestles were first set up, then a canopy was added, and eventually solid walls and a roof were constructed. Next a room would be built over it, jettied outward by two or three feet, creating added space for the occupant.

The process was repeated on each of the succeeding stories, choking the light and air from the street. Just around the corner were dwellings with only one or two rooms on each floor, but rising five and a half stories above ground level.

Pudding Lane was now so narrow that a cart could barely pass through it, and the jetties projected so far overhead that in places the garrets of the facing houses almost touched, leaning toward each other like the heads of two old men nodding over a mug of ale.

The sun penetrated the narrow gap between the buildings for a few minutes around noon, otherwise the lane was in permanent, stygian shadow. The inhabitants counted themselves fortunate to have any light and air at all, for many of their peers lived out their days in closed courts and alleys or dank and verminous cellars, "so full of poor people who live only by their toil that it would be difficult to try to give their exact number."[26]

Only two houses in Pudding Lane were occupied by a single family. All the others were divided into tenements, reached by narrow passages, alleyways, or rickety stairs. Some were home to as many as eight different families.

There were only two brick houses in the street, one the next house below Thomas's in the lane, the other in the Fish Yard, a very small court with a freestone pavement, where part of the catch daily landed at Billingsgate was sold. All the other houses were of timber-frame and lath-and-plaster or weatherboard construction, and dated at least from the reign of Elizabeth.

Some were far older than that. They had drooped and sagged against one another with the years until there was not a true vertical to be seen among the bulging gables, timbers leaning at drunken angles, and cracked and twisted weatherboards rough-coated with pitch. The fierce summer heat had caused every crack to gape wider, and some of the timber cladding was peeling away from the house walls like bark on a dead tree.

There was nothing to mark one house from another save the great gilded and painted signs projecting over the lane at first-floor level. Some showed trades—Adam and Eve signified a fruiterer, a unicorn's horn an apothecary, and a coffin a carpenter—but others owed their origin to the arms of some long-dead king or noble.

On the east side, each visible one above another as they climbed the steep hill, were the signs of the Three Tuns, the two great gilded fish that marked the entries to the Fish Yard, the Rose and the Boar's Head. On the west side were the King's Head, the Golden Bale, the Plasterers' Arms, the George, the Sugar Loaf, the Star, and the Blue Anchor.

High winds and the passage of time had weakened many of the massive iron-framed signs, and they sometimes came crashing down with terrible effect. One in Fleet Street had recently killed "two young ladies, a cobbler and the King's jeweler." City law required the signs to be nine feet above the ground, high enough for a rider on horseback to pass beneath them, but Thomas had never seen a horseman willing to chance his neck by riding over the rough cobbles and mounded filth in the lane, and some of the signs sagged so low that even a man on foot had to look to his hat.

The lane itself was cobbled with flints and oyster shells embedded in dried mud, and there was a shallow kennel—gutter—running down the middle. The uneven surface of the lane was smothered in filth. Horse shit, kitchen waste, dust, cinders, and ashes were piled in heaps that smoked and smoldered, and a midden of oyster shells and fish guts from the stalls in the Fish Yard had been dumped or spilled in the street.

Swill—the contents of close-stools and chamber pots—was also thrown down from the upper stories, and pedestrians often jostled each other and sometimes came to blows over the right to "take the wall"—to walk close to the house walls under the shelter of the jetties.

The swill tipped from overhead was merely one of the hazards of walking the streets of the city. The human and horse shit, fish guts, ashes, and other rubbish were dumped in the lane to lie there until the scavengers swept the street or the next rainstorm washed it down into the river. After ten months of almost unbroken drought, the piles of filth and ordure were knee-high in places.

Thomas walked up the lane and along the entry at the side of his tiny shop. The passage was so narrow that his sleeves brushed against both walls. He paused at his door, resting his forehead against the warm, rough-hewn oak. After a few moments he straightened, squared his shoulders, and went inside.

The maidservant, Rose, was laboring up the stairs with a basket of washing, and the house still reeked from the urine used to bleach the sheets. She had begun the wash as Thomas had left that morning, and even now, past nightfall, the work was not yet done. He watched her sink down to rest for a moment before continuing up the stairs. Her gray hair was plastered to her forehead with sweat, and she looked sick and old.

He walked through to the parlor, where a platter of oysters and a dish of cold mutton stood waiting on the table. The candles made dull reflections in the pewter plates, and the dim light barely penetrated the shadows in the corners of the paneled room. He picked at the food in silence as the night grew darker and the heat more oppressive.

Unsettled, he stood up and walked outside. He paused for some time at the end of the passageway, jingling his coins in his hand, then allowed himself to be drawn by the warm smell of ale and tobacco, the glow of candlelight, and the buzz of talk and laughter filtering down King's Head Gate.

He rejoined the company in the tavern, smoking his pipe and watching the players at the dice and shovel-board tables. Later he moved on up Fish Street Hill. Other inns and taverns—the Hoop, Harrow, Swan and Bridge, Star, Miter, Golden Cup, Salmon, Black Raven, Crown, Maiden Head, White Lion, Sun, and Swan—lined both sides of the street. On the west side, just above Crooked Lane, was the Black Bell—once the great house of Edward, the Black Prince, son of Edward III, but now a common hostelry.

As Thomas walked up the hill, the smell of burning pitch filled his nostrils and two liveried servants ran past him holding torches aloft to light the way for the following sedan chair. Some noble on the way to an assignation sat invisible in the dark interior.

A fiddler was playing in the back room of the Star Inn. Thomas went inside and lingered there well into the night. The bellman patrolling the street with his staff and lanthorn had long since called eleven o'clock when Thomas, stumbling a little, his head fuddled with drink, made his way out. A rat scuttled away into the darkness, and he heard the sound of horses, restless in their stables, as he walked through the darkened yard of the Star and along the entry into Pudding Lane.

As he emerged, a linksman standing at the top of the lane with a blazing brand of pitched rope called to him, but Thomas waved away the offer of a torch to light his way. Guttering candles still burned in two or three lanthorns at intervals down the street, but their feeble glow barely pierced the enveloping darkness, and the moonlight touched only the roofs and garrets high above him.

The street was deserted, but the night was full of sound. The easterly wind had backed a point or two into the north and strengthened into a gale, raising a fog of dust in the streets and carrying the stink of the meaner areas of the city into the homes of the gentry in the west.

There was a crack as a loose slate slid down a roof and shattered on the cobbles. The wind whistled around the chimney stacks and gables, and rattled the shutters. The rusting iron signs squealed in protest as they swung through ponderous arcs overhead, and from every side came the squeaks and creaks of wood twisting and flexing in the gale. Almost lost in the noise, Thomas could hear the faint whisper of a trickle of water in the conduit and the rush and roar of the receding tide as it poured through the arches of the bridge, setting the great waterwheels groaning as they turned.

Dust and ashes whirled on the wind, stinging Thomas's eyes as he crossed the lane and felt his way along the narrow passage to his door. He fumbled with the heavy iron key, then turned the lock and let himself into the hall. The house was dark and silent. He picked up a candlestick and peered into the fireplace, but the fire had burned low in the hearth. He made a halfhearted search for a match or a tinderbox, then walked across the room, leaning on the table for support, and let himself out into the narrow passageway.

He crossed the tiny yard stacked high with bavins and went into the bakehouse. Its walls were stained with soot and grease, and a gray coating of flour and dust clung to every surface like a fall of dirty snow. Three long trestle tables ran diagonally across the floor, and barrels of lard and sacks of flour were piled against the rear wall, muffling the noise filtering through from the roisterers in the alehouse in Botolph's Lane behind the bakehouse.

A stack of wood stood ready on the brick floor next to the oven. Flitches of bacon hung from the rafters, and several pots of baked meat for the Sunday dinner stood on a ledge just inside the oven, above the kindling placed there by his apprentice to dry, ready for the next day's baking. Thomas rested his hand against the warm bricks as he leaned in to rake up the embers of the fire, but he could not produce enough flame to light his candle.

He recrossed the yard and went back into the hall. Squatting on his hands and knees, he managed to blow enough life back into the fire there to light the candle, then raked over the embers. There were five other hearths in the house. He checked each one and made sure that all the windows and doors were closed and barred. Then by the feeble light of the candle he climbed the narrow winding stairs and entered his chamber. As he took off his clothes and pulled on his nightgown, he heard the call of the night bellman passing by: "Midnight. Look to your lock, your fire and your light, and so goodnight."

Thomas emptied his bladder noisily into the chamber pot, and in the next room he could hear Hannah muttering and grumbling in her sleep. He climbed into bed and blew out the candle. He was asleep within seconds.

Chapter 2

The Hellish Design

A Hackney Coachman

Fear you not some plague, some coal blown with the breath of the
Almighty, that may sparkle and kindle, and burn you to such cinders that
not a wall or pillar may be left to testify the remembrance of the City?
Thomas Reeve, *God's Plea for Nineveh*

IN THE BOOK OF REVELATION, 666 IS THE NUMBER OF THE BEAST, whose attributes included the ability to bring down fire from heaven. Sixteen sixty-six had long been heralded by visionaries and hellfire preachers as the year when God's punishment would be meted out to sinful London. The lechery and debauchery of the court of Charles II added to the puritan certainty of divine retribution, and prophecies of doom and gloom, many suppressed by the King's surveyor of the press, forecast "great drought and barrenness, conflagrations or Great Destruction by Fire."

Thomas Reeve's *God's Plea for Nineveh*, published in 1657, warned:

Methinks I see you bringing pick-axes to dig down your own walls and kindling sparks that will set all in a flame from one end of the city to the other. What inventions shall you then be put to when your sins have shut up all the conduits of the City, when you shall see no men of your incorporation but the mangled citizens, nor

THE
VISION
OF
Humphrey Smith,

Which he faw concerning

LONDON,

In the fifth month, in the year 1660. being
not long after her KING came into her.

---

*The Prophet speaking of the pouring forth of the Spirit in the later dayes saith,
That then the young men shall see visions.* Joel 2. 28.

And the wise King said where there is no Vision the people perish. Pro. 29. 18.

*And the true Minister of Christ said, I will come to Visions and Revelations of
the Lord.* 2 Cor. 12. 1.

Concerning the Great City of London.

I Beheld all her waters which belonged to her frozen up, and that exceeding hard, and the vessels which went upon them, so that I and others passed over her waters without the least danger, and over the greatest vessels which had carried her merchandize; For all was frozen with a mighty freezing, whereby all her goodly merchandize were stopt, and her mighty swift waters were turned into a mighty thick frozen ice, which stood still, so that her pleasant streams ran no more.

A   And

One of the many pamphlets predicting a great fire in London.

hear no noise in your streets but the cries, the shrieks, the yells and pangs of gasping dying men?

Humphrey Smith's *Vision which He Saw Concerning London*, also written years before the event, predicted a fire in 1666 "in the foundation of all her buildings and there was none could quench it. . . . The burning thereof was exceeding great. . . . All the tall buildings fell and it consumed all the lofty things therein. And the fire continued, for though all the lofty part was brought down yet there was much old stuff and parts of broken down, desolate walls, which the fire continued burning against."

Daniel Baker also warned where the "evil ways" of London would lead. "A fire, a consuming fire shall be kindled in the bowels of the earth, which will scorch with burning heat . . . a great and large slaughter shall be throughout the land."[1] And Walter Gostello "looked up to heaven and there saw such a cloud of blackness and dirt as could not possibly arise from any place but hell. . . . If fire make not ashes of the City, and thy bones also, conclude me a liar for ever. . . . Repent or burn, you and your city London."[2]

Thomas Ellwood, writing in 1662, foresaw both plague and fire. "In one day shall her plagues come upon her, death and mourning and famine, and she shall be utterly burnt with fire."[3] Even the rather less hyperbolic Samuel Pepys was moved to remark, "Certainly this year of 1666 will be a year of great action, but what the consequence of it will be, God knows."[4]

The close of 1665 had marked the end of a quarter century of constant turmoil and upheaval. In an age when life expectancy was only thirty to thirty-five for the rich and twenty to twenty-five for the poor, few could recall a time when internecine conflict had not poisoned the air. The bloody and bitter Civil War, the regicide of Charles I, the Commonwealth and the Protectorate under the iron hand of Oliver Cromwell, the unrest under the weak and indecisive rule of his son Richard, the suppression of Catholicism and—since the Restoration—Nonconformism all had left scars that would not readily be healed.

As the citizens who had survived the plague prepared to greet the new year, some looked forward to 1666 with hope, some with relief, some with foreboding. There were those who now felt themselves inured to almost every trouble or danger, taking their pleasures where they would with the recklessness of those living on borrowed time. Others retreated deeper into black pessimism, mortifying and scourging themselves, and flaying their weaker brethren with their invective.

Still others went about their business with a dumb fatalism, affecting indifference as to whether the judgment of the plague had been the final terrible burden to be laid upon them, or whether the malign fates might yet hold another, still more dreadful judgment in wait.

As the fateful year dawned, signs and portents of further judgments were eagerly sought. "Comets or blazing stars do portend some evil to come upon mortals . . . as likewise phenomena of new stars, battles fought and coffins carried through the air, howlings, screechings and groans heard about churchyards, also raining of blood, unwonted matter, etc."[5]

On January 6 "Mr Secretary Morris's cistern of water was turned into blood in one night . . . [which] troubled their heads at Court,"[6] and on March 31 a "new blazing star appeared every day since Monday at one or two o'clock in the morning and continuing until daylight obscured it . . . the city was last night setting up to see it . . . mighty talk thereon."[7] Letters from Vienna also brought news of "a brilliant comet and the appearance of a coffin in the air. Watchers heard noises of fires, cannon and musket-shot."

At Easter it was "raining fish" in Kent, and on July 17 hailstones "as big as turkeys' eggs" fell in Norfolk, "one hailstone twelve inches about." The Spanish ambassador claimed that "a deformed monster" had been born in London, "horrible in shape and color. Part of him was fiery red and part of him yellow, on his chest was a human face. He had the legs of a bull, the feet of a man, the tail of a wolf, the breasts of a goat, the shoulders of a camel, a long body and in place of a head a kind of tumor with the ears of a horse. Such monstrous prodigies are permitted by God to appear to mankind as harbingers of calamities."[8]

Not all the portents were as cryptic. "A pyramid of fire was observed rising from the sea which afterwards broke up in flames and sparks. This lasted a quarter of an hour and appeared again in three days." "On Monday last at night was seen by hundreds for about an hour together flames of fire as it were thrown from Whitehall to St James and thence back again to Whitehall."[9]

The hellfire preachers' apocalyptic visions of fire raining down from heaven had been largely ignored in the wet years from 1660 to 1664, but a drought began in the plague year of 1665. A cold, dry winter and a dry spring were followed by a prolonged hot summer. There was some rain in the early autumn of 1665, but every month from November 1665 to September 1666 was significantly dryer than normal.

In Scotland the *Chronicle of the Frasers* was reporting "hot drought" by May 1666, and throughout Britain it became "a very droughty year, the driest that ever man knew . . . so that the grounds where the cattle should have fed were burned like the highways." In Oxford, the rivers were "almost dry . . . to the great impoverishment of the boatmen . . . the like has not been known in the memory of man, or at least for sixty years."[10]

Urban fires were closely linked with droughts. There were groups of fires coinciding with the prolonged periods of drought from 1611 to 1616, 1630 to 1635, and 1653 to 1657. The pattern was repeated in 1665 to 1666; during the course of the latter year one Sussex church alone held nine collections for fire losses in different parts of the country.

In London, this "so long and extraordinary a drought"[11] had lasted unbroken for ten months. Divine intervention was sought to end it. The wardens of St. Margaret's Church in Fish Street Hill paid sixpence to "My Lord Mayor's officer for bringing an order to pray for rains."[12] The prayers went unanswered, and by September 2, 1666, the eve of the anniversary of Cromwell's death, the city was a tinderbox.

Yet despite the drought, the dire prognostications of the preachers and prophets, and the countless previous fires in London, complacency reigned. Many shared the smug assumption of one contemporary observer that "notwithstanding the houses were most of timber very contiguous each to other and had constant and fierce fires kept in the hearths of them night by night" and were lit by burning candles, there was no place "better armed against the fury of fire."[13]

The equipment for fighting fires had barely altered since Roman times. The tools available were wooden ladders, leather buckets, long-handled swabs and brooms for beating out a blaze, and squirts—brass syringes holding only a gallon of water at a time.

Firehooks—iron grapnels attached to twenty- or thirty-foot poles, ropes, or chains—were also used with axes and crowbars to demolish the houses surrounding a fire. The work was difficult and time-consuming; those doing it were liable to being sued for compensation; and unless the timbers and other flammable material from the demolished buildings were removed from the site, they could still ignite and allow the fire to spread.

There were also a few crude fire engines. The Romans had a manually operated fire pump based on a design from the second century B.C. After the fall of the Roman Empire the fire pump was forgotten for a thousand years, and the first "engines to be drawn upon wheels from place to place for to quench fire among buildings" were not brought into use in England until 1625.

The Mayor's *Seasonable Advice for Preventing the Mischief of Fire* required each of the twelve principal livery companies in the city and every city ward to obtain "engines for spouting water . . . this Instrument so useful and necessary to the securing of this City." They were said to have been "found very commodious and profitable in Cities and great towns,"[14] but they were difficult to maneuver and operate, and dependent on the vagaries of the water supply.

At low tide, water was hard to obtain from the Thames, and in periods of dry weather the flow from the aqueducts, conduits, and wells was reduced to a trickle. In the absence of sufficient water, one lord mayor made the serious suggestion that any small fire could be extinguished by "gentlemen gathering together in a circle and pissing on it."

City laws also required ladders, buckets, axes, and firehooks to be placed in every church and barrels of water to be kept by every door between Whit Sunday and August 24, but they were not enforced. The buckets, ladders, and axes were borrowed and not returned, the barrels went unfilled or found other uses. The accounts of St. Margaret's, Fish Street Hill, include a payment "for mending 24 buckets and gathering them up," and another "for carrying the buckets and locking them up again" after they had once more been removed from the church.[15]

Attempts to legislate to control the fire risk were scarcely more effective. The curfew—from the French *couvre-feu,* a metal fire cover to stop stray sparks from igniting a blaze—was first introduced by King Alfred in 872 and unsuccessfully reintroduced by the Normans following the conquest.

In 1189 the first Mayor of London, Henry Fitz-alwyn, passed regulations requiring citizens to keep ladders ready to fight fires and help those escaping them. The danger from burning thatch also led him to outlaw it as a roofing material, and he laid down that all new buildings were to be constructed of stone. Almost five centuries later, despite countless repetitions of the order by succeeding kings and lord mayors of London, wooden houses were still being built.

In the fifteenth century, houses began to be fitted with flues, but since these were formed from hollowed-out tree trunks they produced a fresh rash of urban fires. The problem became so serious by the middle of the century that the Lord Mayor issued a proclamation that anyone lighting a fire beneath a wooden chimney would be fined.

The prohibitions on thatched roofing and wooden chimneys eventually were effective and most of the buildings in Restoration London were tile-roofed, but attempts to restrict dangerous trades to outlying areas were no more complied with than the prohibitions on building with wood. Smoke and sparks continued to belch from the furnaces of foundrymen, metalsmiths, dyers, glassmakers, gunsmiths, brewers, and scores of other tradesmen.

The fire risk was heightened by the narrowness of the streets. "That the buildings should be composed of such a congestion of misshapen and extravagant houses; that the streets should be so narrow and incommodious in the very center and busiest places of intercourse; that there should be so ill and uneasy a form of paving underfoot . . . it is hereby rendered a labyrinth in its principal passages."[16]

In the poorer quarters such as Alsatia there was barely a lane wide enough for a cart to enter, but throughout the city most of the streets, unchanged in layout since Roman times, were "fitter for a wheel barrow than any noble's carriage." "Sure your ancestors contrived your narrow streets in the days of wheelbarrows, before those greater engines, carts, were invented."[17]

Most streets were paved with "unshapely flint stones, which break like glass, or soft rag stone which quickly molders, or too small pebbles." Four-wheeled country wagons drawn by horses in single file also created narrow ruts in unsurfaced roads that made it impossible for a coach and four to pass. The King, the Duke of York, the Duke of Monmouth, and Prince Rupert were in a coach that overturned at King's Gate in Holborn. His Majesty fell in the mud but was unhurt.

There were also even bigger "long wagons" pulled by seven or eight horses and carrying goods or upward of twenty passengers, but hired coaches—"hackney hell carts"—were the cause of even more complaints, not merely for the obstructions they created but for the foul and intemperate language of their drivers.

One of Charles II's first proclamations after the Restoration required all hackney coaches and horses to be kept off the streets in coach houses, stables, or yards until called for hire. It was as useless as Cromwell's 1654 order that no hackney coachman should stand for hire in the street or feed his horses within three yards of any man's door. There were often as many as twenty hackneys standing in the Strand or at the conduit in Cheapside, and the streets remained so congested that accidents were frequent. Pedestrians were often pushed and jostled into the path of carts and iron-wheeled coaches.

Few new buildings of any substance had been erected within the city walls since the reign of Elizabeth, and London remained a medieval city of twisting, congested thoroughfares and timber houses. James I's avowed intention that having found "London of sticks" he would leave it built of brick had had no more effect than Charles II's ordinances such as the proclamation of August 16, 1661, that required new buildings to be constructed of brick or stone and forbade jetties and overhanging windows.

On April 11, 1665, the King again wrote to the Lord Mayor, Recorder, and aldermen warning of the peril of fire from the narrowness of the streets and alleys in London. He authorized the imprisonment of those who continued to break the building regulations and the demolition of the houses, but his strictures had no effect. Indifferent to the fire risk, builders and their customers preferred the cheapest forms of construction, and timber houses and jetties continued to be built.

Chalk was much cheaper than stone or brick, and was used, bonded with mortar, in the foundations of poorer buildings and mixed with flint for rubble walling. When wet it could degenerate into yellow-white, slippery mud, which when dry turned to dust as fine as talc. Cellar roofs were supported by brick or stone arches, or more usually, timber piles.

In those mean districts where even chalk and flint were an extravagance, many dwellings were little more than tar-paper shacks, thrown together around a timber frame that was sometimes prefabricated away from the site. Over the previous two centuries, the size of timbers used in construction had halved, and beech puncheons (studs) were routinely used as a cheaper alternative to oak. Walls were made either from beech laths covered with mud stiffened with mortar and "mixed with the hair of animals; the poor use very finely chopped straw,"[18] or from boards of deal—fir—or spruce, coated with pitch.

The houses were "very narrow in the front towards the street, but built five or six roofs high."[19] They were "small and ill-built . . . the scurviest things in the world,"[20] "dark, irregular and ill-contrived . . . with their several storeys jutting out or hanging over each other, whereby the circulation of air was obstructed, noisome vapors harbored and verminous, pestilential atoms nourished."[21] This style of building caused many "to make reflection on the covetousness of the citizens and connivancy of Magistrates who have suffered them from time to time to encroach upon the street and so to get the top of their houses from one side of the street to touch the other which, as it does facilitate a conflagration, so does it also hinder the remedy."[22]

The central area of the city, where the merchants and wealthy tradesmen had their premises and great houses, was surrounded by an inner ring of poorer parishes, their "alleys . . . pestered with people."[23] These older parts of the city were almost entirely composed of wooden warehouses, crumbling tenements, lean-tos, shacks, and shanties teeming with people, and this overcrowding further heightened the risk of fire. People lived near their place of work, crammed into whatever housing they could find among the densely packed workplaces of the riverside districts by the banks of the Thames and the Fleet, the highways that carried most of the traffic of the city in raw materials and finished goods.

The population of London had more than quadrupled in the space of a century. Some three hundred thousand people lived there. The next five largest towns—Norwich, Bristol, Newcastle, Exeter, and York—could muster only eighty thousand between them. Every available inch of building space in London had been divided, subdivided, and subdivided again to accommodate the burgeoning numbers.

A single small house in Dowgate Ward was home to eleven couples and fifteen single people; a ten-room house in Silver Street was occupied by ten families, many of whom had taken in lodgers. Even these were far from the worst examples of overcrowding. Sir John Parker's house in Whitefriars was divided into twenty tenements, and Francis Pyke's nearby house had been divided into no fewer than thirty-nine tenements.

Slums extended from Bridewell, at the mouth of the Fleet River, in an almost unbroken arc around the city walls. There were sprawling, crowded tenements north of the Strand, and in Holborn and Clerkenwell. They lined the banks of the Fleet Ditch and spread around Cripplegate and Bishopsgate and as far as Shoreditch to the north of the city, and the Whitechapel Road and the Ratcliffe Highway in the east. There were more slums around St. Katharine's and the Minories in the shadow of the Tower, and they extended east along the river through the shantytown of Wapping to the isolated slum village of Stepney.

There were also even less savory quarters full of rookeries, stews, coney burrows, and criminal refuges, where the medieval right of sanctuary had been formally extinguished but where, among the poor and dispossessed, colonies of beggars, debtors, thieves, robbers, and the lowest soaks and harlots still gathered. The thieves and gangs of organized beggars even had their own impenetrable argot, the "canting tongue," and they lived beyond the ineffectual reach of the watchmen and parish constables—who often hired decrepit substitutes to perform their duties for them.

An act of the Common Council in the first year of Charles II's reign had provided for a thousand bellmen or watchmen to patrol the streets of London by night, but assaults on these officers of the watch were common, and even when they did manage to effect an arrest, the suspects were often rescued by their neighbors. "At the cry of 'Rescue' bullies with swords and cudgels, and termagant hags with spits and broomsticks, poured forth by hundreds, and the intruder was fortunate if he escaped back into Fleet Street, hustled, stripped and pumped upon. Even the Warrant of the Chief Justice of England could not be executed without the help of a company of musketeers."[24]

Prudent citizens carried arms or swords at all times for their own protection. Even when the weapons of political suspects were confiscated, they were often allowed to retain some arms for self-defense.

Householders were required to hang out lanthorns—hollow cow horns in which a candle could be placed—to make passage safer at night. Watchmen patrolled "armed with javelins, bills and halberds, covered with rust,"[25] and the night bellmen also walked the streets with lamps and bells, calling the hours of the night, but all took pains to steer clear of the criminal sanctuaries and the gangs of ballers—ruffians—roaming the streets.

Soldiers, recruited from the dross of society, were often criminals themselves, and memories of the conduct of the army during the Civil War were still fresh. Soldiers could be used in political troubles, such as the Venner Rising of 1661, but not to patrol the streets, where they were confronted by the citizens uniting against them, even in defense of the most hated criminal.

The watchmen and bellmen also had the task of watching for fire in the night. London had been ravaged by fire throughout its history and rebuilt again and again on the rubble and ashes of the ruins. It had first been fired in A.D. 61, during Boudicca's uprising against Roman rule. The thick layer of ash, charred wood, broken tiles, burnt clay, and fire-reddened earth from that fire was often still encountered by builders when digging cellars or foundations. Above it was another similar band, the relic of the fire that again destroyed Roman London sixty years later.

Great fires were recorded in 798, 982, and 989—"so great and lamentable a fire that, beginning in Aldgate, it burned down houses and churches all the way to Ludgate, together with the stately fabric of St Paul's." In 1087 the wooden Saxon cathedral was again "quite consumed, together with the greater part of the city."[26]

Blazes among the densely populated houses on London Bridge were particularly dreaded. The houses were all of wood; it was feared that the bridge might collapse under the extra weight if they were replaced by buildings of brick or stone. On July 10, 1212, a southerly gale spread a fire from the Southwark bank, where it had destroyed the church of St. Mary Overy.

"A great multitude of people going over the bridge to see it or help to quench it, on a sudden by blowing of the south wind, the north part of the bridge was set on fire."[27] Thousands of people were trapped in the middle. Many ships came to save them, "into which the multitude so inadvisedly rushed that the ships being thereby sunk. . . . It was found that above three thousand souls perished by this disastrous accident. Whole bodies were found half-burnt besides those who were turned to ashes."[28] Other estimates put the death toll as high as twelve thousand. The blaze was known as the "Great Fire of London" for over four and a half centuries, until it was succeeded by an even more terrible blaze.

One writer at the turn of the thirteenth century described the only inconveniences of life in the capital as "the immoderate drinking of the foolish and the number of fires." By the reign of Henry VIII, the threat was so constant that night bellmen were given the additional duty of watching for fires, and their numbers were substantially increased. Their cry, "Take care of your fire and candle, be charitable to the poor and pray for the dead," echoed through the streets of the sleeping city every night. The King's Briefs detailing the losses incurred in major fires were circulated so frequently to churches to solicit donations for the sufferers that they were allocated a special place in the communion service.

In the seventeenth century, London had already seen a blaze in Southwark in 1630, when fifty houses were destroyed, and in 1633 "a most raging dismal fire" broke out on London Bridge. A servant of John Briggs, a needle maker, left a tub of hot ashes under the stairs when she retired to bed. The heat ignited the wooden stairs and the resulting fire burned forty-two houses over the arches at the northern end of London Bridge and another eighty in the parish of St. Magnus the Martyr, on Thames Street, near the foot of Pudding Lane. "The fire remained glowing and burning for a week after in their vaults and cellars."[29] Some houses were never rebuilt, and thirty-three years later their blackened sites remained as a reminder of the disaster.

There were other, even more recent memorials. On January 4, 1649, there was "a lamentable and fearful fire" in a ships' chandler's house in Tower Street containing twenty-seven barrels of gunpowder. "By casualty and negligence fire came to those in the shop," started by "means which cannot be known because none in the house was left alive to report, and did blow up suddenly many houses and shatter and deface many more." Forty-one houses were destroyed and more than a hundred damaged, and sixty-seven people were killed. The 1650s also saw "great fires" in Thread-needle Street and Fleet Street, causing death and widespread destruction.[30]

Successive lord mayors issued "Seasonable Advice" on prevention of fires, listing the ways blazes had started:

Some have been burnt by bad hearths, chimneys, ovens or by pans of fire set upon boards. Some by cloths hanged against the fire, some by leaving great fires in chimneys where the sparks or sickles breaking, fell and fired the boards, painted cloths, wainscots, rushes, mats, as houses were burned in Shoreditch.

Some by powder or shooting off of pieces; some by tinder or matches, some by setting candles under shelves; some by leaving candles near their beds; some by snuffs of candles, tobacco snuffs, burnt papers and some by drunkards, as many houses were burnt in Southwark.

Some by warming beds; some by looking under beds with candles; some by sleeping at work leaving their candles by them; some by setting candles near the thatch of houses; some by snuffs or sparks fallen upon gunpowder or upon mats, rushes, chips, small coal and in chinks; so Wimbledon was burnt.

Some towns were burnt by malt kilns, some by candles in stables, or by foul chimneys; some by candles among hemp, flax, and cotton warehouses; some by candles falling out of their candlesticks; some by sticking their candles upon posts; some by links knocked at shops, stalls, cellars, windows, warehouses, doors and dangerous places; some by carrying fire from place to place where the wind has blown about the streets, as it did burn St Edmunds-bury; some by warm sea coal, cinders put in baskets or wooden things, as did burn London Bridge.

And some have been burnt without either fire or candle, as by wet hay, corn, straw, or by mills, wheels or suchlike; all which has been done by carelessness; and some have been fired of purpose, by villainy or treason.[31]

The city could scarcely have been in greater peril of fire; it was feared as much and perhaps even more than the plague, but if it were to break out, the wrath of God was far from the only possible cause. Arson was regarded as the most terrible of crimes, and those convicted of it in previous centuries were themselves burned to death, but there was no shortage of people with a motive for setting the city on fire.

Outlawed Catholics and nonconformists, disaffected republicans, former soldiers of Cromwell's armies, agents of the French and Dutch with whom England was at war—any of them could have led a plot to burn London; but in a city built of wood and fueled and lit by open flames, an accident was never more than a stray spark away.

Indeed, the city could easily have been destroyed by accident during the plague the previous year. The means by which the plague was spread was then unknown—the virus carried by rat-borne fleas was not finally identified until the closing years of the nineteenth century—and in the face of a disease that seemed to spread by invisible, inexplicable means, the weight of informed opinion, such as it was, came down in favor of a theory that it was carried through the air as a "pestilential miasma." The Lord Mayor was sufficiently convinced to give audience only when enclosed inside a glass case,[32] and the climate of fear was stoked by stories, such as that told by a music teacher in Westminster, of plague sufferers leaning out of their windows "to breathe in the faces of the well people going by."[33]

One celebrated physician claimed that the death toll from the plague would have been even more savage had not the summer been "refreshed with moderate breezes, sufficient to prevent the air's stagnation and corruption and to carry off the pestilential steams."[34]

The belief in a miasma led to the idea that smoke or pungent odors could drive off the plague, "for there is a marvelous great virtue and strength in fire to purge, correct and amend the rottenness and corruption of the air."[35] It was a remedy handed down from antiquity; Hippocrates claimed that a town in ancient Greece had been saved from the disease by firing the wood that encircled it.

In the plague of 1563 every householder in London had been commanded to lay out wood for bonfires. Pitch and faggots were also burned in the streets to drive off the epidemic that killed thirty thousand people and greeted the accession of James I in 1603. Charcoal, "stare," pitch, frankincense, and incense had again been ignited in 1625, when the accession of Charles I to the throne was the signal for another epidemic that claimed over forty thousand lives.[36]

The "rules and orders to be observed by all Justices of the Peace, mayors, bailiffs and other officers for prevention of the spreading of the infection of the plague" in 1666 required that "fires in movable pans or otherwise be made in all necessary public meetings in churches etc, and the convenient fumes to correct the air be burned thereon."

The wardens of St. Margaret's bought "rosemary and bay for the church," and spirits of sulfur scattered in a room, "a fumigant of brimstone, saltpeter and amber," phials of vinegar on the windowsills, "rue and wormwood taken into the hand, myrrh and zeodary into the mouth," and nosegays and pomanders of bitter herbs were also believed to be effective. Tobacco, either chewed or smoked, was thought to be a particularly powerful prophylactic against the plague.

Lady Giffard "burnt Burgamot Spirit and made as many servants as they could after the smoke was gone, take tobacco for a great part of the day, strewed rue in the windows and held myrrh in their mouths when they came anywhere that they apprehended infection."[37]

When Samuel Pepys came across houses in Drury Lane marked with the red cross and the legend "Lord have mercy upon us," he was at once "forced to buy some roll-tobacco to smell to and chew,"[38] and one Eton schoolboy recollected that he was never flogged as hard in his life as he was when caught not smoking in the street during that perilous year.

The sextons smoked incessantly as they worked—fragments of clay pipes are almost as numerous as skeletons in the plague pits outside the city walls—and the College of Physicians recommended "stink-pots"—braziers or temporary hearths built of firebricks—and "good fires in and around infected houses and the frequent discharge of guns as a means of improving infected air."

Some citizens went beyond discharging muskets and ignited whole pans of black powder inside their houses, blowing out windows and setting several buildings ablaze. More prudent citizens burned wormwood, rosemary, juniper, tamarisk, cloves, and "noxious materials such as tar, brimstone, saltpeter and even old leather and human feces on their domestic fires."

Belief in the value of fires and fumes against disease was curiously persistent. During a yellow-fever epidemic in Philadelphia in 1793, frightened citizens built fires in front of their houses or exploded gunpowder to drive it away. And in the epidemic of the same disease that struck New Orleans in 1853, the city officials burned barrels of tar on street corners and fired cannons at dawn and dusk to "cleanse" the air.[39]

In 1666, despite the endorsement of the College of Physicians, many physicians publicly doubted the efficacy of fires in houses or streets. "As heat is demonstrably a great nourisher of the verminous effluvia emitted from pestilential ulcers, it was highly unreasonable to make fires in every street with a view to purify the air and destroy the plague."[40]

They also decried the wasteful extravagance of the idea at such a time of hardship, but the Lord Mayor was ready to clutch at any straw. On September 2, 1665, as the Bills of Mortality showed the weekly death toll mounting toward ten thousand, he issued a proclamation, endorsed by General Monck, requiring bonfires to be ignited before every sixth house in every street within the city, Westminster, and the liberties, and at intervals of a few yards right around the city walls. The residents of "all streets, courts, lanes and alleys" were "to furnish themselves with sufficient quantities of firing, viz, of sea-coal or any other combustible matter, to maintain and continue fire burning constantly for three days and three nights."[41]

Braziers also were to be lit on ships moored in the Thames. Coal was the preferred fuel, but with Dutch raids on coastal shipping and the plague itself disrupting the sea-coal trade with Newcastle, the fuel was so scarce that wood, faggots, and tar barrels also were used.

At eight o'clock on the evening of Tuesday, September 5, torches and burning links were touched to the huge "city bonfires" at the Custom House, Billingsgate, the approach to London Bridge by St. Magnus's Church, Queenhithe, Blackfriars, the Bridewell, Bow Church, the west gate of St. Paul's, Leadenhall, the Royal Exchange, and the Guildhall.

The chosen night, like the previous weeks, was windless. "There was such a general calm and serenity of weather as if both wind and rain had been expelled the kingdom and that for many weeks together he could not

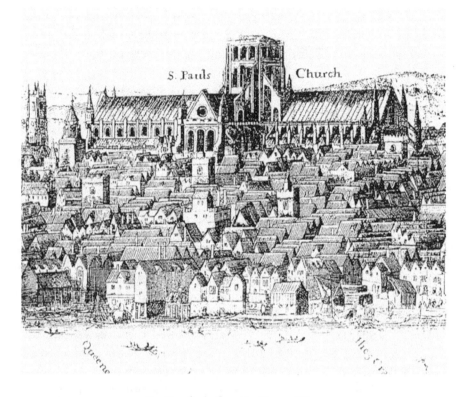

St. Paul's before the Great Fire.

discover the least breath of wind, not even so much as to move a fan, and the fires in the streets with great difficulty were made to burn."

Once alight, fires blazed all the way down the hill and burned the length of the bridge. Flames even rose from ships moored in midstream on the river and speckled the darkness on the Southwark bank. The sky was lit by a glow that stretched from one end of the city to the other. The ramparts of the city walls were capped with fire, and gouts of flame flared from every street, casting a baleful glare on the stone towers and spires of the churches, tall as great oaks, that rose above the huddled houses.

Above them all stood the mighty bulk of St. Paul's, its towering walls and squat, square tower ringed by a circle of fire. Great blazes burned at every angle of the walls, the flames licking at the crumbling stonework.

The smoke from a thousand fires rose ever higher into the still, humid air, obscuring the moon and staining it ochre. It disappeared from sight as the smoke merged with the black clouds gathering in the night sky. A dark pall hung motionless over the city, and the stench of burning pitch and brimstone smelled like the gates of hell.

London lay still and silent, awaiting its destiny. There were no cries of panic, no running feet; only the fires seemed alive in the whole vast panorama of the city. So it stayed as the lowering pall of smoke grew ever more black, dense, and threatening, choking the very air from the streets.

Minutes, hours passed, with no sound but the crackle of flames and no movement save the billowing smoke. Then there was a sudden flash of blinding light and within a heartbeat a deep, rolling rumble of thunder. A fat drop of rain, then another and another, splattered in the dust.

Lightning again forked down. There was another peal of thunder, and then a curtain of rain swept over the street, hissing against the cobbles. Within seconds water was teeming from the roofs, pouring from jetties and spouts, and cascading in waterfalls from the gables. The kennel in the center of the street filled with a surge of brown, foaming water.

The fires burning before every sixth house hissed and spat. The flames shriveled and sank to twists of smoke and steam in the rain, then guttered out, one by one, like snuffed candles. Water swirled around the piles of filth and rubbish in the streets and lapped at the heaps of black, charred embers, then swept them away. Tar barrels still ablaze outside St. Margaret's were lifted by the torrent and borne away, rumbling down the steep hill to expire in the murky waters of the river.

There was now no sound but the rush of water in the streets. Choked by clouds of swirling smoke, the light over the city dimmed and went out, leaving it as black and cold as the grave. The brooding mass and squat, truncated tower of St. Paul's, dimly outlined against the sky, rose from the clouds of smoke and steam like a great death ship cresting the waves.

It was just as well that the prolonged thunderstorm—at once proclaimed by preachers as another sign of God's displeasure with sinful London—had doused the flames. Although two men had been set to tend and watch over every fire, so closely built and combustible were the older parts of the city that the attempt to burn off the plague might easily have reduced the entire city to rubble. But London's reprieve might yet prove to be a temporary one.

The riverside wharves were stacked with wood and coal, domestic fuel for the coming winter. Behind them, running parallel to the river from one end of the city to the other, lay Thames Street. The warehouses lining the street "and others thereabouts were almost nothing else but magazines of combustible and sulfurous merchandises."[42]

If fire were to break out here, with an easterly wind to drive it, all London might be in peril.

Chapter 3

The Lodge of All Combustibles

Bye my Butter milke

It was in the depth and dead of the night, when most
doors and senses are locked up in the city.
Thomas Vincent, *God's Terrible Voice in the City*

IN THE DEAD HOURS OF THE NGHT, SOMEWHERE BETWEEN ONE and two o'clock on the morning of the Lord's Day, Thomas awoke with a start. He heard the whistle of the wind around the eaves, the rattle of the casements, the creak of timbers, and the squeak of the great iron signs as they swung in the gale, and at first he thought that these were the sounds that had awoken him.

Then the noise came again. His servant, Teagh, was pounding at his door, his hoarse shouts ending in a hacking cough. As his senses cleared, Thomas felt a choking sensation. He struggled for breath, his eyes streaming with tears. The room was filled with smoke.

He leaped from the bed, shouting to his daughter. He groped his way to the window, threw the casement wide open, and took a deep draft of the night air. Then he recrossed the room, fumbled for the handle, and opened the door.

The corridor was filled with smoke, but it was less dense at floor level. Thomas dropped to his knees and crawled toward the head of the stairs. The darkness was lit by an orange glow. He heard the crackle of fire and saw flames already licking around the stairs, barring the way. The treads were thin and fibrous from generations of wear, and the flames seized on them hungrily, climbing fast toward the upper floors.

Holding a fold of his nightgown over his nose and mouth, Thomas struggled along the corridor to his daughter's room. Hannah was out of bed and standing huddled by the window, her eyes wide with fear.

He thrust his head and shoulders out of the window. There was a sheer drop of twenty feet to the street, and the jetty of the floor above projected out by a yard, preventing them from climbing to the roof. He looked to right and left, but there was not sufficient foothold on the timber studding for them to escape that way.

The stairs were now well ablaze. He led the way back to his own room and peered down into the yard. In the light from the fire, he could see that the stacks of brushwood in the yard were not yet ablaze and the bakehouse was still in darkness. The wall fell away sheer to the cobbles with no trace of a handhold or foothold.

He ran back into the corridor, followed by Hannah and Teagh. The servant's chamber at the front of the house offered a possible escape. If they could climb out onto the great iron sign hanging from the wall below his window and lower themselves from it, there would be a drop of only a few feet to the ground.

Thomas turned the handle, but the door was stuck fast. Fighting down a growing wave of panic, he laid a hand on the door. It was hot to the touch. It resisted as he pushed, then gave with a crack as he put his shoulder to it. He caught a momentary glimpse of the smoldering hangings around the walls, then there was a blinding flash. He threw himself flat as a sheet of flame spread in an instant from one side of the room to the other. It burst through the door, searing over his head, but enveloping Hannah, standing behind him. Her clothes and hair were ablaze at once, and he and Teagh had to beat out the flames as she clung to them. Her face and arms were left badly burned.

The smell of burning hair filled Thomas's nostrils as he reeled away and crawled back along the corridor. His hair was singed from his head, his ears burned, and his brow blackened and blistered. He croaked to Hannah to follow him and led her and Teagh up the crooked winding stairs to the garret. Every breath he took felt like fire in his lungs.

He closed the door behind them, but the smoke was now so dense and choking that they had to lie full length as they wormed their way across the floor. The maidservant, Rose, lay on her sleeping mat on the bare boards, shaking with fright, the covers still drawn up about her chin.

Thomas hauled himself upright and pushed open the casement. The wind whistled in his ears as he wrenched and tore at the window, forcing it backward and forward against the frame until the rotten wood gave and fell crashing to the cobbles below. He struggled to force his bulky frame through the opening, then perched swaying on the sill as he felt around for the roof tiles, his fingers scrabbling for grip.

He found purchase on the edge of a tile. It shifted a fraction under his hand, but held as he straddled the casement and the roof edge for a moment, then hauled himself out onto the roof. He braced his foot against the ridge gutter and reached a hand around, calling to Hannah to follow him. She hesitated on the brink, backlit by the flames already licking at the door of the garret, then, clutching his hand, she half climbed and was half dragged through the broken casement and onto the roof.

Teagh clambered out next. Only Rose now remained behind. She stood in the window, rooted to the spot. Although Thomas cajoled and entreated, ordered and threatened, she remained motionless, mute with terror. When he grasped her arm to pull her out, she jerked it away.

He teetered on the point of falling for a moment, then hauled himself back to the safety of the roof. He tried once more, telling Rose that she would die if she stayed there. She shook her head, mute, more frightened of falling to the cobbles than of the fire within.

Wreathed with flame and smoke, her face was still framed at the window as Thomas turned away and began to crawl along the gutter, clinging to the uneven, soot-encrusted roof. The wind whipped his nightgown around him, and the coarse roof tiles scraped his knees. As he crawled on, his groping hand dislodged one of the tiles. It slid down the roof and disappeared over the edge, shattering on the cobbles forty feet below.

Thomas felt cold sweat on his blistered brow as he continued to inch his way forward. Hannah's hand brushed his foot as she crawled close behind him, but in truth, if either had slipped, there was nothing the other could have done.

He crawled the last few feet to the garret of his neighbor, Robert Taniton. He reached around, his fingers scrabbling at the glass, and kept banging on the small panes until at last the casement was thrown open and a face appeared.

There was a narrow ledge in front of the casement just wide enough to stand on. Thomas stood there, gripping the frame with his left hand and reaching out with his right to help first Hannah and then Teagh to safety.

Just before he crawled after them, Thomas looked back along the roof to the garret of his own house. He could no longer see Rose's white, frightened face at the window, just a thick, black column of smoke belching out of the gaping casement to be snatched away by the wind.

Still coughing and retching from the smoke, he stumbled down through Taniton's house. His neighbor's household was already roused and at work gathering together their valuables. Taniton's man ran down the street to alert the watchman and find a cart for hire to carry away his master's goods.

It was only then that Thomas thought of the gold locked in his own cabinet. He ran outside and up the street to his house. The door was barred and bolted from the inside, and the windows were smoke-blackened and cracked with the heat. He could hear the roar of flames and the crash of falling timber. His gold and everything else he possessed were already beyond his reach.

He retreated and stood helpless with Hannah as their home and workplace burned before their eyes. The bakehouse, filled with combustibles, its walls and ceiling steeped in decades of smoke and grease, was now an inferno, and smoke was also seeping in thickening streams from between the roof slates. Tongues of fire were scorching the broken casement through which they had escaped. Hidden behind the burning walls, Rose already lay dead, asphyxiated by the smoke and fumes long before the creeping flames devoured her body.

A few moments later, above the howling of the wind and the crackle of the blaze, Thomas heard the cry of "Fire! Fire!" repeated from street to street and echoing through the courts and alleys. There was a thunder of drums, beating to call the citizens to arms against the blaze, and moments later the bells of St. Margaret's on Fish Street Hill started to ring out in a discordant, reversed peal.

More of Thomas's neighbors were now astir. There were cries and shouts, and the sound of running feet. A few ran to the church for the equipment stored there against the outbreak of a fire, but such was the speed at which the blaze was spreading that most hurried to secure their goods, already certain that their houses were doomed.

The men returned from St. Margaret's almost empty-handed. There had been no great fire these thirty years, and the equipment stored there was either damaged or missing altogether. The ladders, axes, and many of the leather buckets had been taken and not returned, and most of the remainder were cracked, split, and useless. The firehooks—grapnels on long lengths of chain and rope, used for pulling down houses—were dragged out of the church entry but then dumped in the middle of the lane for want of the manpower to use them and a leader to take charge.

Thomas stood stunned and helpless, his mouth agape, still staring as the flames burst through the roof of his house. At first the breach was no more than the width of a man's arm, but as more and more laths and timbers burned through, showering down roof tiles into the heart of the fire, the flames spread wider and rose higher and higher into the sky. Sparks, smoldering embers, and flecks of flame caught by the wind were whirled away across the street, some lodging among the gutters and gables of the facing houses, some disappearing over the roofline into the darkness beyond.

Rousing himself at last from his stupor, Thomas took Teagh and two other neighbors and ran up the hill and through the dark passage at the back of Butchers' Hall near the top of the lane. The brass fire squirts stored in the hall were solid as cannon barrels, and the weight made them stagger as they hurried back down the lane.

There was another delay as an ax and spades were found, the cobbles of the street torn up, and the quill—the elm water pipe—broached. The flow was weak, for the engine in the Water House at the bridge was out of order and the cisterns were almost empty, but water filled the hole in the cobbles and began to run away in a thin stream down the kennel.

Thomas, Hannah, and Teagh joined a ragged chain of people, using such leather buckets as could be found, augmented by wooden tubs, earthenware bowls, and even chamber pots to move water to the squirts. But each one took three men to operate, two holding the handles at either side while a third forced in the plunger that sent the feeble jet of water through the broken windows of the house, and there were too few hands for the work.

The early hours of the Sabbath were "a time when most persons, especially the poorer sort, were but newly in bed and in their first dead sleep."

47

Most of those who were awake and might have fought the blaze were too busy salvaging their goods. Men, women, and children ran in an unending stream to and from St. Margaret's, storing their valuables in the refuge that all citizens sought for themselves and their goods in time of peril. If any structure could withstand the blaze, it would be the church, almost the only stone building amid the forest of timber houses.

With nothing left to save, Thomas and a handful of others continued to battle the fire. Their efforts to extinguish it met with no success, but for half an hour thereafter it remained confined within the bakery and Thomas's house, isolated to the south by the stout brick walls of Taniton's house and to the north by the passage leading to the Fish Yard.

During that time the Lord Mayor, Sir Thomas Bludworth, arrived at the scene, roused from his slumbers in his house in Gracechurch Street. Bludworth was also MP for Southwark, a colonel in the Orange Regiment, and the former Master of the Company of Vintners. He was rich, a successful Turkey merchant with interests in the timber trade, and a leading member of the Levant Company who also had influence in the East India Company.

"Firmly grounded in the true religion, and sincerely devoted to the interests of . . . his prince and his country,"[1] he owed most of his influence and position to his unswerving loyalty to the Crown. Arrested on suspicion of Royalist sympathies during the Commonwealth, he was among those who attended the exiled Charles at The Hague and provided a letter of credit to ease the financial worries of the impoverished Court in exile. His reward was a knighthood at The Hague and substantial royal patronage in the years that followed the Restoration.

He had been installed as Lord Mayor on October 29, 1665, but was unusually young for the office and widely regarded as lacking the requisite brains and qualities of leadership, "a young man of little experience,"[2] "delighting more in drinking and dancing than is necessary for such a magistrate,"[3] and "a zealous person in the King's concernments; willing, though it may be not very able, to do great things."[4] Samuel Pepys took an even less charitable view, describing Bludworth as "a silly man, I think" and "a man mean of understanding and despatch of any public business."[5]

Pudding Lane was too narrow for the Lord Mayor's coach to enter, and Bludworth, disheveled and irate, was forced to descend the lane on foot. His scornful gaze took in the fire, the bucket chain, and the procession of

Thomas's neighbors hurrying down the lane, their heads loaded with goods to be deposited in the church or the waiting carts on Thames Street.

His gaze returned to the blazing building. "Pish," he said. "A woman might piss it out."[6] He turned on his heel and strode back up the lane. A few moments later his coach rumbled off into the night. He was "not long ere undeceived of his foolish confidence."[7]

Soon afterward the flames at last breached the brick walls of Taniton's house. They began to jump from garret to garret, as if following the route Thomas had taken to escape the blaze. The fires burning fiercely in the roofs ignited the lower stories, and fanned by the wind, the flames began to move down the lane with gathering speed.

Like the throat of a chimney, the stepped jetties almost meeting overhead further increased the already ferocious updraft. Sparks and burning embers carried aloft on the wind lodged among the stables and outbuildings at the rear of the Star Inn. Its stores of hay and its midden of dung and straw were soon ignited. Flames encircled the courtyard of the inn, running through the timber galleries with a gathering roar, and within minutes the whole building was ablaze.

The terrified neighing of the horses trapped in the stables could be heard above the thunder of the flames. A few were led to safety, a few more broke free and bolted through the blazing archway, galloping away through the darkened streets trailing smoke from their singed coats. Still others, choked by smoke, collapsed and burned to death in their stalls.

The gale, still increasing, drove the flames on. Thomas's house and bakery were still ablaze, though nothing remained but a shell open from ground to sky; all within it had been devoured by the fire. Still the little group kept up their work with buckets and squirts amid the roar of the flames, the crash of falling timbers, and the small detonations of flints exploding within the rubble walls. Then there was a sudden warning shout, half-smothered by the thunderous rumble as the house of the King's baker collapsed into the street. They fled for their lives, leaving the squirts buried under the smoldering rubble.

The buildings on both sides of the lane were now well ablaze, and flames could be seen shooting skyward above the rooftops to the west. The ships' chandler's just below Taniton's house in Pudding Lane was burning fast. Stored in his cellar were a score of barrels of Stockholm tar, used for waterproofing wood and caulking the seams of ships' planking. Blazing roof timbers crashing down through the stories of the house had broken through the floor into the cellar and set the staves of the tar barrels smoldering. Before long they were ablaze. Their contents began to volatilize as the heat increased, but the barrels as yet remained sealed.

The cellar extended some way under the street, and the first signs of the new danger were the cracks appearing in the ground. There was no further warning, just a massive detonation that shook the ground with the force of an earthquake. The lane erupted. Clods of earth, cobbles, masonry, and fragments of blazing tar barrel were blasted outward and upward as a pillar of fire rose as high as the rooftops. Within seconds another dozen houses were ablaze.

Thomas and Hannah had been thrown to the ground by the force of the blast. Deafened, their faces scorched and their clothing smoldering, they dragged themselves to their feet and ran blindly to escape the advancing wall of flames. They fled through the church entry and into Fish Street Hill, where once more they were confronted by another line of fire spreading down toward the waterfront from the inferno raging in the Star.

They ran before it down the hill and away along Thames Street to seek sanctuary where they could. Behind them the fires burned on in two parallel lines down Pudding Lane and Fish Street, the wings of an army advancing toward the bridge.

The "wooden pitched houses . . . old paper buildings and the most combustible matter," all baked dry by the drought, gave themselves up to the fires one by one. The flames slipped from house to house, furtively creeping behind paneling and hangings, then bursting forth with sudden, shocking violence.

Beech laths became flaming brands, cracking and spitting as they burned, and plaster turned to dust and ashes. Great timbers tumbled and fell blazing, bridging courts and alleys, creating flare paths for the consuming fires to follow. Each house, each hovel, made its contribution to the fires, which rose ever higher into the sky and advanced ever faster. A hot, searing wind now traveled before them, and buildings already charred and smoldering erupted as the wall of flame reached them.

St. Margaret's was now besieged on all sides. The flames roared through the desiccated grass of the churchyard and lapped around the walls. The funeral garlands shriveled and crumbled into ashes, the burning parchment cut into the shape of a pair of gloves took flight, trailing smoke as it spiraled up into the sky, borne aloft on a pillar of fire.

For a time the stonework and the stout oak doors of the church held the blaze at bay, but the east window began to bulge and buckle in the heat, and then cracked and shattered. As the flakes of glass fell to the ground, the flames poured through the breach, seizing upon the goods stored inside.

The pews and the aisles in the nave and the vault belowground were stacked with a jumbled mass of furniture, tapestries, paintings, documents, books, clothes, and casks of wine and brandy. Anything that could be moved from the fire-threatened houses had been deposited there. Now it was all more fuel for the fire. Confined within the body of the church, the flames burst out with a roar like cannon fire, wreathing the bell tower in fire and running the length of the roof of the nave in seconds.

Flames leaped into the sky, chasing the billowing swirls of smoke, and for the first time was heard a sound that struck terror into every heart: a roar and rumble like an ocean pounding against a rocky coast. It bore within it the thunder of flames, the crash of stone and timber, the pounding of running feet, and the cries and screams of human beings.

A lead cistern stood in the churchyard against the rear wall of the church. It was one of two—the other was in the Green Yard at Leadenhall—fed by the engine of the Water House at the bridge. As the cistern emptied, its last water trickling out through the broken pipe in Pudding Lane, the heat began to melt the lead. When the flames moved on, the cistern was a wreck, a pool of molten lead solidifying as it mingled with the dust of the blackened churchyard.

Gathering speed as they rolled down the hill, the twin streams of fire in Pudding Lane and Fish Street Hill burst upon Thames Street, "the lodge of all combustibles." Every aspect of the City of London could be found in the narrow confines between Thames Street and the river. There were great churches and guildhalls, cavernous warehouses; and in the narrow lanes running down to the river, crowded together so densely that most lay in almost perpetual darkness, were stores and cellars, docks and wharves, ships' chandlers and rope makers, workshops and manufacturers, containing every material and every trade on which the city thrived.

Among a thousand "wares and commodities stowed and vended in those parts" were oils, pitch, tar, turpentine, brimstone, saltpeter, gunpowder, cordage, resin, wax, butter, cheese, brandy, sugar, honey, hops, tobacco, tallow, rope, hemp, flax, cotton, silk, wool, furs, skins and hides, and the wharves where coal, timber and wood were unloaded.[8] Among these workplaces, between and around the handful of buildings in stone and brick, was a sprawling rookery of houses built of little more than sticks and mud. Clinging to every inch of space, stacked and cantilevered upon each other, stood ruinous tenements, shacks and hovels, cramped garrets, and damp, dark cellars. There, those who gained their living on the river—porters and carriers, stevedores and dock laborers, boatmen and wherrymen—found lodging. They had fed the plague in the previous year, now they were fuel for the consuming fire.

Even if any carters had been disposed to linger in the shadow of the flames, there was no time to load carts with possessions. Those with a boat piled it with whatever they could carry and fled before the advancing fires. Others simply threw their furniture into the river, until the whole surface of it was "covered with goods floating, all the barges and boats laden with what some had time and courage to save."[9] Those without access to a boat carried whatever goods they could manage on their heads or backs, and then fled.

Roaring through the warehouses on Thames Street, the twin walls of flame came together to beat against the stones of the church of St. Magnus the Martyr. Scrambling to escape, the parish clerk left behind the church plate and all the burial money received since Lady Day. All of it melted and was consumed as the fire ravaged the church.

The stones shattered in the heat; and fed by the wooden stairs and staging in the belfry, flames engulfed the bell tower, forming a huge burning torch that lit up the night sky. It sent out a warning across London that few in that hour before dawn had eyes to see.

For those within its compass, the fire already had a dreadful aspect, but from a distance this blaze among the low and mean housing clustered around Pudding Lane and Fish Street Hill still seemed a thing of small consequence.

In Seething Lane, a quarter of a mile distant toward the Tower, the Clerk of the Acts, Samuel Pepys, roused from his sleep by his maid, climbed to the garret to look out on the fire, then returned to bed. The rest of the city slept on, untroubled, as the first traces of dawn began to redden the eastern sky.

Around Bridgefoot it was already bright as day. The flames marched on, laying waste the Parsonage House in Churchyard Alley and devouring the Bear Inn as they spilled onto the approach to one of the wonders of England: London Bridge, "the bridge of the world," 910 feet long and rising from twenty stone arches spanning the Thames.[10] Stately timber-framed houses with intricately carved and gilded facades, and "built with a good deal of woodwork and paneling,"[11] lined the bridge. One, Nonsuch House, claimed to have been built without a single nail, was capped by four great copper-clad onion domes from which gilded weathervanes projected.

The houses crowded in upon a roadway that was nowhere more than twenty feet wide and in places narrowed to twelve. The ground floors of the buildings were occupied by a double row of shops. Above them, the houses stood four, five, and even six stories high, projecting out over the river on each side, supported by a rook's nest of timbers. The greatest buildings filled the bridge from side to side, and the roadway burrowed beneath them, forming dark tunnels filled in the daylight hours with a tide of jostling humanity.

Toward the northern end of the bridge, where most of the houses burned in the fire of 1633 still had not been rebuilt, there was a gap spanning six arches. The iron rail was lined with wooden palisades against which sprawling rows of stalls and shops had been built, further encroaching on the roadway. The only other breaks in the double row of buildings were The Square by the old chapel of St. Thomas between the ninth and tenth arches, where pilgrims once paused to pray on their way to Canterbury, and the drawbridge over the fourteenth arch. Once raised at almost every tide to allow great vessels to pass upstream, it had lain unused for well over a century, for want of the money to repair the mechanism.

Giant waterwheels set in the two northernmost arches used the force of the tides to raise river water into conduits that supplied the lower parts of the city. At the other end of the bridge another pair of waterwheels drove corn mills fed from the Southwark granary.

Unresisted, the fires swept through the gate tower and at once engulfed the houses built since the fire of 1633. Three stories high and projecting fifteen feet over the river on great wooden beams, they tumbled one by one in the wake of the fire. Rubble completely blocked the roadway, barring all entry to the city from the south. The jettied stories and blazing timbers collapsed into the river, the water erupting in cauldrons of smoke and steam as the fire debris, black and silent, drifted downstream with the retreating tide.

The flames raced on among the weatherboarded shops and stalls, devouring the palings lining the gap left by the fire thirty years before. In their path were the great turreted houses surrounding the drawbridge and lining the southern end of the bridge. Hundreds scrambled from their beds and fled for the safety of the Southwark bank, the air above them already thick with sparks and burning brands. Others clambered down from the timbers projecting over the river and huddled together on the stone starlings beneath the bridge to await rescue by watermen.

Greed took precedence over compassion, and the boatmen roused from their beds by the thunder of the fire became the first to profit from it; the fee they charged for safe transport to the Southwark shore was at once twice and then three times the normal rate. Above their heads, a few people on the bridge had the prudence and courage to face the fires, casting down some of the stalls and wooden palisades into the river even as the flames roared toward them, driven by the keening wind.

Burning all before them, the fires met their first check above the eighth arch of the bridge. The remaining stalls and palings offered insufficient fuel to ignite the first of the buildings beyond the gap, the stone-walled tenement that had once been St. Thomas's Chapel. The flames scorched the walls, then guttered and went out, leaving the northern half of the bridge a mass of smoking, twisted ruins. The great houses to the south were untouched, but those who had reached the Southwark shore now faced a fresh alarm.

A blazing ember blown by the wind a full two hundred yards from the bridge had set light to a stable in Horseshoe Alley, near Winchester Stairs. It spread quickly to two neighboring houses, but hooks, chains, and ladders were brought at once from the church of St. Mary Overy and a neighboring house was pulled down before the flames could reach it. Thus isolated, the fire south of the river was extinguished, foiled by the decisive action so wanting on the other side of the bridge.

On the north bank the flames rumbled on with ever increasing appetite, heralded by the rumbling alarm of beating drums and discordant bells, audible as far off as Lincoln's Inn, where they were heard by Francisco de Rapicani.

Dark-eyed, black-haired, handsome, and powerfully built, the thirty-year-old Italian had come to London as an emissary of the deposed Queen Christina of Sweden and a traveling companion to several Swedish nobles, ambassadors to the Court at Whitehall. On Saturday night, he and his friend Baumann had ventured over the river to Southwark to sample the delights of its theaters, bear-baiting arenas, and pleasure gardens:

> I had not crossed the bridge over the Thames before. As we went over, and I looked at the fine great row of houses, I said "Those are fine buildings indeed, and it would be a pity if they should ever catch fire," for they were built with a good deal of woodwork and paneling. I thought no more about it and we went on with our walk until evening.

Coming back in the twilight, we were in the middle of the bridge when blood suddenly poured from my nose. I was very alarmed and said that it must signify something. I went aside to the iron rail of the bridge and bled for the space of a good two Paternosters. Then we went on to a coffee house to smoke a pipe of tobacco until about ten o'clock, when there was no carriage to be had.

As I was lodging in Covent Garden and it was already late, Baumann said I should spend the night with him at Lincoln's Inn. We had hardly been in bed for an hour when . . . we heard a great noise of drums. We jumped out of bed and from the window could see nothing but a great fire beside the Thames, near that same bridge.[12]

The rapid spread of the flames along the waterfront was aided by the "dread and pavid manlessness that seized the inhabitants . . . by this did every man's unmanly example discourage till at last the hearts of men were at their heels and every hand became palsied by terror."[13]

The wooden waterwheels under the northernmost arches of the bridge were utterly destroyed. One burning wheel fell from its mountings and rolled across the mud, toppling into the water and floating away, the upper part still burning as it drifted downstream.

Just west of the bridge was Gully Hole, the narrow passage leading to the Water House. The flames at once fastened on the "lofty, wooden building" and the great engine "which by wheels, iron chains, etc . . . forces water through leaden pipes" into the city was destroyed. The conduits were already low and breached in a number of places as the people sought water to fight the fires. Now they began to run dry.

The flames burning west along the shore were beginning to cut off access to the only other source of water in the lower part of the city, the Thames itself. Even for those still within reach of it, the tide was ebbing and the flow so low after such a drought that water could be fetched from the river only after a long trek across the mud. To the fleeing inhabitants of the waterside districts, it already seemed that an act of God rather than the hand of man might perhaps be the only hope of stemming the progress of the fires.

Soon after dawn the Lord Mayor returned to the scene. He was pressed "that he would give order for the present pulling down [of] those houses which were nearest and by which the fire climbed to go further."[14] Sailors from the Tower stood ready to assist the creation of firebreaks by demolishing houses with barrels of gunpowder, but Bludworth refused to countenance the idea, repeating over and over, "When the houses have been brought down, who shall pay the charge of rebuilding them?"[15]

He well knew the answer. Ancient city law dictated that any man destroying another's house should be at the charge of rebuilding it. Only the express authority of the King in Council would absolve Bludworth of responsibility, and by the time His Majesty had been persuaded to give his assent, the whole city lay in peril. "London, so famous for wisdom and dexterity," could now find "neither brains nor hands to prevent its ruin."[16]

West of the bridge lay a warren of crumbling timber houses, shacks, and shanties spilling across the old fish market quay right down to the water's edge. Hundreds of people lived in these crowded tenements built of lath and plaster bound with horsehair, rotting timber, and rough deal boards, crudely weatherproofed with pitch. The area was honeycombed with filthy, narrow passages—Rood Alley, Fleur de Lys Alley, Black Raven Alley, Stockfishmonger Row, and a score of others—scarce wide enough for two men to pass, but giving ample entry to the fire.

The flames raked them from end to end in minutes. They burned with what seemed a malign purpose, racing to block alleys and passageways, denying escape to the terrified inhabitants. The fleeing residents twisted and turned, ducking into courts and scuttling through passages like rats in the wainscoting, only to find once more their escape route blocked by a curtain of fire.

Some made it to the quays, where boats were already burning at their moorings. Barges stranded on the mud by the retreating tide were also ablaze. Driven before the searing heat, many people jumped from the wharves and floundered away upstream through the mud and swirling water, as the wind drove the flames in pursuit.

Others, their eyes staring white from smoke-blackened faces, clambered from boat-stairs to boat-stairs along the waterfront, or clung to the rotting timbers below the wharves. Coughing and retching from the smoke, they negotiated with the boatmen who stood ready, at an ever escalating price, to take them and their goods up- or downriver, or across to the Southwark bank. Still others straggled away on foot east along the mudbanks beneath the smoking ruins lining the shore.

A few found shelter with friends or relatives in nearby streets, only to move again as the fire burned on. Some moved themselves and their goods "four and five times"[17] in the space of a single day. An unknown number of people died—

S Michaells

the Old Swan

Fishmongers hall

Fishmongers' Hall, the first of the great guildhalls to be destroyed.

the old, the halt, the lame, and the sick, those who lingered a few moments too long as they struggled to save their families, and "those persons who, their eyes dazzled by greed, remained behind for a moment to save their wealth, perished when they found their path cut off by the flames, their eyes now blinded even more by the smoke than they had been previously by covetousness."[18]

So fast was the progress of the fire through this waterside quarter that the engines brought to battle the flames were themselves consumed or tumbled down into the river and were lost. A hot, searing wind came before the flames, full of smoke, dust, and ashes, and the rumble of distant thunder. The heat increased until pitch melted from weatherboarding, and wisps of smoke began to curl from doors and casements, eaves and gables.

The noise grew louder, and a blizzard of sparks, burning embers, and ashes fell from the sky, cloaking the roofs like snow. The eastern face of every building now streamed with smoke, and the air was so dense with it that people groped their way blindly through the streets. The rumbling and thundering grew so loud and the heat so fierce that it seemed a volcano was erupting. Those fleeing pressed their hands to their ears to blot out the terrible sound, snatching them away only to beat out the smoldering embers lodging in their clothes.

Then out of the heart of this maelstrom of heat and noise and wind burst a wall of flame fifty feet high, moving as fast as a running man. Each smoking, smoldering building in its path erupted at its touch. Devoured and picked clean, only the skeletons remained as the fires moved on. Not a wall remained standing. The dark and festering courts and alleys were gone forever, laid bare to the light of the rising sun.

Fishmongers' Hall now stood in the path of the inferno, a range of imposing buildings, some of them pre-Tudor, surrounding a central courtyard. A high arched gateway in the stone facade led from there to a narrow riverside terrace with a watergate. The walls gave barely a check to the flames, which were soon bursting through the roof lantern of the hall. They advanced with such speed and purpose that the fleeing inhabitants could save only themselves.

Fishmongers' Hall and its east and west wings were razed to the ground. Only the imposing stone frontage to the river remained. All the records of the salt-fishmongers and stock-fishmongers and all their gold and silver plate were consumed. All that was saved from the wreckage was a dagger, "an ugly weapon with a twisted steel guard,"[19] said to be the very dagger used by Lord Mayor Walworth to slay Wat Tyler during the Peasants' Revolt in 1381.

Chapter 4

A Lake of Fire

Sunday, September 2, 1666

A Couple of Dray Men

Never was there the like Sabbath in London.
Thomas Vincent, *God's Terrible Voice in the City*

THE EASTERLY GALE WAS STILL STRENGTHENING, BUT THAT Sunday morning, like all those that had preceded it throughout the summer, had dawned bright and cloudless. The pillar of smoke rising from the fires was visible throughout the city, but the sunlight seemed to diminish the flames, and at first the blazes causing such terror on the shore west of the bridgefoot caused barely a tremor elsewhere. Fire was too frequent a phenomenon in the old city to cause much comment or alarm. A blaze would erupt, a few houses would be burned and pulled down, a small note in the *London Gazette* of that week would record the losses and the dead.

For the rest of London, life went on as normal that Sunday morning. Men and women slept late, attended church, and went about their feast day preparations, with little sense of foreboding. Leaving his wife, Elizabeth, dozing, Samuel Pepys rose at eight that morning, and looking out of his casement, saw the fire "not so much as it was and farther off."[1] He dressed for church and broke his fast, and only when his maid, Jane, burst in to tell him that three hundred houses had been burned down in the night by a fire raging all the way down Fish Street Hill to the bridge, did Pepys stir himself.

Before he left, he dressed in the "fine dark suit trimmed with scarlet ribbon"[2] and the velvet cloak he had newly purchased from a mercer in Cornhill, careful not to let Elizabeth discover the price. It was scarcely suitable garb for viewing a fire, but if the blaze was as serious as Jane had said, Pepys intended to be the first to bring a report to Whitehall. Men such as he owed their position and future advancement to the services they were able to render to those persons of quality with whom they came into contact. An opportunity to appear before His Majesty himself was not to be missed.

He walked to the Tower, and gazing westward from one of the turrets, saw for the first time the extent and the intensity of the blaze. He hired a boat and was rowed through one of the arches of the bridge and upstream across water thick with boats, floating goods, and furniture.

They passed the smoking ruins on the bank and the raging firefront, and Pepys then bade his boatman make for Whitehall. As he was rowed upstream, carried on the rising tide, the fire rumbled on behind him, its noise growing like a gathering storm as the force of the gale and the contours of the land conspired to keep it roaring westward along the river frontage.

Pepys alighted at the palace boat-stairs at Whitehall just before eleven o'clock. Approached from the river, the great palace built around the house confiscated from Cardinal Wolsey by Henry VIII had more of the air of a jumble of small houses in a dozen different architectural styles, with the great Banqueting Hall rising behind them.

Pepys went first to the King's closet in the chapel. After describing the fire to the courtiers assembled there, he was escorted up the Privy Stairs to the first floor and through the long gallery hung with paintings and rich tapestries. French furniture and velvet-lined musical instruments ornamented with silver gilt added to an air of opulence designed both to impress and to intimidate visitors with the power and splendor of the Crown.

Above the splashing of a fountain, the song of caged birds, and the soft ticking of endless clocks came the murmur of low voices as courtiers strolled through the long gallery or stepped aside to mutter together in bays overlooking the river. Many of them were far less well arrayed than the room through

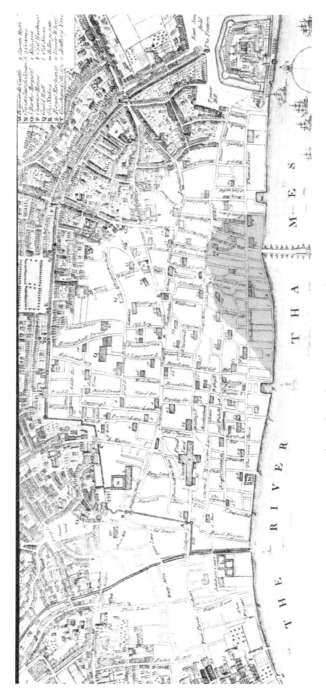

Map of the fire's spread on the first day.

which they moved. For all the superficial elegance of their apparel, most were dirty and smelly, and their clothes, close to, were often patched and worn.

They hovered around the fringes of the Court, hoping always for the chance of advancement, a sign of favor that would lift them above their rivals, but away from Whitehall many lived in as much poverty and squalor as the King's lowlier subjects. "They frequent the palace and sometimes are in the presence of the King, but how they live and rest in their lodgings it is pitiful to relate, and barns and stables are good resting places."[3]

The courtiers eyed Pepys with curiosity as he was led into the Guard Chamber. He stated his business and was admitted at once to the Presence Chamber. Although the canopied Chair of State was empty, passing servants still bowed to it as if the King were actually seated there.

Pepys gave an account of the fire to a group of courtiers gathered in the chamber, and when word was taken to the King he at once summoned Pepys to appear before him. It was a signal honor. Only a select few were permitted to pass beyond the Presence Chamber into the Privy Chamber, the Withdrawing Room, and finally the Royal Bedchamber.

Pepys wrinkled his nose as he entered, then recomposed his features. King Charles delighted in his spaniels, which followed him everywhere and slept in his bedchamber. A bitch had recently whelped, and Pepys could hear the mewling cries of her puppies from their refuge beneath the bed. The smell of dogs and the stink of dog shit was heavy in the air, but then the whole Court was "nasty and stinking."[4]

His Majesty, evidently but recently awoken, lay on the bed. He was tall with a dark, almost olive skin, and such prominent features that he could have passed for a Greek or a Levantine. He had a powerful figure, if a little swollen by dissipation, but as one contemporary acidly observed, it was "hard to determine whether he took more pains to preserve it by diet and exercise or to impair it by excess in his pleasures."

Barbara Palmer, Lady Castlemaine, stood nearby. She was the King's mistress, though if the rumors of the streets were even one part true, there were many, many others who could have claimed that honor, if only for one night. Pepys himself had counted seventeen royal mistresses before the Restoration, and the number had more than doubled since.

"The king does spend most of his time in feeling and kissing them naked all over their bodies in bed, and contents himself without doing the other thing, but as he finds himself inclined, but his lechery will never leave him."[5] Tom Killigrew, the Groom of the King's Bedchamber, was facetiously urged to suggest to His Majesty that he seek employment as monarch, for he spent "all his time in employing his lips and his prick about the Court and has no other employment."

Lady Castlemaine, "with whom the King had lived in great and notorious familiarity from the time of his coming into England," had given birth to "a son whom the king owned."[6] Her compliant husband had been rewarded with a title and a country estate a tactful distance from the capital. She was a strikingly beautiful woman, twenty-five years old, auburn-haired, with a full, voluptuous figure and a piercing, almost insolent gaze. Pepys looked on her with frank admiration, but her deep blue eyes traveled over him as if he were no more than part of the wall hangings.

Charles's most favored courtiers lounged in chairs or leaned against the wall by the casements, awaiting their master's pleasure. The King surrounded himself with wits and buffoons, for "as he had an extraordinary share of wit himself, so he loved it in others."[7] He remained a paradox. He was sharp enough of mind to study the sciences, but though "he had much compass of knowledge . . . he was never capable of much application or study." He excelled "in playing off one faction in Parliament or Court against another," and "no age produced a greater master in the art of dissimulation, yet no man was less on his guard, or sooner deceived in the intentions of others."

"The ruin of his reign and of all his affairs was occasioned chiefly by his delivering himself up at his first coming over to a mad range of pleasures."[8] For the majority of his subjects, "all the King meant and sought was to enjoy a lazy, thoughtless ease in the constant debauchery of amours and in the pleasures of wit and laughter with the most worthless, vicious and abandoned set of men that even that age afforded, and who often made him the subject of their jokes and mirth, even to his face."[9]

A trio of ill-favored men in shabby clothes awaited His Majesty's notice, each with an array of potions in vivid hues. Charles was well known for his patronage of mountebanks and charlatans and seemingly undisturbed by the sums of money they extracted from him for their sovereign remedies. But on the rare occasions that he was genuinely ill, he dismissed every one of them from his presence and entrusted himself only to the care of the royal physicians he at other times ignored.

Despite the early hour, a group of nobles was already gaming at a table laden with goblets of wine and gold coins. Pepys's hungry eyes feasted on this scene of "inexpressible luxury and profaneness, gaming and all dis-soluteness, and as it were total forgetfulness of God (it being Sunday) . . . the King sitting and toying with his concubines . . . whilst about twenty of the great courtiers and other dissolute persons were at basset around a great table, a bank of at least £2000 in gold in front of them."[10]

Pepys bowed low before the King and remained in a half-crouch as he waited to be acknowledged, his face working with barely suppressed excitement and self-importance.

The King's brother, James, Duke of York, Lord High Admiral of the Fleet, stood at the window watching him. He was immaculately attired and aloof both from his older brother and from the gaming of the nobles. Like his brother, he had been "bred with strange notions of the obedience due to princes," but he was a man of proven courage and great application to the business of state, much of which his elder brother delegated to him while he was at his pleasures. "Lacking his brother's ready wit, he had no vivacity of thought, invention or expression, but he had a good judgement where his religion or his education did not give him a bias, which it did very frequently."[11] He was lean and ascetic, his expression permanently dour and his thin lips pursed as if in disapproval of Charles's sybaritic excesses, but in one thing they were united. James was equally relentless in his pursuit of fresh amours among the women of the Court and the city, and his own mistress, Lady Denham, was also present awaiting his pleasure.

He stifled a yawn as he studied Pepys. Such men were valuable to princes, when their own avarice could be coupled to industry and efficiency in the Crown's affairs, and the Duke had appointed Pepys Clerk of the Acts at the Navy Office, though he held few illusions about him. He was competent enough, but a barely concealed air of greed and low cunning clung to him, coupled with an all-too-evident desire to ingratiate himself with his betters, as if by contact with them he could gain the position that his breeding denied him.

The Duke saw his brother's interest kindle as Pepys recounted the ravages of the fire that had sprung up in the night. A clerk was summoned and the King dictated and signed a parchment. He handed it to Pepys, instructing him to find Sir Thomas Bludworth and give him the royal orders. The parchment authorized the Lord Mayor to "spare no houses but pull down before the fire every way."[12] Several companies of the King's Guards were also to be sent to the city.

The Duke of York motioned to Pepys as he bowed and began to back out of the chamber. He told him to send word to the Lord Mayor that he should have any additional soldiers he might require for the task.

Captain Cocke, a colleague at the Navy Office, lent Pepys his coach, and he departed at once, while His Majesty and his courtiers readied themselves to view the blaze from the royal barge. The courtiers were always glad of any temporary diversion from the languor and stupor of the Court, but a few of his closest intimates also seemed to share their King's excitement and high good humor.

In the past the least rumor of a fire had seen him take to the river in his barge to scour the city skyline in search of the blaze. More than once he had alighted to take personal charge of fire-fighting operations, his eyes glowing with excitement, unconcerned for his clothes trailing in the mud or the state of his exquisite cuffs and ruffs as smuts and water rained around him.

While they prepared themselves, Pepys began his search for the Lord Mayor. Such was the press of people now in the streets that he was forced to abandon the coach at St. Paul's. He went on from there on foot, battling against a tide of refugees fleeing from the fire down Watling Street.

Further fueled by the hops and barley malt stored in one of the many riverside breweries, the fire had swept over Ebgate Lane, very narrow because of encroachments, and devoured the three rambling, weather-boarded buildings at the head of the Old Swan Stairs, well used by those who preferred a river crossing to the interminable delays on the bridge, or who chose not to shoot the arches by boat.

Beyond the stairs, across Katharine Wheel Alley, stood Dyers' Hall, an ancient, ruinous building so decrepit that the members of the Company of Dyers were already considering its demolition. The flames spared them the labor, roaring through the hall, melting the suits of armor and much of the gold and silver plate stored there.

They burned on, cauterizing the filthy tenements of Coldharbor around White Cock Alley and Red Bull Alley. Once a sanctuary for debtors and fugitives, Coldharbor was approached by a stinking, dark alley beneath the choir of All Hallows the Less. Like the rookeries in its shadow, the church was utterly destroyed, leaving no memorial but shattered stones and piles of smoking ashes. The Water Gate of Coldharbor still stood, but all else was swept away.

All Hallows the More, a few yards to the west, was next to burn. Those walls not destroyed in the fire were so weakened that they were blown down by the wind after the flames had moved on. The steeple alone survived, but so fierce was the heat within it that the bells melted where they hung. They fell to earth in a stream of molten metal, long before the great oak beams supporting them had burnt through.

The gathering pall of smoke, the sparks and flecks of fire carried on the wind, and the clashing sound of reverse peals of the bells from a succession of churches as the fire spilled from parish to parish now generated the first widespread alarm in the city. People filled the streets and clambered onto the church towers and their own rooftops, straining to see the flames. "We came into Gracechurch Street and there, from the top of an high house, saw it was come as far west as Coldharbor, and as far northward as Crooked Lane. Returning homeward we found a party of forty horse of the Life-guard in Cornhill and met some companies of the King's regiments, and of the Trained Bands and auxiliaries, marching into the city."[13]

Wild rumors began to spread that the city had been willfully fired. Fleet Street was jammed with people, and a horseman thundering through the crowds "with more speed and fear than wit, crying 'Arm! Arm!' frightened most of the people out of the churches."[14] "While we were at church, there was a cry in the streets that the Dutch and French were in arms and had fired the city."[15]

Some people fled their homes at once, while others clung stubbornly to their dwellings until the fire was at their very doors, then ran through the streets with their hair and clothes singed and smoldering.

Pigeons stayed in their roosts in the eaves and gables of the houses even as the fire advanced on them. Many delayed too long. They fluttered about the rooftops trailing wisps of smoke from charred and scorched wings, then plummeted to their deaths. One took flight with its wings fully ablaze. Driven west by the wind, its blackened, still burning body crashed, already lifeless, into a roof, spreading the fire still further.

Every street and lane in the vicinity of the fire was thronged with laden carts and people bent double under the weight of goods carried on their heads and backs. Some of the sick were also carried aloft, still in their beds or blankets.

The streets were a bedlam of noise: the rumble of iron wheels, the cracking of whips, the rattle of carts jolting over the cobbles, the stamp of hooves, the sound of running feet, and a cacophony of shouts and yells, voices raised in curses or prayers, and "the fearful cries and howlings of undone people."[16] "Beside the dreadful scenes of flames, ruins and desolation, there appeared the most killing sight under the sun, the distracted looks of so many citizens, the wailings of miserable women and the cries of poor children and decrepit old people with all the marks of confusion and despair."[17]

Above all rose the deadly, thunderous roar of the fires, the crash of falling stone and timber, and the noise of shattered glass or fractured stone, pierced by explosive detonations as superheated casks of brandy, black powder, and a thousand other combustibles succumbed to the flames.

The surface of the Thames around the bridge was already crowded with boats laden with people who had escaped with no other covering than a blanket. They stared at the fires in stunned disbelief. "No man that had the sense of human miseries could unconcernedly behold the dismal ravage and destruction made in one of the noblest cities of the world."[18]

Unaware that the Royal Authority had now been issued, Sir Thomas Bludworth had nonetheless been so alarmed by the rapid advance of the flames that he had organized a few groups of men from the Trained Bands to pull down houses. They began to do so despite the fierce opposition of "tenacious and avaricious men, aldermen et cetera, [who] would not permit because their houses must have been the first."[19]

As the houses were demolished, clouds of dust swirled through the air, mingling with the smoke from the advancing fires and shrouding every outline in a fog backlit by the diffused glow of flames. But although firebreaks were at last made, "they always began too near the fire, by which they were forced from their work ere finished."[20] The flames either were upon them before the breaks had been completed, or else seized on the timbers and laths among the rubble left mounded in the street and burned unhindered across the gap.

In the confusion and chaos, and the headlong rush to save possessions from the conflagration, almost all other attempts to fight the fires had been abandoned. When Pepys at last came upon Bludworth, who had a handkerchief wrapped around his face like a highwayman to keep the smoke from his nose and mouth, the Lord Mayor was already beaten. "Walking towards the fire, we were stopped in Cannon Street by the abundance of goods and carts with which it was filled. Here we met my Lord Mayor on horseback and with a few attendants, looking like one frightened out of his wits."[21] In that he was far from alone.

When Pepys handed him the Royal Authority, Bludworth exclaimed "like a fainting woman," "Lord, what can I do? I am spent. People will not obey me, I have been pulling down houses but the fire overtakes us faster than we can do it."[22] He told Pepys that he needed no more soldiers, but had to go and refresh himself for he had been up all night. With that he rode away. He was not seen on the streets again for three days.

It was now early afternoon, and the fire ignited twelve hours earlier was still growing. Each burning building further fueled the conflagration and increased the speed of its advance.

Many of those at present beyond its reach remained unperturbed. Francisco de Rapicani had returned to Covent Garden that morning with his friend Baumann "and we spent the Sunday there together. At midday he took me to a meal with some of his friends, where there was a fine company gathered, including some men and women from the city. They were—God forgive us—quite cheerful for so perilous and sorry a time, but some of those who had come to us from the city suffered great loss, for before they could get back home, their houses had gone up in fire and smoke. The fire was spreading with such fury that it was thought that about a hundred houses were being burnt every hour."[23]

It continued its remorseless progress throughout the day, burning a half-mile swath west along the riverfront. The wind also continually scattered flecks of fire far in advance of the main body of the flames, "great flakes carried up into the air at least three furlongs."[24] Lodging in roofs and gutters, they ignited fresh blazes, "breaking out in several places at so great distances from each other," adding to the confusion and panic and fueling rumors that the blazes were "fed by design," by incendiaries casting fire-balls into houses. Several French and Dutch were said to have been "taken with little hand-grenades about the size of a ball which they carried in their pockets." There were "a hundred stories of people taken with fire-balls and others endeavoring with matches to fire other places."

The fires burning along the waterfront through Coldharbor had now set alight Watermen's Hall. The members of the guild were all on the river in their lighters and wherries reaping the harvest of the fire, hiring out themselves and their craft. Not a man could be spared from such lucrative work to save their own company hall. A mere handful of papers somehow survived; all their other records, pictures, plate, and valuables were consumed.

As the hall burned, the King and the Duke of York, attended by some of the courtiers, came into sight, sailing downriver to view the fires. A company of the King's Guards followed in another barge. To some of the royal party at least, they "came to see King Charles I avenged."[25] They landed at the Three Cranes in Vintry and Their Majesties ascended to a roof from where they could watch the destruction of Watermen's Hall.

The King was at once busy giving directions for more houses to be pulled down before the fire, but so fast did it advance that little could be done. Unchecked, the flames swept on to engulf the Steelyard, roaring through the three arched gateways opening onto Thames Street. The ancient hall of the Hansa merchants, dominated by its stone tower, overlooked a site that covered three acres. There stood the Rhenish winehouse and the houses and warehouses of the merchants trading in everything from grains and fibers to cables, masts, and steel.

Every building was destroyed, and so fast were the flames now moving that the master of the hall was forced to flee with his clothes ablaze. Behind him the treasures and paintings of the wealthy guild were left to the mercy of the flames. The warehouses were crammed with goods, providing plentiful fresh fuel, and the fires in the Steelyard raged all that afternoon and deep into the night.

There were still hopes of stopping the fire at the Three Cranes, but the King and the Duke did not care to wait for the outcome of that. They returned upriver to Whitehall, leaving the Earl of Craven with a Royal Command to assist the Lord Mayor and the magistrates. Craven had shown conspicuous courage and charity in the plague year, remaining in his great house at the bottom of Drury Lane and giving large sums of his own money to aid the sufferers and build pesthouses, but such assistance as he could now offer was feeble in the face of the new peril threatening London.

A downpour of rain, a change in the wind, and that peril might yet have been averted, but the skies remained clear and cloudless, and far from abating, the wind continued to blow with steadily mounting force.

Against so fierce a gale, the fires near the seat of the blaze in Pudding Lane and Fish Street Hill were only inching their way eastward toward the Tower and northward up the hill toward Gracechurch Street. More than fourteen hours after the blaze had erupted, "getting round into Little Eastcheap, we came so near as to look into Fish Street and perceived it was then, being four o'clock, within five houses of the upper end of the street.

Thence we went into Pudding Lane and observed not above three houses burnt in that lane on the north side of the house where it began."[26]

Farther west, however, the flames met the rising ground beyond the Walbrook, an open stream in medieval times but long enclosed, its course visible only as the meandering valley between the two hills on which the city stood. The fires began to make a stealthy progress up the hill, seeping into the alleys and courts on the north side of Thames Street. Invisible to watchers at the waterside, they were now starting to eat their way toward the heart of the city.

Once more, thousands of people, bent under the burden of their goods, carried them ahead of the flames to the sanctuary of the churches lining the ridge around Cannon Street. They were soon given dramatic notice of how illusory that refuge could be. A burning brand carried on the wind five hundred feet from the fires still raging on Fish Street Hill lodged in the very tip of the slender, tapering spire of St. Lawrence Pountney Church, one of the tallest in the city.

Stuck fast in a crevice, the brand smoldered and almost died out, but fanned back into life by the wind, it again burned brightly. The lead sheath encasing the spire was cracked and old, and the flames soon penetrated it. Aided by the dust, moss, and lichen of centuries, dried to tinder by the baking drought, the wooden framework caught fire. As it burned, the sheath melted. Molten lead falling down through the steeple and tower ignited the timbers beneath.

The black, needle-sharp shape of the spire outlined against the flames that engulfed it was like a dagger thrust at the heart of the city. It was visible as far as the Temple Gardens to the west. The sight of it and the manner of its ignition created fresh panic in the surrounding streets. Blazing up so far in advance of the main body of the fire, it seemed to offer fresh confirmation that incendiaries were loose on the streets, firing and torching as they went. "Other houses were discovered to be burning which were near no place from whence they could imagine the fire could come; all of which kindled another fire in the breasts of men, almost as dangerous as that within their houses."[27]

The scale of the disaster that was engulfing London had not been evident to most of its citizens until now, but as darkness fell and the black pall of smoke over the city merged with the night sky, the true extent of the fires could be seen. "I was that evening a second time on the water, and it was then it appeared with all the horror and dreadfulness imaginable, the flames afforded light enough to discover themselves, the black smoke and the buildings they so imminently threatened."[28]

The "most horrid, malicious, bloody flames,"[29] dimmed by the afternoon sun, were now revealed in all their terrifying extent, a great arc half a mile in length. The outer edge was marked by a continuous line of fire, sharp as a headsman's ax. Behind it, the ground already conquered, lay a blackened, smoking wasteland, studded with the still blazing remnants of churches, halls, and houses, and the infernos that had been warehouses of oil, pitch, and spirits. The heaps of coal and timber on the quays still burned ferociously, as they would do for days.

A lake of fire covered much of the city, the blackened towers and spires of churches rising from it like dead trees submerged by a great flood. Melted pitch "in flaming cloud," tallow, oils, and animal fats poured in blazing streams down the steep streets and alleys at the waterfront. As they spread over the surface of the river, they ignited the furniture, wool bales, and other flammable materials already thrown into the water, giving the impression that even the Thames was now ablaze, "like nothing so much as a sheet of flame."[30]

All night long, the river was covered with boats emerging from the shadows by the boat-stairs and wharves into the baleful red glare of the fires, as they ferried goods and people to the safety of the south bank. The wharves at Southwark were piled high with goods and merchandise, furniture, and household effects. Other boats held station in midstream while spectators, both fascinated and appalled, watched the onward march of the flames.

"The raging east wind . . . in a moment raised the fire from the bottom to the tops of the houses and scattered prodigious flakes in all places, which were mounted so vastly high into the air as if heaven and earth were threatened with the same conflagration."[31]

Smoke hung like fog over the water, and a downpour of sparks and flakes and drops of fire fell hissing into the river. The watchers and fire fugitives in their boats were constantly beating out smoldering embers lodged in their coats.

More of the goods and furniture thrown into the river for want of a boat were ignited by the falling sparks, adding their smoke and flames to the infernal glare. The three-quarter moon was stained a livid red, then hidden completely behind the billowing clouds of smoke, but its light was not needed. The glow of the fires illuminated the night streets of the city more brightly than they had ever been lit before. The clouds of smoke were so densely charged with sparks and blazing embers that it was almost impossible to tell them from the flames.

As the night wore on, so the fires advanced even further, moving up the hill away from the mean waterfront districts into the commercial heart of the city. The Steelyard was still blazing, but the vanguard of the fire had moved on, burning its way through Cougar Lane, around Dowgate Dock, and roaring on up Dowgate Hill, devouring the half-demolished houses that were being pulled down to make a firebreak. As the flames swept through from Emperor's Head Alley and Pisspot Alley to Three Cranes Lane, the magnificent Skinners' Hall and the halls of the Tallow Chandlers and Innholders were consumed. The master of Tallow Chandlers' Hall escaped to Hampstead in a coach, bearing with him the guild records and plate, but the medieval building, arranged around a small courtyard, was completely destroyed.

By eight that night, the fires by the waterfront had burned their way as far as the Three Cranes at Vintry. The great cranes, driven by rumbling treadwheels and used to haul hogsheads and casks of wine and brandy from the holds of ships clustered around the wharf, burst into flames and toppled one by one. The Three Cranes tavern, one of the oldest in London, was also burned to the ground. The flames rose to engulf the rooftop where only a few hours before the King and his brother had stood to view the then distant blaze.

So long confined around the northern end of Fish Street Hill, the fires had also now broken out from there. The church of St. Michael in Crooked Lane, a long, low building with a crenellated roof, surrounded by a "filthy plot by reason of the butchers in East cheap, who made the same their laystall,"[32] was burnt to a cinder. The steeple above its squat tower crashed in flames through the roof of the nave. A few yards away, the tiny church of St. Martin Orgar was also razed to the ground.

As the flames traveled on, ever hungry, in the dead of that Sunday night, they burned Eastcheap, destroying the Boar's Head Tavern, where Shakespeare had caroused and imagined the revels of Falstaff, Mistress Quickly, and Doll Tearsheet.

Raging westward, engulfing everything in their path, they advanced toward the blaze spreading from St. Lawrence Pountney. At the same time, flames were also burning up the hill from above the ruins of All Hallows on Thames Street. The three fires joined forces, and united, they swept forward with a rush to destroy Suffolk House and the Merchant Taylors'

School. John Goad, the schoolmaster, snatched a few volumes from the library in the teeth of the flames, but all the rest were lost.

During the daylight hours on Sunday, people had moved themselves and their possessions a little way from the flames into the houses of friends or acquaintances, or piled them in the churches. Those outside the immediate area of the fire merely watched and waited. After nightfall, when the flames grew more visible and the scale of the blaze was more evident, a general panic ensued. The alarms until then had been chiefly about the papists and the fears of invasion by the Dutch or the French, but now people's only concern was to save their goods and valuables.

Buildings were now burning only a few yards from Cannon Street, and the possessions lodged in the churches there were moved north again to Lombard Street and beyond to Cornhill, until the nave of every church was filled to the rafters with goods.

Chapter 5

A Hideous Storm

Monday, September 3, 1666

bye pyppins good

Bowels of bells a yearning fall
And melting weep at the black funerall.
Lo, stately marble monuments become,
Instead of others, their own smoakie tomb:
Noe other epitaph you can espie,
Save only this ... Here Dust and Ashes lie.
England's Lamentation for the Dismall Conflagration of her
Imperial Chamber of the Citie of London

T HE GLOW OF THE FIRES AND THE SPURTS OF FLAME SOARING
into the heavens had lit up the windows of the Palace of Whitehall
during the night. Citizens gathering outside the walls of his palace, held
back by the company of Guards stationed before the gates, had woken
Charles with their pleas of "God and the King save us."[1]

If he needed any further intimation of the danger that London now faced, the dawn breaking dim and baleful that Monday morning provided it. It was cloudless once more, but the blue sky and rising sun were obscured by the pall of smoke extending across London to the western horizon. Charles had risen at a far earlier hour than was his custom, and from the windows of the Royal Bedchamber he could see that the gale still blowing from a few points north of east was sending the smoke from the burning city directly over Whitehall. It was a signal he could no longer ignore. What had seemed at first a fire to cauterize the meaner quarters of the city and extirpate the lingering menace of the plague now threatened the whole of London, and its richest as well as its poorest citizens. If the fires were not stemmed, the King himself would be burned from his home.

On the previous day he had returned to Whitehall after an hour's inspection of the fires, having made no more than token attempts to control them. Now, sensing that not just his palace but his throne was in peril, he summoned his Council. In place of the Lord Mayor, the King gave James, Duke of York, supreme control of the city. A string of seasonable commands was issued at once, bringing some order and direction to the haphazard attempts that had so far been made to control the fires.

Handpicked nobles, each in command of a group of men, were put in charge of the fire stations, and more troops were sent into the city. The justices of the peace for Middlesex were summoned to Ely Place in Holborn to deliberate on the means of subduing the fire. Meanwhile an arc of fireposts was set up outside the city walls, some distance ahead of the flames, running from Cow Lane in Smithfield through Shoe Lane, Fetter Lane, and Clifford's Inn Gardens to Temple Bar.

A further ring of fireposts was also set up closer to the firefront in Aldersgate, Coleman Street, and Cripplegate. Each was provisioned with beer, bread, and cheese, and the parish constables were ordered to attend with a hundred men and thirty foot-soldiers "with a good careful officer and three gentlemen" to direct the work. Any man "diligent at night" was to be rewarded with a shilling of the King's money. Whatever fate should befall the city itself, their tacit orders were to find means to ensure the survival of Whitehall and Westminster.

Instructions were sent to the Lord Lieutenants of the surrounding counties to draw their militia in around London, to relieve those soldiers and citizens already exhausted by their battles with the flames. Seamen

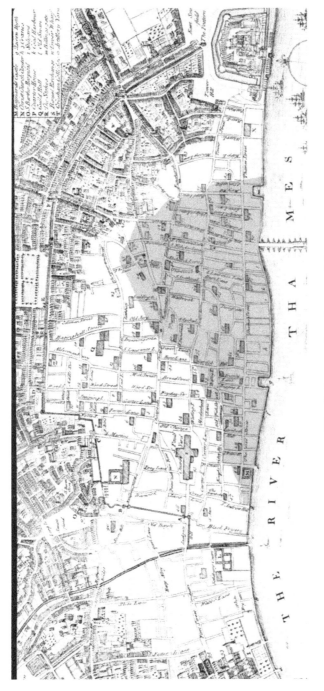

The fire's spread on the second day.

were called up from the dockyards at Deptford and Woolwich and from the ships of the Fleet in the Thames. They began the work of pulling down houses before the fire, demolishing them with rope and chain.

The task they faced was growing greater with every passing hour. Fierce fires were burning along Eastcheap and Cannon Street, raging north on Gracechurch Street, and still burning west through the waterfront districts flanking Thames Street, where Joiners' Hall and Vintners' Hall, with its wharf and the almshouses built around its quadrangle, had now been destroyed.

More churches were erupting in flames, including three within yards of one another on the hill above Thames Street: St. Martin's Vintry, St. James's Garlickhithe, and St. Michael Paternoster Royal above Elbow Lane. In the last of these, the marble tomb of Richard Whittington, four times Lord Mayor of London, shattered in the heat as the church and its almshouses were razed. Cutlers' Hall, higher on the hill, burned a short while later.

Thomas Farriner and his daughter had found temporary refuge with a friend, a fellow baker, in one of the lanes running south from Cannon Street, but once more they were forced to flee as the approaching rumble of flames and the crash of falling buildings told its own grim story.

As they hurried away, Thomas saw an old couple sweeping the dust and dirt from their door with brooms. Never was there more pointless work. Thomas shouted to them, but they waved him away and continued with their sweeping even as the sparks from the advancing fires rained down around them, setting their clothes smoldering. As the sparks struck the ground, they spilled outward in rings of fire, merging and fading like ripples on a pond but continually renewed by the fireflakes falling from the heavens.

The old couple were lost to Thomas's sight as thick smoke billowed around them. His own lungs filled with acrid fumes and he sank to his knees. A moment later a house wall collapsed with a roar, almost burying him in the debris. He dragged himself up and took Hannah by the arm, and they fled before the flames again, the air still burning in their lungs. They ran into any street that looked darker than its neighbors, hoping that there the fires might burn less fiercely or even pass them by.

Wraithlike figures appeared out of the swirling clouds of smoke and dust, laboring to draw breath as they staggered through the streets. Others, blinded by smoke and burning sparks, groped their way along the walls, fleeing the heat and noise. They saw people stumble and slump to the ground, or crawl on all fours to get away from the flames. Hands grasped at Thomas and tried to cling to him, but he brushed them away.

The smoke lifted for a moment, and he filled his lungs with drafts of still hot but sweeter air. Then the billowing clouds closed in again, and the stench of smoke and sulfur once more flooded his nostrils. In the next street, an oak chest and a looking glass stood abandoned against a wall. As he hurried past, Thomas caught a glimpse of a reflection, a wild-eyed face, the skin burned red, blistered, and covered with tiny, pitted black marks, and so swollen that the eyes were no more than narrow slits. He could have been looking at a stranger. He turned away and hurried on.

Their ragged course took them northward, though they had only the most vague awareness of that. They sought only whatever sanctuary they could find, praying all the while for some relief from the judgment of fire upon them. As they ran, a horse went careering through the streets ahead of them, its eyes wild with terror, its coat and mane ablaze.

Each fresh outbreak of flame as the wind hurled flakes of fire overhead caused consternation and panic. Every street and lane was piled high with goods and choked with traffic. Carts and coaches jostled for space with people on foot staggering under their burdens. Thomas and Hannah found streets blocked with rubble from isolated fires or from houses pulled down to make firebreaks. The roads were left cratered as freestone pavements and cobbles were torn up and pipes severed in search of water to fight the flames, and these became yet another obstruction to those attempting to flee. Horses fell and broke their legs, carts overturned, blocking the street, and were abandoned to burn where they lay.

Soldiers also held back the crowds at many points, keeping the streets free for those fighting the fires. Each time, Thomas and Hannah were caught up in the panic-stricken retreat of the mob, further choking the lanes and streets to the west and north of the fires.

In the confusion, many of the carters and carriers and the thousands of people fleeing for their lives found themselves taking any unblocked street or lane as they sought a way around the obstructions. Driven by the wind and the fire to parts of the city unfamiliar to them, many became grievously lost in the warrens of narrow, winding alleys and dead-end courts. Not all who entered those mazes emerged again.

The traffic was not only out of the city. As news of the great fire spread, every cart owner and boat owner within reach of London was making his way toward the city. "It seems the whole country, ten miles round from London, came posting in with their carts, wagons and teams, and all very ready to help these deplorable citizens in their great distress away with their goods."[2] Laborers who had no carts poured into London on foot to offer themselves as beasts of burden.

For the second time in the space of a year, the established order of the city was turned on its head. In the plague year, the drunk, the vagrant, and the hitherto unemployable had been put to work, their wages undreamed of, though the ultimate fate of many was death.

Now the fire had once more made the poor all-powerful, and the rich their helpless pawns. The wealthiest merchant of Lombard Street might be forced to beg like a supplicant seeking alms for the muscle to carry away his fine goods and his riches.

"I am sorry to be the messenger of so dismal news," Lady Hobart wrote from her house in Chancery Lane. "There was never so sad a sight, nor so doleful a cry heard, my heart is not able to express the tenth, nay, the thousandth part of it. . . . All the carts within ten miles round, and cars and drays, run about night and day and thousands of men and women carrying burdens. I am almost out of my wits. We have packed up all our goods and cannot get a cart for money, they give five and ten pounds for carts. I have sent for carts to my Lady Glascock if I can get them, but I fear I shall lose all I have and must run away. Oh, pray for us now, the cries make me I know not what to say, oh pity me. . . . Oh I shall lose all I have, we have sent to see for carts to send to Highgate and cannot get one for twenty pounds to go out of town."[3]

The hire of a cart—a couple of shillings on the Saturday before the fire began—rose to five, ten, twenty, and even forty pounds. One rich merchant paid £400 for the removal of his goods.[4] "Some of the country men had the conscience to accept of the highest price which the citizens did then offer in their extremity. I am mistaken if such money do not burn worse than the fire out of which it was raked."[5]

Even those prices did not yield profit enough for some. "In this pinching extreme occasion, the carters stood for ten and twenty pounds a cart to take up their goods; and after they bargained (with grief I tell it) they would not trust, but required their money beforehand and then went fairly away with the goods and the money and were never heard of more."[6] "Certain persons, assuming the character of porters, but in reality nothing else but downright plunderers, came and offered their assistance in removing our goods. We accepted, but they so far availed themselves of our service as to steal goods to the value of forty pounds."[7] It became "a removal out of the danger of the fire into a den of thieves. The riches of London and the substance of the inhabitants thereof were as well devoured by suburban thieves and by the country men's extortion for their carts and conveyances as by the fire."[8]

The great crowds fleeing London and those moving into it clashed repeatedly at the narrow city gates. Huge backlogs of people and carts filled all the surrounding streets; blows were exchanged and swords drawn.

By Monday afternoon the magistrates had been persuaded to order that the city gates should be shut and no further carts be admitted to the neighborhood of the fire. By so doing they hoped to compel people to abandon their attempts to salvage their own goods, and "while the gates were shut, that, no hopes of saving any things left, they might have more desperately endeavored the quenching of the fire,"[9] by assisting the troops and Trained Bands. In this the magistrates were disappointed. The order succeeded in neither aim and was rescinded the following day, having "occasioned the loss of much goods. Some pressed carts, others for want of them lost all; and sometimes their numerousness would hinder one the other."[10]

The fires raced on through the shoreline, ravaging the rest of the Vintry district, its breweries and brandy and wine stores so much fresh fuel for the flames. By ten on Monday morning the fires had crossed Townsend Lane and were within a few yards of Queenhithe Dock, lined with the houses and stores of merchants, and "a place of much trade for ground corn or meal which is brought out of the West Country."[11]

The huge dock had once shared with Billingsgate all the shipping traffic into London from overseas, but its trade had declined and Billingsgate's increased when the drawbridge on London Bridge fell out of use, preventing larger vessels from passing upstream. A great marketplace remained behind Queenhithe, and here it was hoped a stop could be put to the fire.

The King himself traveled down from Whitehall in his barge and landed at Queenhithe to encourage the men employed in removing the market stalls and demolishing the houses to create a firebreak. He remained there for half an hour before returning to Whitehall, but "all those endeavors were slighted by a leap which the fire made over twenty houses upon the turret of a house in Thames Street."[12] The house burned to the ground and the flames roared on.

The King and the Duke of York were frequently in the city throughout the rest of the day. "The Duke of York and many of the nobility were as diligent as was possible. They commended and encouraged the forward, assisted the miserable sufferers and gave a most generous example to all by the vigorous opposition they made against the devouring flames."[13] The Duke continued to "ride with his guard up and down the City to keep all quiet," traveling as far east as the Navy Office in Seething Lane.

The King had already made arrangements to begin the transport of his treasure upstream, but he concealed his anxiety as he also traveled around the perimeter of the fire, encouraging and exhorting the soldiers, members of the Trained Bands and such civilians as had been pressed to the task to extinguish the fires or create firebreaks ahead of them. He gave "orders for pursuing the work by commands, threatenings, desires, example and good store of money which he distributed to the workers out of a bag of one hundred pounds, carried for that purpose."[14]

Few stood ready to take the King's shilling. The fire was left to do what it might, and the only concern of the vast majority was to escape with their lives and whatever goods they could carry. The great exodus from the city, begun in the dark hours of Sunday night, continued throughout Monday.

Samuel Pepys had been up at four that morning, loading "all my money and plate and best things" into a cart Lady Batten had sent him. He traveled to Sir William Rider's house in Bethnal Green, "riding myself in my nightgown in the cart, and Lord, to see how the streets and the highways are crowded with people running and riding, and getting of carts to fetch away things."[15]

He continued to move his goods away throughout that day, hiring a lighter to take them downriver. "We did carry them, myself some, over Tower Hill, which was by this time full of people's goods . . . and down to the lighter which lay at the next quay above the Tower Dock. And here was my neighbor's wife . . . with her pretty child and some few of her things, which I did willingly give way to be saved with mine, but there was no passing with anything through the postern, the crowd was so great."[16]

Few now thought to seek refuge for themselves within the city walls, where the surviving churches and company halls were already stacked high with goods and thronged with frightened people. Most instead sought the safety of the open fields. Those finally free of the burning city laid themselves down in Goodman's Fields to the east of the Minories or Moorfields north of the city. There they settled themselves among the mounds and hummocks of earthworks thrown up to protect London from attack during the Civil War. They kept watch on their goods and snatched a little rest in the dark hours that the fire lit as bright as day, while more and more of the dispossessed crowded around them.

These were the medieval tenterfields where the cloth weavers had spread their fabrics to dry, still used as the drying ground of the city's laundresses. Two years before the fire Sir William Davenant saw "acres of old linen making a show like the fields of Carthagena when the five month shifts of the whole fleet are washed and spread."[17]

Now those same fields were littered with the distraught and dispossessed, while never-ending streams of their fellows still poured from the city gates, seeking out a few yards of open space where they too could lay down their burdens.

The east wind continued to howl, sending smoke swirling around them, half choking them as rains of sparks fell at intervals from the sky. Lit by the glare of the flames, their rest was constantly troubled by the noise of the firestorms: the crash of falling masonry, the thunder of collapsing walls and towers, and the crack of explosions as stones heated in the furnaces of the fires shattered and blew apart.

Not all the citizens had been so quick to flee. The troops and Trained Bands maintained what order they could near the periphery of the fire, but around them all was chaos and confusion. "The goods lodged in the fields, guildhalls and churches, or abandoned in houses as the fire approached, offered rich rewards" to looters. "In the forsaken shops of the wealthy inhabitants, numbers of thieves and pilferers greedier of booty than the fire, villainously skulked,"[18] "to prog [scavenge] for themselves and to pilfer from them whom the fire sufficiently threatened and at last preyed upon."[19] Risking their lives, they raided houses even as the flames licked around them and prospered so much that "the thieves had not the strength to carry all their booty."

One great arm of fire continued to rage westward along the waterfront, devouring everything on either side of Thames Street, but another was now developing. The flames had been slow to consume the buildings north of

Eastcheap and Cannon Street, but as the wind shifted a couple of points
farther from the north during the morning and the raging fires swelled into
firestorms, these densely packed districts gave themselves up to the inferno.
Half a dozen churches stood among this warren; all were burned. The
parish register of St. Mary Abchurch was snatched so late from the flames
that the scorch marks are still visible upon it.

Mr. Langley, the warden of St. Mary Woolchurch Hawe, was at work
with a couple of men and a hired cart moving his own possessions when the
sexton and a group of parishioners came running to his house bearing "the
new great Bible . . . embroidered bear cloths and cushions,"[20] the register and
the sacramental plate from the church. The warden bade his men load the
church property onto the cart and take it to safety before returning for his
own goods, but the fires arrived before the men came back and he could only
stand and watch as his house and all his goods were consumed by the flames.

A burning arc was also extending up Gracechurch Street, threatening
Lombard Street and Cornhill. The lower end of Gracechurch Street, the city's
original grass market, still served as a market for herbs and fruit, but houses,
shops, and stalls had steadily encroached on the once broad, open space. The
fire swept across the remaining gap and burned both sides of the road, climbing the hill away from the poorhouses, workshops, and tenements and into an
area lined with "divers fair houses," the residences of merchants and bankers.

The old conduit in the middle of Gracechurch Street and St. Benet's
Church on the corner with Fenchurch Street was destroyed, but driven on
by the gale, the fires raged with even more ferocity through Lombard
Street. It was narrow and twisting, and lined with great Elizabethan and
medieval houses three and four stories high, crowned with richly worked
jetties and casements projecting above a forest of painted and gilded signs.
There were more fine houses in the streets and alleys running north and
south of Lombard Street, the financial heart of the city, where the wealthiest men of the land had residence.

Sir Robert Vyner, showing the characteristic prudence of the richest of
them all, took alarm earlier than his neighbors. All his papers and bonds
were moved out of his great house next to St. Mary Woolnoth Church
twenty-four hours before the fire consumed the street.

The other great merchants were also able to safeguard their gold, bonds,
and securities, moving them just before the fire reached the street. Nothing
else could be saved as the flames swept from one end of the street to the

other like a tornado. By four o'clock the whole of Lombard Street, from the churches of All Hallows and St. Edmund King and Martyr at the eastern end to St. Mary Woolnoth at the western end, had been laid in ruins.

There was now nothing to halt the flames' progress through the densely packed streets to the north of Lombard Street, and they soon were threatening Cornhill. "Coming back and taking a melancholy dinner, we went into the city about three o'clock. We got into Thames Street and so round by the skirts of the fire, though with much difficulty, through the streets barricaded with goods, carts and coaches. By the time we had reached Cornhill, the fire had consumed Lombard Street and was within forty yards of this. The Duke of York was in another part of the city. We came home at five o'clock and seeing little probability in a desired stop, three of us of this house packed up our books, etc, and put them aboard a barge."[21]

Cornhill was one of the most broad and spacious thoroughfares in the city and one of the most fashionable, packed, like the streets and lanes opening off it, with the shops of mercers, glovers, and merchants selling a host of other luxuries. As the fire raged nearer, a company of the King's Guard under the command of the Duke of Monmouth forced the crowds of desperate people out of Cornhill. The young and handsome Duke, just eighteen years old, had only recently been acknowledged by the King as his bastard son, despite the opinions of those who argued that for a man to recognize his bastards was to "shit in his hat and then clap it on his head."[22]

Monmouth had been elevated to the peerage with precedence over all other peers not of the Blood Royal. He would end his days a score of years later on the executioner's block at Tower Hill, after leading a rebellion against his uncle, James II, during which he accused him of causing the Great Fire.

For now, though, his sole aim was to extinguish it, and soldiers and men of the Trained Bands, together with a few civilians, began pulling down the houses on the south side of Cornhill, trying to broaden the already wide street into a firebreak that would halt the flames.

It was the only hope. There was no water to fight the fires; the wells were almost dry, and the conduits bringing water from the New River Head at Islington were empty. The elm quills—pipes—under the streets had been severed in a thousand places to fill fire buckets in unavailing attempts to stem the blazes. During the night what water remained had drained away, running uselessly down the streets and lanes to the river. As the fire burned on up the hill into "the very bowels of the city,"[23] almost every pipe and cistern was dry.

The great stone churches of St. Michael Archangel and St. Peter in Cornhill were almost hidden by the ranks of shops that over the years had advanced right up to their walls and porches. Squads of men and teams of horses heaved at ropes and chains attached to iron firehooks embedded in the gables and roof timbers of the houses. As they came crashing to the ground, the two churches stood revealed for the first time in centuries. Within hours both were destroyed.

The attempt to create a firebreak merely hastened the destruction of Cornhill. Scores of narrow alleys, unchanged since medieval times, opened onto the street, like bellows feeding a furnace, and the fires burned right through them. The mounds of rubble, timber, laths, and plaster left by the destruction of the houses had not been removed. The fire fastened on them and bridged Cornhill without even a momentary pause.

The church of St. Peter was razed to the ground and only the tower of St. Michael's was left standing. So fierce was the fire within the body of the church that it roared through each of the four timber stages in the tower in minutes, and burning through the supports, sent the great bells crashing to the ground. They sounded one final funereal knell as they tumbled, then were forever silenced.

The thunder of the fires could now be heard from one end of the city to the other, and their heat was so fierce that none could approach within a hundred yards, or look for long into the burning white heart of the flames.

The Royal Exchange, the "glory of the merchants," just north of Cornhill, now stood square in their path.[24] It was a cathedral of commerce, its trading floor swarming with merchants, the galleries and broad passageways full of shops patronized by people of quality.

A bell tower rose above the double-arched entrance, with a huge clock set in its southern face. The tower was capped by a cupola on which stood a golden grasshopper, the symbol of the builder of the Exchange, Sir Thomas Gresham. In the great courtyard, five thousand merchants struck their bargains, "buying, selling, bearing news" in English and a babble of foreign tongues—French, Spanish, German, Italian, Dutch, Swedish, and Portuguese. Among them was a merchant with three teeth fashioned from diamonds, "which he had inserted in India and which provided a glorious spectacle when the sun shone on them."[25]

The niches at first-floor level held statues of every English sovereign since the Conquest, and the vast quadrangle was surrounded by vaulted, marble-pillared colonnades that formed whispering galleries, where even soft-spoken words echoed and spread outward like ripples in water. Nobles, gallants, and fine ladies lingered in the cool shadows.

Two balconied galleries ran right around the building, full of shops and merchants' offices, each timber-framed with stout oak brought from Gresham's own Suffolk estates. They were filled with every luxury the wealth of a great trading nation could command:

> Here if anywhere, might a man have seen the glory of the world in a moment as the Devil showed it to Christ upon a high mountain. Was it not the great storehouse whence the nobility and gentry of England were furnished with most of those costly things where-with they did adorn either their closets or themselves? What artificial thing could entertain the senses and fantasies of men that was not there to be had?
>
> Such was the delight that many gallants took in that magazine of all curious varieties that they could almost have dwelt there, going from shop to shop like bees from flower to flower, if they had that fountain of money that could not have been drawn dry. I doubt not but a Mahomedan, who never expects other than sensible delights, would gladly have accepted of that place and the treasures of it for his heaven and have thought that there were none like it.[26]

Now the merchants and the gallants had fled, and the marble and stone proved no obstacle to the fire. A wall of flame swept along the encircling galleries and exploded out of the stairwells and walks, filling the whole courtyard with fire. Flames burst from the bell tower and devoured the gilded emblem of the grasshopper, which tumbled into the inferno below.

The Exchange was razed to the ground, the flames sparing only the wreckage of the tower and a fragment of a single marble pillar. Every statue fell from its niche to shatter on the ground below. Only that of Gresham himself survived, to be found intact among the ashes when the fire had moved on.

The flames even penetrated the crypt beneath the flagstone floors where the East India Company's stores of pepper and spices were held. An extraordinary scent—the incense of the merchants' cathedral—filled the air, and flames of blue, purple, and green shimmered over the crypt. When the fires moved on, only burned husks and a black, sticky residue were left behind among the ashes.

By the riverside, the fire was now well beyond Queenhithe, tearing across Broken Wharf and Brig Lane. The wood wharves stacked with timber were engulfed at once, and the fire swept on, devouring Woodmongers' Hall and Paul's Wharf. By nine on that Monday evening the flames were beating against the walls of Baynard's Castle, a great, gray riverside fortress, standing sentinel over the west of the city as the Tower did in the east. Within its walls Richard III had taken the Crown, and there the Council of State had declared against Jane Grey and proclaimed Mary Tudor queen.

Three principal towers and seven lesser ones broke the monolithic facade it presented to the river, each pierced by tall, narrow windows. The crumbling masonry of the upper levels of the ivy-clad towers was the haunt of ravens. Those people huddled in the lee of the massive walls thought themselves safe from the fire, for here surely the flames would break and fall back like waves against a rocky headland. Yet even these "flinty walls . . . yielded like a paper building to the fire."[27]

It was flanked by weatherboarded structures built out over the river on wooden piles. They were instantly consumed, and their blazing ruins collapsed into the water in hissing clouds of steam, but the fires had already bridged the gap to Baynard's Castle. Flames ran from window to window along the river frontage until it was clothed in fire from end to end, and tongues of flame leaped high above the battlements.

The castle burned all through the night. "At one o'clock in the morning, the wind at east-by-south, we went up the river and leaving our trunks, etc, at a little unknown house in Battersea, we were at London again by seven, and understood the fire had nearly mastered Baynard's Castle, about which it had been employed at least ten hours."[28] At daybreak, only two turrets remained.

The front line of the fire was now a mile across, extending in a curving, broadly northeasterly line from Baynard's Castle to beyond Leadenhall, a great reaping hook or "a dreadful bow . . . such as mine eyes never before had seen, a bow which had God's arrow in it with a flaming point."[29] Aligned with that flaming point, though still distant from it, lay St. Paul's.

Fires burn fastest with the wind and uphill. After nightfall, having conquered the lower Walbrook, the fires along Thames Street began an accelerating ascent of the ground rising toward Cheapside on the ridge, sweeping up Garlick Hill into Bow Lane, and up Lambeth Hill, destroying Blacksmiths' Hall by the churchyard of St. Mary Magdalen.

The parish of St. John the Evangelist, the one city parish to escape the plague the previous year, was utterly destroyed and Old Fish Street burned from end to end. The flames swept on into Knightrider Street and began climbing Friday Street, named after the principal trading day of the fish-mongers who once congregated there, and Bread Street, named for the bread market held there in the time of Edward I.

One of the occupants fleeing with his goods once more claimed incen-diaries were at work:

> When a man at the furthest end of Bread Street had made a shift
> to get out of his house his best and most portable goods, because
> the fire had approached near them; he no sooner had secured them,
> as he thought in some friend's house in Holborn, which was
> believed a safe distance, but he saw that very house and none else
> near it, in a sudden flame. Nor did there want, in this woeful dis-
> temper, the testimony of witnesses who saw this villainy commit-
> ted, and apprehended men who they were ready to swear threw
> fire-balls into houses which were presently burning.[30]

Flames were also approaching from due east, moving fast along Can-non Street, razing everything in their path as they burned down the slope, driven on by the wind. They ripped through St. Swithin's Church and burned up St. Swithin's Lane to destroy the Salters' Hall. Its great garden was turned to a wilderness of ash. Painter-Stainers' Hall also vanished without trace. Its Binding Book of apprentices survived, its covers badly charred as it was snatched from the flames.

The Church of St. John the Baptist upon Walbrook was engulfed, and the fire raged on through the slopes above Cannon Street, a dense mass of houses intersected by narrow foot-passages that only acted as chimneys for the flames. The noose of fire around St. Paul's was beginning to tighten.

As the westward arm raced onward, the northern arm was extending steadily farther away from the river. It threatened even more destruction for the city, for each yard gained northward by the flames broadened the firefront offered to the easterly gale.

With the Royal Exchange gutted, Threadneedle Street immediately behind it now offered little resistance to the fires. The churches of St. Benet

Fink on the south side and St. Bartholomew Exchange on the north were consumed within minutes of each other, and the whole of St. Bartholomew parish was destroyed save three small houses in Copthall Alley. By some unaccountable means, the inferno swirling around them left the houses untouched, though all around was laid waste.

The flames burning Threadneedle Street and Cornhill came together with those roaring up Walbrook Street to form a raging inferno at Stocks Market. The force of the firestorm sucked the very air from the streets. The fire "broke in like waves of the sea and raged like a bear robbed of her whelps. . . . What a hell of confusion and torment in the rage of fire and wind. . . . The fire carried the noise of the whirlwind in it and was so informed with terror that it surprised the eyes and hearts of men with fear as well as their houses with flame."[31]

Within minutes Bucklersbury and Poultry were also ablaze. The flames raced through the scores of taverns in Poultry, and the apothecaries in Bucklersbury. The windows full of bottles of vividly colored powders and liquids, skulls, dried toads, and ancient-looking texts in Greek or Hebrew were wreathed in fire, and the fumes of a thousand potions and strange ingredients momentarily added their exotic vapors to the inferno.

The fires raked the north side of Poultry without a pause and engulfed the Poultry Compter, a fetid stone lockup where a venal crew of turnkeys, keepers, yeomen, and sergeants preyed upon the unfortunate miscreants incarcerated there. Every prisoner, from those confined in the dank and air-less Hole deep belowground to those in the privileged cells on the master's side of the jail, paid "garnish" for every privilege.

The raging fires burned on up Three Crowns Court and ravaged the Grocers' Hall, built in 1427, leaving only a single stone turret in the elaborate gardens. They also destroyed the tiny church of St. Mary Colechurch, where Thomas à Becket was baptized, but then were checked by the Mercers' Hall at the eastern end of Cheapside. The Mercers were one of the richest guilds, and their hall occupied almost all of the land between Old Jewry and Ironmonger Lane.

The stout stone walls of the Mercers' Hall and "the fair and beautiful chapel, arched over with stone" gave stubborn resistance. Even when the flames at last broke through to burn with a ferocious intensity within the great walls, they could yet make no progress beyond them. Almost all of the mercers' plate was destroyed; two hundred pounds' weight of molten silver, fused with the dust and ashes of the great hall that once had housed it, was recovered from the rubble after the fire. The stained glass windows of the chapel, twisted by the crucible heat of the blaze, also fell among the ruins. Samuel Pepys retrieved a piece of the glass after the fires had passed and kept it as a curiosity.

Although Mercers' Hall checked the westward march of the flames for several hours, they continued to creep north from Threadneedle Street toward Lothbury and Throgmorton Street, threatening to outflank the obstruction. The Post Office in Posthouse Yard, north of Threadneedle Street, now lay in their path.[32]

The Postmaster, James Hickes, had stayed at his post throughout the previous year as the plague raged through the city. With the fires now approaching, he waited with his wife and two small children as long as he dared before the fear of being cut off drove them out. "This night past at past twelve o'clock, Sir Philip and his lady fled from the office for their safety. I stayed so long as one, until my wife and children's patience could stay no longer, fearing of being quite stopped up."[33]

Burned by the searing wind, the roar of the pursuing flames always in their ears, Hickes and his family ran for their lives, stumbling through the streets. The night was harshly lit by the glare of the fires, but clouds of choking smoke and dust swirled around them, shrouding familiar landmarks like fog. They blundered their way north and west, the children close to exhaustion but driven on always by the terror they read in their parents' eyes, until they reached Cripplegate and found sanctuary beyond the walls at the Golden Lion Inn in Red Cross Street.

Early the following morning Hickes began setting up a temporary Post Office at the inn, saving such packets and letters as he could, but the abandoned Post Office was gutted and the bulk of the mails destroyed. "How we shall dispose of our business," he wrote, "only the wise God knows."[34]

Also left behind and consumed by the flames was "a complete secret apparatus for tampering with, copying and forging letters in the interests of the State." It was the invention of Sir Samuel Morland, who first persuaded Lord Arlington to test its effectiveness. He wrote a letter, sealed it, and handed it to Morland. Within minutes he received two letters, his own and a copy, each with an identical seal, and confessed that he could not tell which was which. A further demonstration before the King so impressed His Majesty that considerable funds and two rooms at the Post Office were placed at Morland's disposal to aid him in the task of spying on or compromising the King's enemies "with great advantage to the Crown."

Seals were opened and resealed undetectably, writing and seals counterfeited, and copied so fast that "even when a whole sheet of paper was closely written on both sides . . . little more time than one minute was required." Years later Morland tried to persuade William of Orange to adopt his system, but His Majesty "thought the secret should die with him [Morland] as too dangerous to be encouraged."[35]

With the Post Office destroyed, no means remained of communicating the fate of London to the nation, for though that day's *London Gazette* had contained a few lines recording the outbreak of the fire—"It continues still with great" violence—by Monday night the *Gazette*'s printing presses had also fallen victim to the flames. In the absence of reliable news or the mails, ever wilder rumors circulated.

As the fires raged north and west, they also continued to burn back slowly to the east, into the teeth of the ferocious gale. Nicholas Corsellis, a general merchant dealing in "indigo, copperas, lead, Spanish and Virginian leaf tobacco, china roots, olibanum, striped linen, Colchester bays, etc," fled as the fires engulfed his house in Love Lane, just two streets east of Pudding Lane.

He later wrote to James Ward, a merchant in Amsterdam:

I thank God I have saved all my papers and monies, though I was constrained to remove them three times from one place to another. My packer's house in St Nicholas Lane is burnt down to the ground together with a great many goods, especially packs, which by reason of the bulk could not be carried on men's backs . . .

Carts were few to be had so that £60 sterling has been given by a friend of mine for three carts but the greatest difficulty was the obstruction caused by the goods thrown into the street and the crowds of people so that the carts could not possibly be brought into the lane. That little which here be saved was carried on men's backs to London Wall and then thrown over and taken up by country carts and carried away, the City gates being too much obstructed . . .

Your four bales were [lost] I much fear, though I cannot positively say what has become of them because he cannot give me an exact account until he has removed his goods to a house he has taken here in the city. I hope well though I have more of fear than hope. I can assure you that he is an honest man and has done his endeavor for you as for himself, in so much that he protests he could not save his own household stuff because his time and servants were taken up by rescuing merchants' goods he was entrusted with.[36]

It was dusk on that Monday evening before the flames reached Billingsgate, just beyond the foot of Love Lane and barely four hundred feet from the seat of the fire. Sheltered by the rising ground farther from the river, the flames advanced faster and were already threatening the church of St. Dunstan's in the East just below Tower Street. There John Dolben, Bishop of Rochester and Dean of Westminster, led a stand against them.

A soldier priest twice wounded in the Royalist cause at Marston Moor and York, Dolben again gave his monarch great service, leading a column of boys from Westminster School in a march right across the city to the easternmost extremity of the fire. In the shadow of St. Dunstan's they worked for hours to douse the flames in the mean housing crowded around its walls, fetching water in a bucket chain from the river at Young's Quay. Although the fire still reached the church and burned fiercely enough upon it to melt the lead from the steeple, the damaged building survived.

Higher on the slopes, the flames were raging through Fenchurch Street. Near the summit of the high ground above stood Leadenhall, a great fifteenth-century building used as a storehouse for arms during the Civil War. The city apprentices had besieged it, seizing the magazine in 1648 "for God and King Charles."

It was saved from the flames by an alderman of the city. His name went unrecorded but his deeds were witnessed. Filling his hat with money, he scattered it among those working to save the building, urging them to greater efforts. "He alone there under God gave a check to the fire,"[37] and Leadenhall survived with only its western facade damaged. It was the first halt that had been made to the flames anywhere in the city.

East India House just to the east also was saved by the preservation of Leadenhall. The company's pepper and spices had been destroyed in the Royal Exchange and their saltpeter warehouse had also erupted in flames with a terrible roar, but the rest of their vast storehouse of wealth was preserved.

The reverse it suffered at Leadenhall served only to speed the fire's progress elsewhere. The gale continued to howl and even strengthened further, driving the remorseless advance of the blaze across its broad fronts and hurling flaming brands far ahead of the wall of fire.

Death stalked every street in a multitude of forms: burning, breaking, poisoning, suffocating, or killing from sheer terror alone. Those frozen by the sight of the walls of flame bearing down on them might turn to find themselves outflanked, encircled, and cut off by fire sneaking through the alleys or sparks and flames showering down thick as hailstones from overhead, igniting roofs a furlong distant from the front line of the fires. Men thinking themselves safe in their beds awoke with their roof ablaze and smoke filling their rooms.

The fires had barely entered a street before gouts of flame were issuing from every door and window along it. Whole lanes seemed to disappear in an instant, burning as one as the flames reached buildings already charred and smoking from the wall of searing heat that traveled in front of the main body of the fire.

On every hand, blazes erupted as if from nothing. Few thought to blame the wind or the intensity of the fires themselves. To the mob in the streets, ruled by fear, unreason, and panic, each fresh blaze and even the lack of water in the conduits spoke only of the malign intent of fire-raisers and incendiaries at work in their midst.

Such was now the developing power of the firestorm, as the vortex rose ever higher into the sky, that air was sucked in to feed the flames from every point of the compass.

To the bemused and terrified onlookers the wind "blew equally to the right and to the left, and caused the fire to burn on all sides which persuaded many that this fire was miraculous. I myself remember that going into the streets at that time and having the wind impetuously in my face, I was in hope that at my return I should have it in my back, but it was all one."[38]

The force of the blast was enough to hurl debris, sticks, birds, and even timbers and people to the ground, dragging them toward the inferno. A man able to stand his ground might find the fires possessed of an apparently malign intelligence and purpose. Out of the inferno a tongue of flame would suddenly lick toward him. As he turned and ran, the flame—shielded by his body from the draft roaring into the fires—would pursue him, mimicking his movements as he weaved from side to side, reaching out to caress his back and set his clothes ablaze. Only when he fell would the wind sweep the flame back into the maelstrom of fire.

The flames also shifted shape and form. They split and came together again, their tendrils reaching into each street, lane, narrow alley, or suffocating passageway, seeking always another hold, another way of advancement, fastening on the least scrap of timber, dust, or rags.

At times they roared a hundred feet into the air, at others they crept along the rooftops or wormed like snakes across the ground, licking at timbers and pitch-coated planks as if tasting them, and insinuating themselves into cracks only to burst forth with a dragon's roar and devour the next victim whole.

"The noise and cracking and thunder of the impetuous flames, the shrieking of women and children, the hurry of people, the fall of towers, houses and churches was like a hideous storm."[39] It was so loud it overwhelmed the senses of the panic-stricken people flying before it and seemed to carry deep within it every sound dredged from the nightmares and race memories of man. Stones exploded like cannon, timbers snapped like broken bones, and flaming arrows of fire fell from the skies. The noise of the inferno, "as if there had been a thousand iron chariots beating upon the stones,"[40] was heard as far away as Oxford, over fifty miles away, where it sounded like the thunder of huge waves against a rocky coast.

Where the fires had passed on their relentless march, they left nothing behind but smoking rubble, crumbling walls, the blackened towers and spires of churches, and a few chimney stacks strong enough to withstand the holocaust. They still stood, though the buildings they had served were laid waste all around. The faces of the surviving steeples and towers reflected back the glare of the flames, shining like beacons above the black wilderness surrounding them. These were the only landmarks remaining. Already half the city had been put to the torch.

When the daylight faded, the glow of the fires seemed to grow brighter and the transition from day to night effected no visible change. The moon, three-quarters full on the Sunday night, was invisible behind the clouds of smoke still covering the heavens, but the glare of the blazing fires below lit the underside of the pall so that the clouds shone all over, bathing the city with an awful bloodred light.

At midnight the magistrates, led by "Lord Manchester, Lord Hollis and others," inspected Fleet Street, beyond the Fleet Ditch. The gouts of flame still soaring above the ramparts of Baynard's Castle gave fresh urgency to their deliberations. "Taking a view of those parts, an hour after [they] ordered the pulling down of some houses in Whitefriars, though some earnestly urged what had been proposed in the morning, that the houses on each side of the River Fleet should be pulled down from the Thames to Holborn Bridge."[41]

The aim of the King and his Council was no longer to save anything of the old city within the walls; that had already been consigned to the flames.

Chapter 6

Outlandish Men

Friday, August 31, 1666

Rats or Mice to kill

*A ship comes sailing up the Thames to London and the master of the ship
shall weep, and the mariners shall ask him why he weeps, being he has made
so good a voyage, and he shall say "Ah what a goodly city this was, none in
the world comparable to it; and now there is scarcely left any house."*
Mother Shipton's Prophesies

O**N THE FRIDAY BEFORE THE FIRE BROKE OUT, CAPTAIN LAW-**rence Petersen had been belowdecks in his cabin, nine days out from Stockholm, when he heard a cry for All Hands and, a moment later, the thunder of a cannon. He hurried on deck to see an English man-of-war bearing down.

The mate, who had the helm, was already shouting the order to reef the sails. Petersen waited, his face impassive but his mind racing as his ship lost headway and the warship closed on its port bow. Beyond it he could see the rest of a battle fleet, a hundred ships or more, stretching almost to the horizon.

The English were at war with the Dutch and the French, not the Swedish, but a fat merchantman laden with iron, copper, and steel was a tempting prize,

97

and in any event, as long as the war continued, no ship bound for the port of an enemy would be allowed an easy passage through the English Channel.

He watched his men clustering at the rails as the man-of-war closed. Among them was the ship's only passenger, Robert Hubert, a thin, pinched-looking young man with a sallow complexion and lank black hair. He wore the high collars and drab, dun-colored clothes of a Calvinist preacher, but he was in fact a watchmaker, or so he had said in his slow, halting speech.

Petersen had raised an eyebrow at this, for the young man's right arm and leg were palsied. The arm hung wasted and near useless at his side, and he walked with a twisted gimping motion, struggling to climb the steps of the companionway even in a flat calm.

How he had come to Stockholm, Petersen did not know, for Hubert was French by birth and had lived much of his adult life in London. Mr. Haggerstern, a merchant and neighbor of the captain, had approached him, asking if he would give Hubert passage, "he being not well in mind and being very poor."[1] Hubert's parents in Rouen, where the *Maid of Stockholm* was bound, would pay a generous price for the safe delivery of their long-absent son.

A sea captain's pay was not so lavish that he could turn down such a welcome bonus, and Petersen agreed at once. He had offered Hubert the use of his day cabin and shared his meal with him on their first night out of Stockholm, but he found the young man morose, slow of speech, and dull of wit, and he soon left Hubert to his own company.

He turned his attention back to the approaching warship. Seamen swarmed aloft to reef the square-rigger's sail. It lost headway at once but slid closer through the greasy swell until it towered over the *Maid of Stockholm*.

The warship's captain cupped his hands to his mouth and hallooed across the gap between them, asking their identity, nationality, and destination. He digested Petersen's reply for a moment, then required him, by order of Prince Rupert, to make course for London. The courtesy with which the request was phrased did not altogether conceal the threat behind it.

Petersen glanced up at the pennant streaming from the mast-top. The strengthening northeasterly wind would have given him a swift and untroubled run through the Channel; now he would be delayed in London while the Dutch and English fleets maneuvered and postured on the high seas. When at last free to resume his voyage, he would be lucky if the pre-vailing westerlies had not begun to blow, condemning him to a further wait of days or even weeks for a fair wind to carry him onward to Rouen.

He cursed under his breath, but one look at the rows of cannon jutting from the gunports of the warship showed him there was no alternative but to comply. He bowed his head in acknowledgment and ordered the mate to set a new course.

Signal flags were run up on the man-of-war, and one of the smaller warships at once detached itself from the battle fleet and tracked the Swedish ship as it headed for the Thames estuary. Driven on by the scud-ding wind, the merchantman and its escort soon left the fleet far behind, and within an hour Petersen felt the rhythm of the deck beneath his feet begin to change. They left the rolling swell of the open sea for the shorter, tidal chop of the estuary, and brown water swirled and bubbled around the stern.

As they sailed on, the shorelines, at first gray-brown smudges like low fogbanks lying on the sea, sharpened into mudflats flanked by seas of wav-ing marsh grass that seemed to stretch to the horizon. Seabirds wheeled and cried overhead, and waders and herons made a grudging retreat from the mud before the rising tide.

As the estuary narrowed further, the first houses appeared along the banks, the cottages of fishermen and oystermen thatched with reed and walled with flint and chalk, and the rude shacks and hovels of the mudlarks and scavengers who patrolled the shoreline at the turn of each tide, swoop-ing like seagulls on the bounty of the sea. Inland, Petersen saw the spires of isolated churches rising from the huddles of cottages surrounding them.

The grass and vegetation on either bank was burned brown by the drought, and even the trees seemed to droop in the burning heat. Many had already shed their leaves and stood stark and skeletal against the cloudless sky. A great drove of cattle plodded wearily along a track to the north of the river, raising a cloud of dust that hung like smoke in the air. "Besides other animals, three thousand oxen" were slaughtered in London every day.[2] Carts laden with fruit and the produce of the fields followed in their wake, drawn onward by the insatiable appetite of the distant capital.

The ships traced the meandering curves of the river westward. Clumps of refuse and debris for which even the scavengers could find no use now littered the shoreline, marker posts announcing the presence of the great city upstream long before they reached it. The houses lining the banks grew more dense and mean, and a pall of sulfurous yellow-black smoke hung over the sky ahead. It streamed away to the southwest before the wind but was so constantly renewed that it appeared to hang motionless in the sky.

The riverbank was now lined with shipyards and slipways surrounded by ranks of hovels and tenements reaching down to the high-water mark and in places built out on piles sunk deep into the mud.

Carried on the rising tide, the two ships drifted on past the ranks of dry- and wet-docks, ropewalks, and warehouses of the great naval yards at Woolwich and Deptford. They passed Execution Dock, where as a warning to all outward bound seamen, "pirates and sea-robbers" and others who had committed crimes upon the high seas were hung "on a gibbet erected at low water mark."[3] There they were left until three tides had washed over them.

As they rounded the bend below Wapping, the Pool of London opened out before them. The *Maid of Stockholm* docked at an empty berth at St. Katharine's Wharf, near Corsellis's brewhouse in the shadow of the Tower, and the man-of-war that had escorted the ship upriver now joined the warships and tenders crowding Tower Wharf. Petersen scanned the city skyline. The prospect was a familiar one to him, but for many of his crew lining the rail it was their first sight of one of the greatest cities of the world. Robert Hubert stood silent alongside them, his eyes hooded, his gaze fixed. Even when the seamen, tiring of the sight, went belowdecks to rest and eat, Hubert remained motionless, staring into the heart of the city, muttering to himself as he rocked on his heels like a man at prayer.

Three days later, the *Maid of Stockholm* still lay alongside St. Katharine's Wharf, though the wind shrieking through its rigging set it pitching at its mooring as if it were riding the ocean swell.

Soon after dawn on Sunday, Lawrence Petersen had seen the devastation on the bridge and the pillars of smoke and flames rising from the waterfront to the west. He had watched with mounting horror through that day and the next as the city was engulfed and the heavens blackened with smoke, but his sympathy for the plight of London was also tinged with fear as the fire burned slowly back into the wind, closer and closer to the Tower.

The warship that had escorted him into London had departed, its sails furled, carried downstream into the wind by the ebb tide and the sweat of its seamen at the oars of the ship's boats. Petersen might have been tempted simply to cast off and escape in the confusion, but he had already seen mobs touring the dockside, seizing and beating foreign seamen. If he was caught attempting to leave the port, he and his ship might be further victims of the rampant xenophobia.

The Trained Bands had been summoned and assembled in the city, but instead of fighting the fire or pulling down houses before it, most of them were set to watch at every quarter for "outlandish men" because of the fears of fireballs and incendiaries.[4] Rumor and wildfire raced each other through the streets, the rumors growing wilder as the panic spread. The French and Dutch were invading and had cut off the water from the bridge and the New River Head at Islington. As word spread of thousands of Frenchmen and papists in arms, citizens bearing every sort of club and improvised weapon filled the streets ready to repel "this chimerical army."[5]

Foreigners and Catholics, always targets in any London disturbance, were at once seized upon. Papists were the object of particular fear and hatred, suspected of wishing to force Protestant Englishmen "to fly destitute of bread and harbor, your wives prostituted to the lust of every savage bog trotter, your daughters ravished by goatish monks, your smaller children tossed upon pikes or torn limb from limb whilst you have your own bowels ripped up . . . or else murdered with some other exquisite tortures and holy candles made of your grease."[6]

In this heated atmosphere every stranger was equally suspect, and every victim handed over to the guard or beaten down in the street seemed to confirm the worst fears of the mob. A French painter was robbed of his goods and his house destroyed by a rabble convinced he was intent on burning it to spread the blaze. Michael Marsh, a company officer of the Trained Band, arrested a Walloon in Leadenhall Street. The man was carrying "a dark lanthorn made, as it is conceived, to lay a train of powder and it was filled with gun powder."[7] Dawes Weymansel, a justice of the peace, said that a man he stopped at the Temple Bar had his pockets stuffed with flax, tow, and other incendiary material, and certain "long things of a black figure which he could not endure to hold in his hand by reason of their extreme heat."[8]

"Amid this welter of extreme misery the greatest crimes and most execrable atrocities were committed, particularly against the large numbers of foreigners who dwelt in London, many of whom were murdered. Others saved themselves as best they could from falling into the hands of the infuriated populace."[9]

Instances of terrible violence were legion. A blacksmith battered a Frenchman, "felling him instantly to the ground with an iron bar . . . the innocent blood of this exotic flowing in a plentiful stream down to his ankles."[10] The man was left for dead. Another Frenchman was beaten in Moorfields and almost torn limb from limb. He was carrying "balls of fire" in a box; upon examination they were revealed to be tennis balls.

Cornelius Riedtveldt, a Dutch baker living in Westminster, lit his oven ready to bake bread. "The people seeing smoke issuing from the chimney cried out that the rogue was setting the town on fire at that end and they dragged him into the streets, severely wounding him and then beat him nearly to death."

His house and bakery were wrecked and plundered, and a rope placed around his neck ready to lynch him. "The Duke of York happened to pass the house just in time to save the man from being murdered."[11] His life was saved but he was imprisoned in Westminster Gatehouse and everything he possessed was looted from him.

The belief that the fire was "a design of our enemies . . . kindled such a rage in the multitude that they killed one poor woman . . . and badly wounded and maimed divers others."[12] The murdered woman, who had been "walking in Moorfields [with] chickens in her apron, was seized by the mob who declared that she carried fireballs. And not only did they violently abuse her but they beat her with sticks and cut off her breasts. . . . It will be a long time before the people of London forget their wild rage against the foreigners."[13]

In this mob rule the women were as violent and rapacious as the men. One Dutch resident of London was "half dead by the word of killing all French and Dutch. Yet I have no reason to complain of any Englishmen . . . but only of English women, who only caused that tumult, having their corps de garde in several streets and did knock down several strangers for not speaking good English. Some of them were armed with spits, some bread-staffs, and the captain with a broad sword."[14]

Petersen also faced a practical problem. Even with the tide to aid him, while the easterly gale blew, his ponderous, heavy-laden craft would make little or no headway into the wind. If the fire approached too close he could cast off, but he would only drift into midstream, his ship at the mercy of the downpours of sparks and blazing embers he could see sweeping over the surface of the river on either side of the bridge. That offered more hope than leaving it to burn at its mooring, but for the moment Petersen could only watch and wait.

He had allowed neither his crewmen nor his passenger to disembark, fearing not only the danger to them from the mobs roaming the quayside, but that they might seize the chance to jump ship. Finding new crewmen would be all but impossible in the chaos of the burning city, and he had no intention of losing his passenger before the charge for his voyage had been paid.

He glanced toward the midships, where Hubert was at the rail, watching the flames. He had barely moved from his vantage point since the fire began. He had been at the rail when Petersen went to his bunk late the previous night to snatch a little sleep, he had been there when the captain rose early that morning, and he was still there now, staring into the flame-lit darkness. He was twisting from side to side at the rail and muttering to himself, his features showing more animation than Petersen had ever seen from him.

Curious to overhear him, Petersen moved down from the stern and advanced across the deck, the sound of his footfalls lost in the thunder of the flames and the howling wind. A fresh burst of flames exploding into the sky lit the scene bright as day. By its light Petersen saw Hubert's face twisted into a lopsided smile. He was repeating "Very well! Very well!" and "Yes! Yes!"—the only English he could speak.

The captain heard the mounting excitement in Hubert's voice, and disgust and fury possessed him in equal measure. He shouted for the mate and ordered him to shut Hubert belowdecks in the hold. Rough hands seized him, and he was dragged across the deck and pushed down the companionway. His palsied leg gave beneath him and he fell sprawling at the foot of the wooden steps.

As Hubert got to his feet he was seized again, dragged along the passageway, and thrown bodily into the hold. There was the thud of a door and the scrape of a barrel being pushed against it. He was left alone in the utter darkness of the dank hold, hearing the slop of bilgewater as the ship heeled with the wind.

When he screwed his eyes tight shut, he could still see the afterimage of the fires he had been watching. A lopsided grin again spread across his face. He opened his eyes and looked around. A faint red-orange light seeped around the edges of the hatch covers, and as his eyes became used to the gloom, he could see the bluish glint of stacked plates of iron and steel and the warmer glow of copper sheet. His gaze took in the closed door and the sealed hatches. As he stared, he heard the slow measured tread of Captain Petersen endlessly pacing across the deck above him. His smile widened.

He groped his way to one of the stacks, folded his coat to insulate him from the coldness of the metal, and squatted down to wait, his eyes tracking back and forth across the boards above his head, following the movements of Captain Petersen as he walked the deck.

Even after the pacing feet at last ceased their tread, Hubert remained motionless. In the silence he heard the muffled voice of the night bellman calling the hour from the quayside, a reassuring sound of normality in a city descended into chaos and madness. Hubert resolved to remain a further hour before attempting his escape. He waited, still as the grave, until he again heard the bellman's voice, then stood up, easing the stiffness from his cramped limbs.

He eased himself between the stacks of metal, feeling his way along the rough surface of the bulkhead dividing the hold from the rest of the ship. He found the door set in it by touch, pressed his cheek against the damp, soft-splintered wood, and listened intently. There was no murmur of voices, no sound of pacing feet, no scrape of chair legs, not even the tap of a clay pipe against the galley stove. The silence was broken only by the far-off rumble of the fires consuming the city.

He held his breath and pushed against the door. It gave an inch, then stuck fast. He pushed again, bracing the shoulder of his good arm against the wood. It held, then yielded another grudging inch, but the barrel wedging it scraped against the wooden deck with a noise that seemed to Hubert as loud as a shout in the darkness.

He waited, his heartbeats thundering in his ears, expecting at any moment to hear the curses and rough voices of the crew, but no sound came. He drew a juddering breath, then bent again to the door. It took all his strength to win another couple of inches, but he could move it no more. He let his head fall forward against the door and felt a draft upon his face.

Amid the faint tang of pine resin, the dank smell of wet wood, and the stale odor of the bilges, he caught the stink of smoke and burning pitch.

At once he renewed his efforts, straining and scrabbling at the door, his breath coming in gasps as the veins on his good arm knotted with the effort. The door gave a few more inches as the barrel shifted away from it, but then wedged against the bulkhead. It would go no farther.

Hubert paused once more, wiping the sweat from his brow, and then squeezed his lath-thin body into the gap. His hips caught for a moment, and though he turned his head sideways, the edge of the door still scoured his cheek and scraped his forehead, but then he was through and limping off down the narrow passageway.

He inched his way between the slung hammocks in which the crew were sleeping, the rasping snores of a deckhand covering the faint noise Hubert made as he stole by them and eased past the galley. The ruddy glow of light strengthened as he reached the foot of the companionway, but he did not try to climb it, knowing that a watch would be kept on deck.

Instead he inched his way past and reached the door of the captain's cabin. No sound came from beyond it, and after a moment he grasped the handle and began to turn it. The door was unlocked. He eased it open a fraction of an inch at a time. The cabin was in darkness, the lamp extinguished, but the fire's glow faintly lit the darkness. The captain's bunk was empty.

As Hubert digested this, he heard a faint noise over his head, the scrape of feet on the planking. He turned and hurried across the cabin toward a small hatch set in the side of the ship, the captain's private scuttle, by which he could enter or leave the ship without being observed by his men.

He pulled back the hatch cover, swung his legs through, and began lowering himself awkwardly down to the quay. He inched out of the shadows cast by the ship, craning his neck to look up toward the deck. Petersen was in profile, staring upstream toward the heart of the fires, but as if by instinct he stirred and turned to glance down at the wharf. His eyes locked with Hubert's, then he straightened up, shouting for his crew.

The noise broke the spell holding Hubert. He bared his teeth in a smile, then turned and hurried away across the wharf, his gimping footsteps striking a hollow, irregular tattoo on the planks. He had only a few yards to cover before he could lose himself in the maze of alleys and courts flanking Corsellis's quay.

As he reached the edge of the wharf, his way was barred by a group of citizens emerging from the shadows. They were smoke stained and disheveled, and as they surrounded Hubert, their faces were full of suspicion and hostility.

He shook his head, unable to understand their shouted questions, and was punched, kicked, and beaten. Through the crowd of hate-filled faces surrounding him, he saw Petersen still watching from the stern rail of the ship as the mob dragged Hubert away.

Chapter 7

A Sign of Wrath

Tuesday, September 4, 1666

Any Milke heere

*Whoever was an eyewitness of that terrible prospect, can never have so
lively an image of the last conflagration till he beholds it.*
Clayandon (Edward Hyde, First Earl of Clarendon),
*Selections from the History of the Rebellion and the
Life by Himself*

IN THE COURSE OF MONDAY THE FIRES HAD DESTROYED AROUND
five times as many houses and churches as on the first day of the fire, but
if the two days and nights preceding it had been terrible enough, the dawn
breaking over the city on Tuesday morning heralded the most fateful day in
London's history.

The gale was still blowing hard from the east, and the day again dawned
hot and dry, though most Londoners had no way of knowing if it was cloudy
or fair, so dense and widespread was the smoke now hanging over the city.
The firefront moved always onward, but behind the lines the warehouses
and cellars continued to burn, feeding flame and yellow-brown sulfurous
smoke into the sky. An immense pall stretched over the whole of London,
far out over the countryside to the west, trailing fifty miles downwind.

The smoke was now so dense that it even darkened the noonday sun, so obscuring it that men could stare directly at it. "The smoke (driven by the wind) made an arch in the heavens (a sign of wrath, as the rainbow was once of peace) . . . to the western part of the horizon, and the sun shining through it seemed perfectly red and might easily be looked on with a naked eye, yielding a fainter light than in an eclipse."[1] For many, the baleful red disk glowing through the pall seemed a portent of the end of the world.

At Oxford, although the sky was cloudless, the "unusual color of the air without cloud made the sunbeams of a strange red dim light," and "the fire or flame made noise like the waves of the sea."[2] Even as far away as the Scottish borders, almost four hundred miles away, the smoke and turbulence of the superheated air over London created mirages like "an abundance of ships in the air."

The fires had burned steadily closer to Cheapside during the night. They were held back only by the stone walls of the Mercers' Hall and the chapel at its eastern end, but flames were also creeping up almost every side street and lane to the south. Embers hurled on the gale from the fires around Cornhill and Threadneedle Street had also created separate, smaller blazes to the north, and they too were now converging on Cheapside. The roar of the fires grew ever louder, echoing along the broad street, the widest in London.

Square in the middle of the western end, where it narrowed and split into Blowbladder Street and Paternoster Row, was the church of St. Michael le Querne. The street divided around its sharp eastern frontage like the waters parting before the prow of a ship.

Spaced at intervals along the rest of the street stood the Standard, the Great Conduit ("a gilt tower with a fountain that plays"),[3] and a square stone plinth bequeathed to the city during the Commonwealth by "Russel, a porter and well-minded man"[4] so that his fellows could rest their burdens there. This prosaic monument had replaced the historic and beautiful cross erected by Edward I in commemoration of Queen Eleanor, and torn down on May 3, 1643. "The populace demolished it . . . in context of the Popish anniversary. . . . A noise of trumpets sounding the while."

Cheapside was the great processional route of the city. English kings on their way to be crowned at Westminster and visiting monarchs and nobles welcomed with pomp and pageantry had all passed along this great thoroughfare lined with magnificent houses. Charles II had ridden along it on his

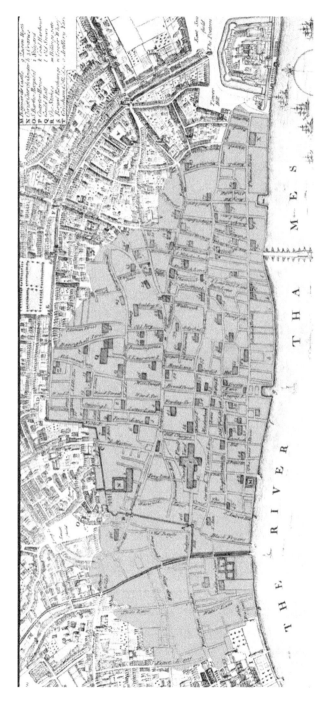

Map of the fire's spread on the third day.

triumphal progress through the city at the Restoration, past cheering crowds and houses hung with tapestries while the water conduits flowed with wine.

On the south side, at the heart of the street, was St. Mary le Bow, named for its bowed—arched—crypt, one of the most distinctive and beautiful churches in London and "more famous than any other parish church of the whole City or suburbs."[5] In medieval times lamps were lit every night in the four graceful lantern pinnacles rising above the domed tower, beacons visible from afar to guide weary travelers home.

Cheapside, home to the goldsmiths, "surpasses all the rest. There are to be seen in this street all sorts of gold and silver vessels exposed to sale, as well as ancient and modern medals, as must surprise a man the first time he sees and considers them."[6] Houses in the busiest parts of the street rose six stories above the ground, and Goldsmiths' Row, just west of the church, was the most opulent part of all, a group of ten houses and fourteen shops built in the late fifteenth century by Thomas Wood, a Master of the Goldsmiths' Guild. The elaborately carved timber facades rose four stories above the street, decorated with the arms of the goldsmiths and painted and gilded lead casts of wood men riding upon monstrous beasts. The Row was "the most beautiful frame of fair houses and shops that be within the walls of London or elsewhere in England."[7]

Throughout the night the goldsmiths and silversmiths had joined the throngs hurrying away, bearing their goblets and plate, rings, necklaces and pendants, ceremonial swords and coronets, and their stores of unworked precious metals and jewels. Their treasures were taken under heavy guard through the unburned streets of the north and east of the city and deposited for safekeeping in the Tower of London.

The goldsmiths were not a moment too soon. During the night the fire had doubled in size and grown ever more intense as it devoured the fresh fuel before it. As the sun rose, the flames burst upon Cheapside. No street in London had played a greater role in the city's history. Now in the space of a few hours it was utterly destroyed.

Fires burning up from Soper Lane, Bow Lane, Bread Street, Friday Street, and Old Change broke through as one onto the south side of the street. There they were met by a wall of flame roaring onward from the east after at last overcoming the mercers' chapel.

The whole south side of Cheapside was at once aflame, and as the tall houses collapsed, hurling burning debris across the gap, the north side also erupted. Goldsmiths' Row was gutted. Fires licking up the jetties burned the balconies where men had crowded together to watch the King's progress to his coronation at Westminster. The great iron sundial projecting from the front of one of the buildings hung there for a moment and then fell, the point driven deep into the ground. A moment later, the entire timber facade peeled away and crashed down.

The gilded and painted signs projecting over the street on long iron poles sank to the ground in succession. As the upper stories collapsed, the great brick chimneys still stood. Black smoke from the fires raging below gouted from them as if in mockery of their former use.

Cheapside's historic taverns were all razed to the ground: the Half Moon, the Mitre, the Standard, and the Bull's Head, where General Monck made his headquarters as he waited for the entry of Charles II into the city.

The Mermaid, between Bread Street and Friday Street, was also destroyed. Shakespeare and Ben Jonson had been habitués of the inn, so renowned for the wit and elegance of its conversation that Francis Beaumont was moved to write to Jonson, "What things have we seen done at the Mermaid. Heard words that have been so nimble and so full of subtle flame as if that every one from whence they came had meant to put his whole wit in a jest, and had resolved to live a fool the rest of his dull life."[8]

The church of St. Mary le Bow was left a blackened wreck, its roof collapsed, its choir destroyed, the pinnacled tower smoke-blackened and crumbling. Only the crypt survived. The baptismal register kept there escaped the flames. It records the birth of Cassia, daughter of Morgan Dandy, who was born "the day the dreadful fire began in London and baptized in the country."[9] Even as the flames raged through Cheapside, the child had been carried through the streets to safety beyond the walls.

No one sought to oppose the fires. "When Cheapside was on fire, not ten men stood by helping or calling for help, I have been an eye witness and can verify this and 100 times more."[10]

Thomas and Hannah had spent the second night of the fire in the church of St. Mary le Bow. Their fitful sleep was further disturbed by the rumble of the fires and the ceaseless noise as more and more people pushed their way into the church, stacking their goods and furniture in the nave and finding room for themselves to huddle down among it to await the dawn.

They were roused by the roar of approaching flames, the crash of falling timbers, and the thunder of collapsing houses, and ran from the church, clambering over piles of goods and still-sleeping bodies in their panic to be gone.

They fled west and then north throughout that day, wandering without aim under the burning sun, the smell of smoke in their nostrils and the thunder of the flames always in their ears. They were often lost in the warrens of streets and lanes, but found themselves drawn back always, without any volition of their own, toward the periphery of the fire.

Unable to find a cookshop or a tavern, or even a milkmaid or water seller, they had eaten nothing since Saturday night and drunk only a few mouthfuls of water scooped from a broken conduit. Eventually, skirting round to the north of the flames, they found themselves on familiar territory not far from their ruined home and made their way along Fenchurch Street and down Mark Lane to Bakers' Hall.

Several other members of the guild and their families and apprentices had already taken refuge there, sprawling around the tiled, rush-strewn floor of the hall, and all that remained to slake the Farriners' thirst and break their fast was a little sour ale, water, and some scraps of mutton already rotting in the heat. In the Bakers' Hall, with a score of members of the craft beneath its roof, there was not even a handful of flour with which they could bake bread.

The easterly gale was blowing harder than ever, carrying the smuts and soot and charred fragments for miles downwind. The walks and gardens of Kensington were almost buried beneath the ashes of linen, papers, and pieces of burnt plaster thrown there by the gale. "Had your Lordship been at Kensington you would have thought . . . it had been Doomsday, and that the heavens themselves had been on fire; and the fearful cries and howlings of undone people did much increase the resemblance. The loss is inestimable. I believe there was never any such desolation by fire since the destruction of Jerusalem, nor will be till the last and general conflagration."[11]

Richard Baxter "saw the half-burnt leaves of books near my dwelling" at Acton,[12] five miles west of the city, and scraps of burned paper were driven by the wind as far as Eton and Windsor Great Park.[13] Lady Carteret picked one up on the grounds of her house on which the only words visible were "Time is; it is done."

"Little pieces of scorched silk and paper were taken up in very many places near Windsor, Henley, Beaconsfield, etc,"[14] over thirty miles west of London. They continued to drift down from the sky for days after the fire.

So powerful was the storm that the English fleet still seeking to engage the Dutch was scattered before the gale down the Channel and forced to find shelter in Portsmouth harbor "rather than lie abroad to be battered by wind and water." Several "had their masts and sails blown away" and a number of Dutch ships were blown aground on the Kent coast between Deal and Walmer.[15]

The great arc of fire cutting a swath through London was no longer discernible. The flames were now advancing on half a dozen different fronts, but were still traveling fastest through the waterside districts. The fires raging along the riverbank were hurled by the wind across Puddle Dock, where once "horses used to water," and raced on through a warren of once fine Tudor buildings. The great houses built on the ruins of Blackfriars following the Dissolution had been subdivided again and again as fashionable London moved elsewhere, and had long since degenerated into slums. These crumbling tenements quickly succumbed to the flames roaring on toward the Fleet River.

The city walls ended on the banks of the Fleet Ditch some three hundred yards from the Thames. Covering almost all of the opposite bank was the Bridewell. It was once a great royal palace of Henry VIII, with high walls and hexagonal turrets of patterned brick capped by battlements rising forty feet above the ground. They surrounded two great courtyards.

The hall was sixty feet long, and the once lavish quarters for the King and his consort also included a long gallery and a great chamber of audience. The palace had been abandoned by Henry VIII in 1529 after an epidemic of the plague and fallen into disrepair, but it had found service down the years in a multitude of guises: as a "hospital" for poor boys, a house of correction for harlots, vagrants, and vagabonds, a school, a bedlam for lunatics, a workhouse, and a prison for apprentices. So large was it that parts of it were also used as a granary, where fifty tons of corn were kept, and as a storehouse for coal. "John Bromfield, yeoman of the woodwharf," extracted £40 from the city for "preserving and removing [some of] the City's coals at Bridewell" before the flames consumed the rest.

Though the walls were too stout to collapse, the Bridewell, like Baynard's Castle before it, blazed from end to end, with flames bursting from the windows and the roof. The corn and coal fueled the fires which, confined by the walls and burning with furnace heat, shattered brick and fused lead and iron together.

Cobbles and paving blocks glowed red, and molten lead from the roofs ran down the gutters like rainwater, setting the waters boiling in the Fleet Ditch. So fierce were the fires that the dead were burned in their graves six feet belowground in the yard surrounding the chapel.

Dorset House, the Earl of Dorset's former mansion behind Bridewell, had survived an alarm earlier in the day when the Duke of York, coming downstream in his barge, had seen a burning brand lodged in its roof. That fire was quickly extinguished, but when Bridewell burned, Dorset House was also destroyed.

Nearby, another suspected incendiary was seized and roughly treated. A citizen, John Stewart, was retreating from the flames when he saw

near Bridewell . . . a man sadly bemoaning the great loss he was like to sustain, the fire then being within five or six houses of him. [He] did beseech the people, for God's sake, they having no goods of their own in danger to come in and help him to throw out trunks, chests, beds, etc, out at a window, having procured two carts or wagons to carry them away.

Whereupon I ran into his house with several others, broke down his windows, threw out his goods and loaded the carts; and there being some interval of time before the return of the carts, and seeing a room wherein were many books and loose papers, which seemed to be a library, I went in and took down a book, which proved to be Ovid's *Metamorphoses*, and while I was looking upon it, there came into the same room an old man of a low stature with a white frock. . . . I took him in my mind to be some groom come out of a stable.

In the meantime there broke forth a fire among the papers which were behind us, there being none in the room but he and I. Whereupon the rest of the people . . . rushing in upon us, put out the fire with their feet. There was a small thing of a black matter, which looked like a piece of link burning, which questionless set fire on the papers, but was immediately trod out.

[They] cried out we had set the room on fire, whereupon I took hold of the old man by the buttons under the throat and said "How now, father, it must either be you or I that must fire these papers." . . .

He said "Parce mihi, Domine." The people, which did not understand it, cried out "He is a Frenchman, kill him," and with pulling of him, his periwig fell off. Then appeared a bald skull and under his frock, he had black clothes, I think of bishop's satin, whereupon he seemed to be a grave ecclesiastic person.

I had much ado to save him from the people, but at last brought him before the Duke of York. We found in his pocket a bundle of papers closed up with wax like a packet, which was delivered to the Duke of York. I know not what was written in them, neither do I know what countryman he was, but methought he looked something Jesuitical like.

This I am certain of, that when I went into the room there was no fire in it, and it was fired when there was none but he and I in it, yet I cannot say I saw him do it, though I cannot but suspect he did it . . . because there were several houses untouched betwixt this house and where the fire was coming on. . . . What became of this fellow after we had delivered him to his Royal Highness, the Duke of York, I have not heard.[16]

The fires ravaging Bridewell burned on. Around the walls of the former royal palace were grouped some of the foulest tenements and rookeries to be found anywhere in the city and the liberties. The sanctuaries of Upper and Lower Alsatia—named for the lawless, disputed territory between France and Germany—and Sharp Island had grown up on the site of the White Friars' priory sprawling over the whole of the riverbank between Bridewell and the Temple.

The fine houses built by noblemen on the ruins of the priory had long been abandoned and divided into tenements where the inhabitants maintained their ancient but now extinguished right of sanctuary by force of arms alone. Neither the writ of the King nor that of the city ran in Alsatia, and brothels, low taverns, and dram shops catered to the frauds, debtors, thieves, robbers, and murderers who congregated there.

The "fogs and damps of the Thames" often hung over the low-lying ground on which Alsatia stood, and the buildings crowded close upon one another. "The wails of children, the scolding of their mothers, the miserable exhibition of ragged linens hung from the windows to dry spoke the wants and distresses of the wretched inhabitants, while the sounds of complaint were mocked and overwhelmed in the riotous shouts, oaths, profane songs and boisterous laughter that issued from the alehouses and taverns which, as the signs indicated, were equal in number to all the houses."

In the whole of this verminous area south of Fleet Street, there were only two streets wide enough even to admit a cart. The shacks and hovels were like paper to the flame, and in the space of a few hours the fires burning on through King Tudor Street into Magpie Alley, Hanging Sword Alley, and the rest of the warren of alleys, foot passages, and courts swept the whole stinking slum away and scattered its inhabitants to the winds.

Immediately beyond this wild, lawless territory was the great wall shielding the lawyers at the Temple from their neighbors. The flames were scorching its stones well before nightfall. The wall and the newly built brick houses of King's Bench Walk gave a temporary check to the fire, but before long these defenses too were breached.

The few lawyers remaining within the Temple, where "neither boat, barge, cart nor coach is to be had,"[17] fled before the flames. "Despairing then of ever seeing this place more but in ashes, we went to Hornsey four miles off, and in our way at Highgate we might discern with what rage and greediness it marched up Fleet Street."[18]

The Templars were entirely unprepared for the blaze. Neither the water from the Thames nor the supply from the New River was of any use to them, for there were no buckets or engines. To their added misfortune, the fire occurred during the long vacation when most of the lawyers were away and their chambers locked. "Whatsoever was there, their money, books and papers beside the evidences of many men's estates deposited in their hands, were all burned or lost to a very great value."

The Sergeants' Inn off Fleet Street at the northeast corner of the Temple was consumed in minutes, and after resisting for a while, King's Bench Walk was devoured along its entire length. Mitre Court, the Master's House, the Exchequer House Office, and all the houses facing Fleet Street were razed to the ground, and the fine trees in the gardens were left as split, blackened hulks by the flames.

Terrified by the rapid advance of the flames toward their residence in the Strand opposite Somerset House, and fearing also the violence of the mob, the Swedish ambassadors had "requested the king that they and the suite that they maintained might be moved from their present accommodation. . . . It was immediately ordered that everyone who was in their suite or under their protection should stay together and follow the ambassadors' coach."

Francisco de Rapicani had set off with the rest on Tuesday afternoon

about fifty strong, [and] followed the ambassadors on foot, as well armed as possible . . . and what an angry mob there was to be seen, young and old, men and women, all together, running, riding, walking, shouting, cursing and praying—we could scarcely pass through them. The burning of Troy came to my mind, and I fancied that it might have looked just like this.

When we had come to the house at Westminster, the king gave the ambassadors a guard at the door and the ambassadors ordered that, so as to keep out of harm, no one was to stir from the house. My room-mate, however, a Swedish nobleman whose name I will not mention, became so impatient at staying away from a lady-friend that he had, that he risked going out. When he wanted to come back again and was just walking or standing in the street, he was seized by a furious mob, together with the steward who was with him, and hung up from the projecting sign of a house at a street corner.

The steward, however, proved his salvation, for he made such a commotion with the crowd that they could not decide which of them to hang first. Thus a little time was gained, and they had hardly got the nobleman strung up when a mounted troop of the Duke of York's bodyguard came by. They saw what was going on, rode up and cut the rope with a sword, threw the crowd's victim onto a horse and brought him away. The next day our good gallant came back home but he was dreadfully teased about the blue ring which could be seen around his neck.

With this notable example before our eyes, we could see without being told what atrocities the maddened people were committing against foreigners; however there was also something in store for the court chaplain. When he heard that the fire was lessening, and from where we were it no longer seemed so terrible, he was seized with curiosity and wanted to see for himself how things were. But he got short shrift, and some people brought him back home with his whole body full of [bruises,] his head and face covered in blood, his sleeves and collar all in rags round his neck and hands, and his cassock turned back to front and tattered at the edge.

When the ambassadors heard about it, they wanted to see him in this state and had him come into the long ante-room. When they asked him what had led him to go out among the mob, he replied, "Why, Your Excellencies, the whole time of the fire I prayed God on my knees that he would keep it away from these rogues; and now what sort of thanks do I get? Oh, may the fires of hell burn them for ever." When he began to give vent to his sort of priestly ardor, the ambassadors turned round and laughed and let him alone.[19]

Chapter 8

The Fires of Hell

Courſe cloth for Tow.

God grant mine eyes may never behold the like, who now saw
above 10,000 houses all in one flame.
John Evelyn, *Diary*

IN THE NORTHEAST OF THE CITY THE FIRES WERE STILL ADVANCING
from Fenchurch Street. They destroyed the church of St. Gabriel,
Fenchurch, and Pewterers' Hall. One of the few relics to survive was a glass
pane, etched with the images of a sundial, a spider, and a fly.

Burning steadily east, the flames ignited Clothworkers' Hall, where the
cellar filled with barrels of oil burned constantly for three days and three
nights. Where the ground fell away from the ridge, the flames could make
little more progress into the wind, but they burned on eastward closer to
the river, entering Tower Street, "the fire coming on in that narrow street
on both sides with infinite fury."[1] The "trays and dishes and shovels, etc,"
of one occupant, Mr. Howell, "were flung all along Tower Street in the kennels,"[2] as panic seized those carrying his goods away.

Seeing the eastward march of the flames, Samuel Pepys and Sir
William Batten dug a hole in the gardens of the Navy Office and buried
Sir William's wine and all the papers of Pepys's office that he "could not

otherwise dispose of." Later in the day he and Sir William Penn dug a second hole "and put our wine in it and I my parmesan cheese."[3]

At the northern fringes of the fire, the Merchant Taylors' Hall, due east of the still smoldering ruins of the Royal Exchange, was burning. The crypt escaped with little damage, but the medieval hall—so vast that a thousand guests were said to have dined together at one city feast with a further three hundred in an adjoining apartment—was completely destroyed. As it burned, the hexagonal turret rising above it, capped with a dome and a great weathervane, collapsed with a roar that was audible even above the scream of the wind and the thunder of the flames. The merchant tailors' charters and papers were saved by being moved to the master's house in Seething Lane, but all the plate of this rich company was destroyed. Three hundred pounds was later paid for the lumps of melted silver found "in the dust."

The gale had now become so fierce that the fire could make little further progress into the teeth of the wind. The merchant tailors' kitchen and the almshouses just beyond the hall were only partially burned, while the church of St. Martin Outwich a few yards farther to the east was unscathed.

Bishopsgate Street was also untouched, but the fires continued to rage northward, consuming the French church, granted to the French congregation by Edward VI. It was the sole surviving relic of St. Anthony's Hospital, the medieval foundation whose swine, St. Anthony's pigs, had the curious right to roam free about the city with bells hung round their necks, while all others were confined.

Burning on across the face of the gale, the flames swept on, crossing Broad Street and Throgmorton Street to engulf the vast Drapers' Hall. Built by Thomas Cromwell, it was the most beautiful Tudor building in London. A turreted gateway opened onto a broad paved courtyard, and the great hall along one side, lit by bay windows and clerestory lights, also had a dark chamber with lattice windows from within which, unseen, the occupants could gaze down on the revels below.

The great roof timbers cut from oak that had stood before the Conquest were burned to ashes. Four hundred and forty-six pounds in coin was forgotten by the Renter Warden in his haste to flee. Left in a cupboard, it was so melted and defaced that when salvaged from the ashes it could be sold only for the scrap value of its metal. The drapers' gold and silver plate was saved, however. Thrown into a sewer running beneath the gardens, it escaped damage in the blaze and was recovered intact.

These vast gardens, extended by Thomas Cromwell by the simple, ruthless expedient of confiscating the land to the north of the hall—"no man dared go to argue the matter"[4]—proved too large an open space even for these fires to cross. Although they also lapped around the Dutch church at Austin Friars, they were rebuffed by the wind and the thickness of the stone walls, and the great nave of the church survived. A few yards to the east, the humble church of St. Peter-le-Poore, "bearing the appearance of a tavern rather than a place of worship with its clock hung out in the center of the street like the sign of a country inn,"[5] also escaped destruction.

The fires had reached their northward limit in this part of the city, but nothing could halt their westward march. St. Margaret, Lothbury, was utterly destroyed save for a single chapel. The entire district, full of smoke-belching foundries and workshops where the makers of "candlesticks, chafing dishes, spice mortars and the like" created "a loathsome noise,"[6] was razed to the ground.

Only a single block in the whole parish survived. A city alderman desperate to save his property produced a hundred pounds in gold and began distributing coins among the bystanders, promising them more if the buildings were saved. Fortified by the promised reward, his makeshift band of workmen pulled down the houses around the "new buildings" and extinguished the flames.

At other places, "the extraordinary offers made by the owners of the houses encouraged the workmen, as at Pie Corner, where one gave them fifty pounds,"[7] but not all were so generous in defense of their property. Sir Richard Browne had a chest with ten thousand pounds in it "taken out of the fire, for which service he gave the men who ventured their lives £4."[8] Alderman Sir Samuel Starling, "a very rich man, without children . . . after our men had saved his house did give two shillings and sixpence among thirty of them, and did quarrel with some that would remove the rubbish out of the way of the fire, saying that they came to steal."[9]

For many, no amount of money could now save their homes. Beyond Lothbury was a merchants' quarter stocked with goods garnered from every corner of the known world. At its heart was the Guildhall, the great palace of the city government, flanked on all sides by company halls. The firepost set up in Coleman Street yards east of the Guildhall was now square in the path of the advancing flames. In the face of heat so intolerable that it could not be endured at a distance of a hundred yards, the post had to be abandoned.

The firestorm, growing in noise and appetite by the second, thundered out of King's Arms Court and Bell Alley and crossed Coleman Street to ravage the church of St. Stephen Coleman. Augmented by fresh torrents of flame pouring out of the top of Old Jewry, the inferno then swept on across Basinghall Street and broke against the walls of Blackwell Hall, the cloth market just east of Guildhall.

The vast building was piled high with huge quantities of cloth brought into London ready for the Michaelmas market. Great stores of paper, tobacco, books, and almost every other merchandise were also destroyed as the flames surrounded and then engulfed the hall. The fires paused to gorge themselves on these rich stores of combustibles and then moved on.

A narrow passage between Blackwell Hall and the church of St. Lawrence Jewry gave access to the Guildhall yard. The fires burst upon it with the force of a bomb, and within minutes the Guildhall was a sea of flame. But even those ferocious, ungovernable fires could not destroy the massive stone walls of the building. Blackened and fire-scarred, they still stood as everything around them was utterly destroyed; but confined within those great walls, the flames burned with renewed ferocity, casting down the gallery and bursting out through the windows and the roof.

All through the night the hammerbeam roof of the Guildhall was in flames, "a fearful spectacle which stood the whole body of it together in view for several hours together after the fire had taken it, without flames (I suppose because the timber was such solid oak) in a bright shining coal, as if it had been a palace of gold or a great building of brass."[10]

The Council Chamber, the Mayor's Court and Parlour, the Town Clerk's Offices, the Hall Keeper's House, and the Sheriff's Court were all destroyed, but the crypt below Guildhall withstood the savage heat and even the impact of the massive roof timbers as they at last burned through and crashed down.

Safe in the stone-arched cellars deep underground, all the records and parchments of London since its foundation survived. Among them was the *Liber Albus,* the city's white book compiled by Richard Whittington and his clerk, gathering together the City Laws and Precedents from centuries of documents and thousands of other ancient records kept in the vaults.

Aboveground all was burned to ashes. Having no hall of their own, the basket makers were accustomed to meet in a room at the Guildhall, and "their chest, with carpets, cushions, silver spoons, books, writings and other things standing in the same room were consumed by the dreadful and lamentable fire."[11] The company halls surrounding Guildhall fared no better, and the halls of the coopers, masons, weavers and girdlers—this last "a very handsome building with an open courtyard and a garden behind it"[12]—were all razed to the ground.

As the Guildhall burned, the streets around it were also engulfed. Flames roared along Basinghall Street, Aldermanbury, and Milk Street, and on into Wood Street and Gutter Lane. As the inhabitants of Milk Street fled before the flames, a tall, lean figure, wrapped in a cloak as black as a raven's wing, stood immobile, apparently oblivious of the heat and danger, his gaze fixed on the church of St. Mary Magdalene. Thomas Vincent had been rector there until ejected after the Act of Uniformity and "did not escape prison for his nonconformity."[13] He had retired to Hoxton, where he preached privately, but the plague year had seen him return to the devastated city, preaching the word in pulpits vacated by ministers fleeing for their lives.

Now once more he strode the streets of the city, apparently without fear, nodding to himself with satisfaction as the fires roared and the buildings tumbled. "God seems to come down, as he did on Mount Sinai, when the Mount burned with fire; such warm preaching those churches never had; such lightning dreadful sermons were never before delivered in London."[14]

The fires advanced with such headlong speed that isolated pockets of housing, pitifully few in number, survived. While the Sheriff's Compter in Wood Street and the nearby hall of the haberdashers' company were burned, a small group of houses nearby somehow escaped destruction.

The flames gained yet greater impetus as they fed on the densely packed timber houses in the warren of narrow alleys extending north from Cheapside all the way to the city walls. They roared through foot passages as narrow and dark as tunnels, with jetties almost meeting overhead, purged the tenements and courts with fire, and then burst with explosive force into lanes and streets already threatened by blazes burning from the east.

The terrified occupants escaped by any way they could find through the maze. How many were left behind to perish trapped in that warren can never be known. The rest, hotly pursued by the ravening fires, fled through the reopened city gates at Moorgate, Little Moorgate, and the postern at Cripplegate, to the open spaces of Moorfields and the Artillery Ground.

Behind them the inferno raged on. The flames broke like storm seas against the city walls and swept westward along them, ravaging the quarter of the city in the angle where the walls turned south and then west again. They lapped around the Barbican, set on the highest point in the city, but were held back from Cripplegate by a firebreak created by blowing up the surrounding houses with gunpowder. It could not be used nearer to the flames for fear of spontaneous detonation in the heat.

Burning on toward Aldersgate, the fires threatened to cut off another line of retreat for the panic-stricken citizens. They had burned so far along the riverbank that escape that way was now impossible, and there was a terrified stampede toward the remaining western city gates of Newgate and Ludgate.

Loaded carts rattled over the cobbles, trying to force a way through the fleeing crowds, and there was "scarcely a back either of man or woman that hath strength but had a burden on it in the streets. . . . Such throngs of poor citizens coming in and going forth from the unburned parts, heavy laden with some pieces of their goods, but more heavy laden with weighty grief and sorrow of heart so that it is wonderful they did not quite sink under their burden."[15]

The streets were "barricaded with goods, carts, coaches and distracted crowds."[16] Some had abandoned their possessions to save children, the old or the sick, carrying them aloft on their backs and shoulders. "They were bringing forth their wives, some from their childbed, and their little ones, some from their sickbed, out of their houses and sending them into the country or somewhere into the fields."[17] "As they ran they made a heartrending murmur; one would have need to have been a Nero to have watched such a spectacle without pity."[18] Thousands and thousands more spilled through Ludgate and Newgate as the waves of flame beat ever closer to them. But ten times that number were still trapped inside the city.

As the firefront thundered on, the halls of the wax chandlers, broderers, saddlers, and scriveners and the churches of St. Mary Aldermanbury, St. Albans, Wood Street, St. Mary Staining, St. John Zachary, St. Anne Aldersgate, and St. Olave in Silver Street all were consumed. One great house in Noble Street survived, the former residence of Robert Tichborne, Lord Mayor in 1657, who subsequently was executed for high treason. All the other buildings were destroyed.

When Parish Clerks' Hall burned, the press on which the weekly Bills of Mortality were printed was destroyed. No bills were published for the following three weeks. The dead went unrecorded and unburied, most cremated where they fell in the ashes of their own houses.

The flames beating against the city walls found the release they were seeking at Aldersgate, rebuilt in 1616 in honor of King James I. A massive equestrian figure of the King stood over the central arch, flanked by the arms of England and Scotland, and the figures of the prophets were set in niches on the side towers.

The fire burst through the gate in a fiery blast that destroyed thirty houses around the gate, but the city walls rearing high above the rooftops and extending to west and north of the great tower by Noble Street shielded the area from the full force of the east wind. The fires made little further progress up Aldersgate, and barely thirty yards from the gate, St. Botolph's Church was scorched but unburned.

Inside the crucible formed by the city walls, the fires remained invincible. The goldsmiths' workshops clustered around Foster Lane, supplying the fine shops of Cheapside, were razed to the ground, and though the ancient square tower of St. Vedast's Church resisted the flames, all around it was leveled.

Goldsmiths' Hall, rebuilt only thirty years previously and the seat of the Parliamentary Committee sequestering the estates of Royalist supporters during the Civil War, was overwhelmed. Most of the gold plate had already been carried to safety, but the silver plate and the tables containing the goldsmiths' marks were lost. The south wall of the hall alone survived the fire, but it was left in such perilous condition that it blew down in a gale the following winter.

Still gathering speed, the flames roared on beyond Foster Lane to burn the foul tenements and dismal rookeries sprawling around St. Martin's le Grand, a medieval foundation and sanctuary seized at the Dissolution and dismantled stone by stone. Just to the south the fires were also racing along Blowbladder Street and into Newgate Street, cutting off St. Paul's from the north.

On the slopes below the cathedral, they were burning up St. Benet's Hill, Addle Hill, and Puddle Dock Hill. The King's Printing House, from where royal proclamations were issued, was burned as the fire climbed the slopes above Oak Tree Court. The King's Wardrobe, on a sprawling site on Puddle Dock Hill just below Carter Lane, was also destroyed. There were kept "the ancient clothes of our English kings which they wore on great festivals, so that this Wardrobe was in fact a library for antiquaries caring to read the mode and fashion of all ages." The loss to the fire would have been greater but for the avarice of King James, who at the beginning of his reign had sold the contents of the Wardrobe to the Earl of Dunbar, "by whom they were sold, resold and re-resold." The church of St. Andrew in the Wardrobe also perished.

Burning their way on up the steeply rising ground, the fires crossed Shoemaker Row and Carter Lane, destroying the Bell Inn, from where Richard Quyney had once written "to my loving good friend and country man, Mr Wm Shakespeare."[19] The flames roared up St. Paul's Chain, Prerogative Court, Black Swan Court, Mitre Court, and through Creed Lane, to burst upon St. Paul's churchyard. The densely packed houses clustered around St. Paul's ignited like dried sticks, and the fires began to lap against the dilapidated cathedral.

Flakes of stone lay everywhere around the foot of the walls. Among them were larger fragments broken off in the winter gales and frosts, and sent crashing to the ground below. Only by divine providence had no one been killed. Settlement of the foundations had caused the great tower to lean from the vertical, and the weight of the massive roof had spread the walls of the nave. "Those pillars, vast as they are, even eleven foot in diameter, are bent outwards at least six inches from their first position."[20]

The spire of the cathedral, capped by a great golden cross and eagle, had been toppled by the fire of 1561, occasioned by "a marvelous great fiery lightning" in one version and "the negligence of a plumber who left his pan of fire there while he went to dinner, as he confessed of later years on his deathbed"[21] in another. It had still not been replaced more than a century later. Elizabeth and James I had conspired in benign neglect of the church, and when Archbishop Laud, under the patronage of Charles I, made attempts to restore it, he found it "like a great skeleton so pitifully handled that you might tell her ribs through her skin," and ready to "sink into its own ruins." Under Laud's promptings, much of the portico was refaced with Portland stone "excellent against all smoke and weather, and the tower scaffolded up to the top with a purpose to . . . rebuild it more fair and of a greater height with a stately pinnacle at each corner and . . . the biggest and most tunable bells in the world."[22]

At the outbreak of the Civil War all funds for repairs were confiscated, and the scaffolding was given to Colonel Jephson's Regiment as compensation for arrears in pay. When it was pulled down, part of the south transept and its roof fell with it. The ruins were left where they lay, save the lead from part of the roof, which went to build water pipes in the city.

The great cathedral was also much despoiled inside. Henry VIII had gambled and lost its peal of "four Jesus bells" to Sir Miles Partridge on a single toss of the dice. "Thus [Sir Miles] brought the bells to ring in his pocket, but the ropes afterwards catched about his neck and for some offence he was hanged in the days of King Edward VI."[23]

St. Paul's suffered far worse desecration under the Commonwealth. Anything smacking of popery—painted glass, wood carvings, statues and tombs—was destroyed, and more lead from the roof was taken to be smelted down for use as bullets and pewter. Whores used part of the cathedral as a bordello, and horses were ridden up the steps and down the nave— one soldier fell and broke his neck while doing so—and stabled in the canons' stalls. A colt foaled in this cathedral stable was baptized by the soldiers with blasphemous rites. Saw-pits were dug in the floors and a blacksmith's forge was set up, its chimney poking through the roof.

The Restoration ended the worst of the abuses, but the work of repair and rebuilding had been desultory and stifled of funds by the King's always pressing need for money. As the fires closed in, the wooden scaffolding that again cloaked the tower was more of a threat than a safeguard to St. Paul's.

The great cathedral was now cut off from three sides, the south, east, and north, and the fires burning up from the river along the city walls were close to completing its encirclement, being almost at Ludgate at the foot of the steep hill rising from the Fleet.

The narrow single arch of Ludgate, made even more cramped by St. Martin's Church jutting out into the roadway, had been choked with people. Now they were fleeing north through the courts and alleys, rushing to reach Newgate before the fires racing in from the north and east sealed the last escape route in the west of the city.

St. Paul's was as yet untouched by the flames surrounding it, but Stationers' Hall at Amen Corner, the Dean's great house to the southwest of the cathedral, and Dean Colet's School to the east were all consumed. Samuel Cromlehome, the High Master of the school, lost his personal library, reputedly the finest in the kingdom. "The loss of these books, I verily believe shortened his days, for he was a great lover of his books and spared no cost in procuring them from all parts of Europe."[24]

The Royal College of Surgeons at Amen Corner had been ransacked when locked up and abandoned during the plague; now it was razed to the ground. Dr. Merritt, the librarian, had just sufficient warning of the fire's advance to cut the portraits of two eminent physicians from their frames. Together with the charters and annals, a case of surgical instruments, and a few volumes from the library, they were all that was saved from the flames.

The stationers had lost their buildings, their printing presses, and all the printed volumes stored in their warehouse, but they, like the booksellers and mercers in the lanes and courts around Little Britain and Paternoster Row, had had enough warning of the onrush of the flames to carry much of their goods into St. Paul's itself. The mercers' finest cloth went into a great strong-room belowground. The rest was heaped in the open churchyard against the walls, a safe distance, or so they hoped, from the surrounding buildings.

The booksellers and stationers took their stock to St. Faith's in the crypt beneath the floor of the eastern part of St. Paul's. It was their own church and the safest refuge from fire in the whole of the city. There they piled their books, papers, and parchments from floor to ceiling. They were neatly stacked like pots in a kiln, separated from the others by a gap just sufficient to allow the free circulation of air, and bore the owner's tags, crest, or mark, ready to be reclaimed when the fire had passed.

Even as the fires burned closer to the cathedral walls, the firefront was sweeping on, tearing down Ludgate Hill with a terrifying roar. Where the city walls stood proud above the surrounding buildings, they had been a formidable barrier for the flames. Here, with the slopes rising steeply above them, they proved no obstacle at all.

The Duke of York had been directing efforts to construct a firebreak on the banks of the Fleet, and had "won the hearts of the people with his continual and indefatigable pains, day and night, in helping to quench the fire, handing buckets of water with as much diligence as the poorest man that did assist; if the Lord Mayor had done as much, his example might have gone far towards saving the city."[25]

During the previous night the Duke of York had sent orders to the Deputy Lieutenants and justices of the peace of the neighboring counties summoning workmen with their tools to be in London by daybreak. All the firehooks, ropes, axes, and ladders that could be found were brought into the city, and the ironmongers' stocks of spades and axes, pails and brooms were also requisitioned. One ironmonger, Starkey, provided thirteen dozen pails and sixty brooms, "which was the means, under God, of stopping the fire at that place."[26]

Such desperate measures still seemed a feeble response to the relentless onward rush of the fire. Around midday Lord Arlington sent a despairing dispatch: "The fire has burnt as far into the body of the City as St Paul's with such violence that no art or pains can meddle with it. All our hopes are now under God in cutting off a part of the town along by Holborn Bridge and so down to Bridewell, to see whether we can save this."[27]

Since the fire began, seamen from the fleet had been urging the wholesale use of gunpowder to demolish houses. It "had been proposed the first day by some experienced persons; then esteemed a desperate cure,"[28] and their advice had largely been ignored. Finally, when much of the city already lay in ruins, they were set to work without restraints. More sailors and dockyardmen were brought in to augment the exhausted forces of soldiers and militia, and the wholesale demolition of houses began.

Connected by a trail of powder, barrels of gunpowder were placed on the ground floor of each house to be demolished. They were detonated in sequence, and the force of the blast was enough to dislocate the timber framing of the building and send it crashing to the ground. "It was first lift[ed] up a yard or two and then fell down flat, without any danger to the bystanders."[29] Any fires caused by the blast were quickly extinguished, but the sound of the explosions on top of the thunder of the fire and the crash of falling buildings "did frighten the people more than anything else."[30]

Panic had seized the King and his Court as much as his subjects. The Queen Mother fled Somerset House in the Strand for Hampton Court, and the King issued a warrant for the removal of the Exchequer to Nonsuch in Surrey, commandeering carriages and lighters for the task, "all Mayors, Bailiffs, etc, to assist at their peril," and sent many of his choice goods by water to Hampton Court.[31] Having secured the safe disposal of his money and treasure, the King traveled downriver by barge to the burning city.

Surrounded by a small company of the King's Guard, he toured the fire stations at the western fringes of the fire, "twice every day and for many hours together on horseback and on foot."[32] He urged the exhausted soldiers and members of the Trained Bands to yet greater efforts, once more encouraging them by words and the golden guineas he dispensed liberally from a pouch across his shoulder, and sometimes even by his own example, descending from his horse to take his place in the line of sweating, smoke-blackened men working with ax and shovel and bucket.

"The King and Duke, who rode from one place to another, and put themselves into great dangers among the burning and falling houses, to give advice and direction what was to be done, underwent as much fatigue as the meanest, and had as little sleep or rest; and the faces of all men appeared ghastly and in the highest confusion."[33]

"When the citizens had abandoned all further care of the place and were intent chiefly upon the preservation of their goods, [the King and the Duke of York] undertook the work themselves and with incredible magnanimity rode up and down giving orders for blowing up of houses with gunpowder to make void spaces for the fire to die in, and standing still to see those orders executed, exposing their persons not only to the multitude but to the very flames themselves and the ruins of the buildings ready to fall upon them, and sometimes laboring with their own hands to give example to others."[34]

It was the first honest toil those soft white hands had ever seen. The King urged his courtiers to the same task, the Duke of York at his side, "handling the water in buckets when they stood up to the ankles in water and playing the engine for many hours together."[35]

Even after the King had returned to Whitehall, the Duke of York remained in the streets until almost midnight. His exertions won him admiration not just from court sycophants but from other, more dispassionate observers. None were "so active and stirring in this business, he being all the day long, from five in the morning till eleven or twelve at night, using all means possible to save the rest of the city and suburbs."[36]

"Had not the Duke been present and forced all people to submit to his commands . . . I am confident there had not been a house standing near Whitehall. The citizens for the first rank minded only for their own preservation, the middle sort so distracted and amazed that they did not know what they did, the poorer they minded nothing but pilfering, so the City was abandoned to the fire."[37]

All day long, a huge force of soldiers and militia had labored on the fetid banks of the Fleet Ditch. The Duke of York directed operations between the Thames and Fleet Bridge, while the Earl of Craven took the northern section up to Holborn Bridge. Civilians worked alongside the soldiers, pressed to the task or bribed with gold. Together they pulled down sheds and wharves, and blasted apart houses and workplaces, clearing a broad firebreak running from the Thames as far as Holborn Bridge.

Even as the exhausted men toiled to complete their task, the fires mocked their efforts. Blazing embers, carried on the gale high above their heads, ignited buildings the length of the Fleet and started fires as far distant as Salisbury Court, more than a hundred yards away. The Duke of York found himself almost completely "environed with fire"[38] as wind-borne burning debris set fire to the buildings behind him. Forced to flee for his life, he was nearly overcome by heat.

Abandoning their tools, the men working on the Fleet fled after him, as flames bursting through Ludgate and spilling in floods of fire over the walls "rushed like a torrent down Ludgate Hill."[39] As the flames approached, the swine still rooting in the baked mud of the ditch lumbered up the banks and ran squealing through the streets.

The jailers of Ludgate had thrown open the cell doors and let the debtors incarcerated there flee for their lives.[40] The flames moved so fast that the statue of Elizabeth over the arch at Ludgate was barely touched by them, and those of King Lud and his son also survived, though much damaged, but St. Martin's just inside the gate was utterly destroyed. The church plate was saved, but so impoverished was the church after the fire that the wardens twice were forced to raise money by pawning it.

At the ditch side below Fleet Bridge, at the bottom of Ludgate Hill, the fires cauterized the site of the Rag Fair, the market where old clothes and bedding were bought and sold. Most of the clothes and bedding traded there were stolen. The dead were swiftly stripped of their clothes, but thieves also broke into houses, robbed fellow lodgers in tenements and boarding houses, and took clothes from washing lines. Even wigs were stolen, sometimes by small boys leaning over walls to snatch them from people's heads as they went by.

Beyond the bridge lay Fleet Street, narrow and twisting, and for much of its length fronted by tall timber-framed and jettied houses. Once more the flames tore through them like a brush fire. By five o'clock it was "advanced as high as Fleet Conduit."

At the foot of Shoe Lane was the Standard, where water from Paddington and Tyburn Brook was piped "for the poor to drink, the rich to dress their meats." It was capped by a stone tower decorated with images of angels. "Sweet sounding bells" set in it sounded the hours of the day and night.

The bells were silenced by the roar of the flames. They swept up Shoe Lane and consumed John Ogilby's printing house in King's Head Court, destroying every copy and the original manuscript of his epic twelve-book poem, *Carolies,* exalting Charles I. The heartbroken poet called it "the pride, divertisement, business and sole comfort of my age."[41]

A little farther up Shoe Lane the fires devoured another victim. Paul Lowell, a watchmaker living behind the Globe Tavern, "being about eighty years of age and dull of hearing, was also deaf to the good admonitions of his son and friends and would never desert the house till it fell upon him, and sunk him with the ruins in the cellar, where afterwards his bones, together with his keys were found."[42]

In the north of the city, channeled by the walls, the fire sweeping west from Aldersgate was roaring along Bull and Mouth Street. It crossed Butcher Hall Lane and laid siege to Christchurch. Second in size only to St. Paul's, the church of the Gray Friars had been almost alone in surviving the Dissolution little altered.

By grant of Henry VIII, the choir remained a parish church and the nave found use as a storehouse. Three English queens lay buried beneath its flagstone floor, and though desecrated and with a public footway passing between the nave and the choir, the church still stood.

To the north, sheltered by its great walls, was Christ's Hospital, where 260 children were schooled. As the fire approached, they were formed into columns and marched off first to Clerkenwell and later to Ware and Hertford. They alone had cause to remember the Great Fire with something other than horror. The school did not reassemble for another fourteen months, and September 2, the anniversary of the day the fire began, was long afterward kept as an annual holiday for the boys.

In the angle of the city walls, which again turned south above Newgate to track the Fleet Ditch to the river, this rambling complex of buildings lay full in the path of the flames. The great church survived, little damaged, but the rest of its buildings were razed.

The fire swept on, devouring the stalls and sheds of the butchers and tripe sellers in the Newgate Shambles, and ripping through the surrounding courts and alleys, it fell upon Newgate itself, bursting through the barred windows and setting the gatehouse and both wings ablaze. The jailers and their charges fled before the flames. Attempts were made to march the prisoners off to the Clink in Southwark, but in the panic and confusion the guard was "not strong enough to hinder the most notorious from escaping by the way."[43] If any were left behind, trapped in their cells, the fires obliterated all trace before they moved on. The thick stone walls of Newgate withstood the flames, but so fierce was the heat that the great iron bars and padlocks of the jail and the manacles and chains in the cells were melted.

With the wind still driving the firefront westward, the flames burned only a little way north outside Newgate. They were checked at Pie Corner on Cock Lane, and just to the east, the great hospital of St. Bartholomew escaped unscathed. St. Sepulchre's lay almost downwind of Newgate, however. The tall tower capped with four pinnacles survived the blaze, but within it the wooden staging was consumed and the bells crashed to earth and melted.

The wardens later paid twenty-two pounds and eighteen shillings "for cleansing the bell metal from the dust." The ingots cast from the molten lead from the roof, gathered after the fire, were refined, "wherein it is supposed the parish plate may be found."[44] The only bell saved from the church was the small handbell with which the Elizabethan merchant tailor Robert Dove rang a death knell before the cells of condemned felons in Newgate. On his own death he left fifty pounds to the church for the felons' knell to be rung in perpetuity.

Still driven on by the gale, the fires raged on down Snow Hill, burning the Holborn Conduit and roaring through the liberties where the war wounded were housed. They could make little progress farther north of Holborn Bridge and were stopped again at Green Dragon Court in Cow Lane and in George Yard, but flames also were burning down Turnagain Lane, New Castle Street, George Alley, Seacoal Lane, and Fleet Lane.

This area between Newgate and Ludgate down to the banks of the Fleet was the oldest part of London outside the walls. The flensing pits of the tanners were dug into the side of the hill above the river, and skinners, dyers, and a multitude of other trades were based there. The waste they threw down into the ditch clogged its banks, blocking the flow, poisoning the water and tainting the air.

The fires cauterized this foul ground and ravaged the Fleet Prison, the oldest in London, sacked by Wat Tyler's men in the Peasants' Revolt but rebuilt on the same site. The prisoners scrambled to escape from its underground cells, nicknamed with leaden irony Bartholomew Fair, for nowhere was less reminiscent of the jollity of the great fair that took place within sight and sound of the Fleet. The flames barely paused to consume the prison before sweeping on and over "the Rules" that surrounded it, where bankrupts and debtors with the funds to pay the wardens their garnish were permitted to live untroubled by their creditors.

In the wake of the fire, the warden of the prison, Sir Jeremy Whichcote, showed a charity and humanity displayed by few of his fellows. He housed the debtors himself, purchased Caronne House in Lambeth for their temporary accommodation, and later had the Fleet rebuilt on its ancient site, all at his own expense.

The easterly gale was still increasing in force, but the hungry fires were sucking in the wind from every quarter, drawn by the terrible, irresistible power of the holocaust now raging at its height. As darkness fell, the light from burning London could be seen fifty miles away.

For miles around, the citizens lay huddled on the bare earth of the fields, their bundles of belongings scattered around them, trying to take what rest they could. Moorfields and Finsbury Fields were now buried under the tide of humanity, but any piece of open ground from St. Giles and Soho Fields in the west to Islington and Highgate in the north and St. George's field in Southwark was also filled with homeless citizens.

The fires had now destroyed the entire city save a small section to the north and east, yet St. Paul's still stood like a great castle, its walls unbreached. Around it all else was laid in ruins, as the blazes conquered the hill on every side and came together on the summit, surrounding the cathedral and licking at the walls.

The pall of black, oily smoke over the city grew more and more dense, forming clouds so thickly charged with particles that a thunder storm broke out, but it was unlike any storm the watchers below had ever seen. Out of the lowering pall of smoke, lightning began forking down around St. Paul's, the bolts stabbing into buildings that already were ablaze. The peals of thunder were lost in the roar of the flames and the screaming of the wind, and though the storm raged for several minutes not a single drop of rain fell from the skies, only the endless torrent of sparks and flaming brands.

Hundreds of people had taken refuge in the cathedral, sure that whatever befell the city, great St. Paul's would stand unharmed. Many lost their nerve and fled as the fires closed in. Those who remained had to make what escape they could, seeking some gap, some chink in the encircling wall of flame, or perish where they stood. Among them were several dogs cowering among the goods piled against the outside of the walls. As the flames came nearer they set up a desolate, terrible howling, which was not extinguished until the smoke and flames overwhelmed them.

An old woman also huddled in the angle of the walls at the southeastern corner of the cathedral. Burned out of her home the previous day, she had wandered the streets, driven before the flames, unable to stop and rest, her mind enfeebled by shock and fear. She had sought refuge at last under the sheltering walls of the cathedral, but now even that sanctuary was threatened by the devouring fires. Her eyes darted to left and right, seeking a break in the wall of flames. Several times she took a few hesitant steps forward, but as the heat seared her face, singed her clothes, and set her hair smoldering, she retreated back to the shadow of the walls.

She cowered there as the fire moved closer, her skin red and blistering. Then she sank to the ground and closed her eyes. The smoke and fumes had done their work even before the flames reached her and turned her tattered rags into a fiery shroud. In death her body crouched, and she thrust out her bony, blackened fists as if fighting the flames that engulfed her.

Now there would be no escape for anyone. The wall of fire completely enclosed St. Paul's, blackening the walls. Only a week before, a group under Dr. Wren had carried out a survey in order to draw up plans and prepare estimates for the repair of the dilapidated cathedral. The fire now rendered those plans irrelevant.

At eight o'clock that Tuesday evening a live brand, one of hundreds driven by the bellowing winds of the firestorm onto the roof of the cathedral, lodged against a board laid over a part of the roof where the lead was missing. Fueled by the dust, soot, and cobwebs accumulated over six centuries, the fire ignited the board, and flames then spread to the timbers supporting the roof. The wooden scaffolding erected around the cathedral for the repair work being carried out that summer hastened its demise.

The jackdaws huddled in their roosts among the pinnacles, niches, and buttresses of the tower had watched as the smoke and flames grew closer, showing their unease by the frequent circling flights they made, but always returning to the great stone tower. Now they fled, their screeches of terror echoing the cries of the people trapped in the cathedral below them. Buffeted by the gale and seized by the updraft from the raging firestorm, the jackdaws disappeared into the pall of smoke, their singed forms almost indistinguishable from the blackened papers and burning embers carried aloft with them.

Streams of smoke wreathed the roof timbers and flowed down the inside of the stone walls, filling the body of the church with a vapor more dense than any incense. An eerie light shone through it, as the flames raging across the roof cast their light through the painted windows above the choir.

A cracking, spitting sound could be heard amid the ceaseless tumult of the fires, as the flames penetrated the roof timbers and sparks and embers began to rain down into the nave. As their goods took fire, the people trapped there fled in panic, fighting to find a way down into the vaults or bursting out of the doors, to be confronted by flames rising as high as the cathedral itself. Some found gaps in the wall of fire and fled through them, their clothes igniting from the heat as they ran. Others did not.

The ancient roof beams, desiccated by the ten-month drought, and the mountains of goods stored inside St. Paul's burned with such ferocity that an hour later William Taswell, a boy standing at a landing place on the riverbank a mile west of the cathedral, was able to read by the light of the flames.[45]

The King and the Duke of York, still riding between the fire stations in the west, saw the cathedral burn. "The fire was now universal like Death himself and respected neither sceptres nor crowns. In the very sight of the King himself it proceeded to crown itself the conqueror of the highest parts of the great building . . . and in a few hours left this marvelous building, the labor of many years, a smoking mass of lamentable ruins."[46]

The cloth of the mercers piled around the churchyard and stored within the nave, the stock of the stationers and booksellers, and the furniture and goods of hundreds, perhaps thousands, of terrified citizens stacked in the cathedral were merely more fuel for the inferno.

The gale from the east was indistinguishable in strength from the winds dragged in from every other direction by the ferocious appetite of the flames. Dust, dung, hay and straw, rags, laths and lumps of wood, pigeons and jackdaws still clinging to their roosts in the tower, all were sucked into the vortex and then spewed out, blackened and burned, from the fiery pillar of smoke and sparks rising miles into the sky.

A strange hissing sound, like rain sweeping across the roofs, made itself heard among the tumult of the fires. The lead of the cathedral roof, six acres in extent, was melting. Terrible in its beauty, bright silver in color and sparkling, hissing, and flashing as it fell, the molten lead tumbled in lava streams into the body of the church and cascaded from the spouts projecting from the outside walls. Everything it touched erupted in flame and fury. A tide of molten metal swept outward over the cobbles, "the very pavements glowing with fiery redness, so as no horse nor man was able to tread on them."[47] The molten lead ran down the kennels in floods, sweeping down the hill in a boiling, bubbling torrent toward the Thames, and suffocating, poisonous fumes filled the air.

The great stones of the church began exploding "like grenados," and the sound of their detonations struck fresh terror into the fleeing citizens. Shattered fragments hurtled in all directions, and pieces of stone "weighing 20, 40, 100 pounds"[48] were blasted off, hurtling over the churchyard to smash into the rubble of the still burning houses surrounding it. Every stone that remained was white and calcined, the skin burned from the face of St. Paul's.

As the cathedral burned, parts of the aisle walls collapsed, and air rushing through the gaps further fanned the furnace inside. The holes gaping in the walls offered a vision into the fires of hell. None could approach, for even if rubble had not blocked every street and alley, the stones were glowing red and the very air seemed on fire, the heat so intense that even at a furlong distant none could face the flames.

The great rose window at the eastern end melted, and the burning roof collapsed inward with a rumble that shook the earth. The falling timbers and masonry smashed through the flagstone floor, opening the roof of the crypt of St. Faith's.

When the booksellers had finished carrying in their volumes, they sealed each door and window to ensure that the fire would not penetrate the crypt. Starved of oxygen but already heated far above ignition point, the smoldering stacks of books and papers needed only air to make them explode into flame. A wall of fire flashed over the roof of the crypt, while molten lead still dripping from the roof burned down through the piles of books, igniting the lower tiers and offering fresh pathways for the flames.

The books were still blazing a week later. Among them lay the toppled, unrecognizable tombs, statues, and effigies of dukes and earls, knights and nobles, chancellors and bishops, all shattered in the heat. Only the shrouded effigy of Dean Donne, tumbling into the crypt below and buried at once in rubble, survived.

The cathedral, begun within twenty years of the Conquest, had seen the meeting of the Barons before the signing of Magna Carta at Runnymede, the murders of Richard II and Henry VI, and the Virgin Queen,

Elizabeth I, on her knees to give thanks for the defeat of the Spanish Armada. Now it lay destroyed, a wreck.

The three greatest buildings in the City of London—the Royal Exchange, still burning twenty-four hours after it was ignited, the Guildhall, and St. Paul's—were now in flames together. The sight of the cathedral ablaze and the march of the flames through the Temple threw the King into even greater panic. The fires were now no more than two hundred yards from Somerset House, the home of Henrietta Maria, the Queen Mother, where the Duke of York and his exhausted men were already at work on a fresh firebreak.

"At ten o'clock at night we left Somerset House, where they began to pull down some houses in hopes to save Whitehall . . . nothing can be like unto the distraction we were in, but the Day of Judgement."[49]

Buildings from the Temple as far west as Charing Cross were either unroofed or demolished altogether. Few remained to argue against the destruction of their properties, for the rich residents of the great houses in the Strand had long since sent their goods upriver and departed London in their wake. Many more had drawn similar conclusions. "We who live in the suburbs preparing for the same fate, fled from our lodgings and have hardly yet recovered our goods or our wits."[50]

Fleeing back to Whitehall, the King planned his own escape from the flames, giving orders to prepare to leave for Hampton Court at six the next morning. The Duke of York also "went home to take some rest, not having slept above two or three hours since Sunday night."[51]

Then in the darkest hours of Tuesday night, with the firestorm raging at its height, came the first faint sign of hope. After howling unabated for four days, the chief engine of destruction, the easterly gale, was at last blowing itself out. It began to ease and veer southerly, and that, more than any work with firehooks and gunpowder, offered hope that the Great Fire might at last be contained.

It only increased the danger to the Tower, however, by aiding the advance of the flames in that direction. The entire stock of the navy's gunpowder—between five hundred thousand and six hundred thousand pounds in weight—was held in the magazine at the White Tower. Had it detonated, "it would not only have beaten down and destroyed all the Bridge but sunk and torn all the vessels in the river and rendered the demolition beyond all expression for several miles about the country."[52]

Frantic efforts were still continuing to remove the vast store of powder. Staggering under their burdens, a procession of seamen and citizens press-ganged from the surrounding streets carried the barrels from the magazine down the ramps to the quay. As sparks rained down from the sky and the sweltering night grew even hotter at the approach of the fires, the barrels were loaded onto ships and carried away downstream to Woolwich and Deptford.

"Above one million two hundred thousand pounds" of the goldsmiths' money, gold, silver, and jewels, moved to the Tower as the fires reached Cheapside, were also now moved again, carried upstream to Whitehall on barges.

Tower Street was on fire from end to end, with flames leaping from Trinity House and igniting the Dolphin Tavern. Below Thames Street the fires wormed their way onward through the warren of warehouses and tenements to cross Water Lane and reach the Custom House. The great Elizabethan buildings were completely destroyed. The streets were now ablaze a mere hundred yards from the western bastion of the Tower.

Bakers' Hall at the head of Horse Shoe Court was also ablaze, driving Thomas and Hannah from their refuge. As it was engulfed they fled eastward ahead of the flames, battling through the crowds, so weary and disoriented that they scarcely knew where their feet were leading them.

When at last they reached the eastern city walls, they found the Tower postern closed against them and the streets guarded by soldiers. There was the constant thunder of explosions, and rumors swept through the choked streets that the cannons of the Tower were firing a barrage at an invading fleet. As Thomas pressed closer, he saw that the houses lining the banks of the Tower Ditch were being blasted apart with gunpowder by seamen charged to do whatever was necessary to save the Tower.

"It burnt down to the very moat of the Tower," but "the old timber dwellings there were blown up with gunpowder." Houses were demolished the length of Watergate, and a wine shop and warehouse in Seething Lane were also detonated, stopping the flames at the foot of the lane. The rubble and timbers were carted off and dumped into the Thames.

There was a thunderclap as the blast of each explosion echoed from the great, gray walls, followed by a brief silence, and then from deep within the Tower came a wild roaring and howling. The sound chilled Thomas's blood.

In the maelstrom of smoke, heat, and noise, the panic of the people had communicated itself to the animals in the King's Menagerie. Mad with fear, the elephant, lions, bears, and great apes roared their terror, dashing themselves against the walls and iron bars that confined them. No man dared to go near them. If the fire swept the Tower, the beasts would be burned with it.

Thomas and Hannah worked their way north, swept along with the flood of terrified people. They tried to fight their way through the crowds choking Aldgate, but the press of people and carts was so heavy that they turned aside. They trudged on, weak from hunger and stumbling from exhaustion, the fires always at their heels, past Bishopsgate, where the mobs were even more dense.

Beyond the walls they could hear the dreadful howling of the inmates of Bedlam. Flogging and chaining up were the only remedies ever offered to those incarcerated there, who also had to endure the stares of citizens amusing themselves by watching the antics of the lunatics, "who often give them cause for laughter." Now, as the fires approached, their keepers had fled, and the deranged creatures were left to fend for themselves as the roar of flames grew closer and dense smoke filled the air.

Thomas led his daughter on in the shadow of the walls until at last they came to Moorgate. The crowds were fewer there, for the fires raged so close that the heat blistered Thomas's cheek as he hurried past the few houses still standing in the shadow of the walls, and reached the gate. Men of the Trained Bands blocked the way, interrogating each fugitive from the fires, seeking papists, foreigners, strangers, but even some of the honest London citizens were too shocked and distraught to answer.

So suddenly had the fire come upon them "and thereby caused such distraction, that several forgot their names when they, with their money or goods under their arms, were examined. Others . . . forgot the day of the month and the month of the year. Others quite distracted for the general loss they have received. Thousands utterly undone."[53]

Almost exactly a year earlier Thomas had stood before this gate to send his son away from the plague-ridden city. Now he and Hannah were also fleeing for their lives. As he looked back into the city, the terrible vision returned to him from that night: once more the city was in flames, St. Paul's ringed by fire and even the river seeming to burn. But these were no feeble bonfires and braziers to be extinguished by rain. The sky stood clear and cloudless save for the pall of smoke, and not even the greatest storm could have extinguished these flames burning in the night.

As they emerged from the shadow of the arch, they saw the Moorfields smothered in humanity, with tens of thousands of people huddled among their mounds of goods and possessions, "where yet they felt such intolerable heat and drought, as if they had been in the middle of the fire."[54]

They walked through the fields for another hour before they found sufficient space to lay themselves down. Thomas and Hannah, her white face scarred with burns and streaked with soot, gazed back toward the skyline of the burning city. The fires still raging there sent flames shooting high above the level of the walls.

As they looked away, their eyes met. The fire starting in their house and bakery had engulfed the whole city. When it was at last extinguished, there would be a reckoning.

Chapter 9

Clamor and Peril

Wednesday, September 5, 1666

*Those that had a house today were the next glad of the shelter of
a hedge or a pigsty or stable. Those that were this day riding
wantonly in coaches were the next glad to ride in dung-carts to
save their lives. Those that thought the ground too unworthy to be
touched by their feet did run up to the knees in dirt and water to
save themselves from the fury of fire or the falling of houses.
Those that fared deliciously this day and nothing curious enough
to satiate their palates were within few days following glad of a
brown crust. Those that delighted themselves in down beds and
silken curtains were now glad of the shelter of a hedge.*
The Life & Times of Anthony a Wood

I N THE EARLY HOURS OF WEDNESDAY MORNING THE FLAMES
reached the walls of All Hallows, Barking, at the foot of Seething Lane.
The stones of the church were blackened and the face of the clock set in
the tower was burned, but though the fire swept on around the edge of the
churchyard, the church itself sustained no further damage.

Samuel Pepys had taken a boat to Woolwich in the dark hours before dawn, carrying his store of gold, "which was about £2,350," and accompanied by his wife and their servants Hewer and Jane. Sailing back upstream, he saw the whole city apparently ablaze, lit as bright as day. As he approached Tower Wharf there was the thunder of explosions as more houses in Mark Lane and Seething Lane were demolished to bar the progress of the fire.

He picked his way through the smoldering churchyard of All Hallows and climbed the blackened tower. From there he saw "the saddest sight of desolation that I ever saw. Everywhere great fires, oil cellars and brimstone and other things burning."[1]

Daybreak that Wednesday morning had strengthened the hopes that the fires could at last be contained and eventually extinguished. The wind was still lessening and backing south and west, but along the western limits the densely packed weatherboarded and pitched houses of the liberties still fed fresh fuel to the blaze.

The Duke of York was again riding the streets by six that morning. He found the fires still burning toward the riverbank but reduced to smoldering remnants on both sides of Fleet Street. Having satisfied himself that the fire there was under control, the Duke and his entourage made for the Rolls Chapel near Clifford's Inn and set every man to work to preserve the Court records stored there. He "caused all people, men, women and children that were able to work to come, and those who refused he beat them to it."[2]

"It pleased His Majesty to command" John Evelyn "among the rest, to look after the quenching of Fetter Lane end, to preserve if possible that part of Holborn."[3] Houses at the bottom of Fetter Lane were blown up with gunpowder, and "preserved by the assistance of some brick houses and garden walls," the flames made no further progress westward. In this the fire itself conspired with the firefighters.

Few of the deliberate attempts to make firebreaks had been successful, for always the wind fanned the fires and drove them on over the gap, but on occasions the speed with which embers were hurled ahead of the main body of fire proved its own undoing.

Near Fetter Lane, a blaze ignited by brands borne on the wind had already burned down a group of wooden houses fifty yards ahead of the firefront. The smaller blaze extinguished itself against the brick walls of the next house; when the main firefront arrived, it was unable to bridge the gap and "its greediness was the cause of its own destruction."

Aided by the labor of the seamen with their gunpowder, the breach was widened enough for the fire to be extinguished. As a result, St. Dunstan's Church and Clifford's Inn, just north of Fleet Street to the west of Fetter Lane, escaped unscathed.

Pushed by the southerly wind, the fires still climbed north on Fetter Lane and Shoe Lane, but by noon they were burning themselves out in the wasteland left by the sweeping advance of the flames on Holborn the previous day.

The breeze was soon abating to a dead calm. The smoke that for four days and nights had streamed away to the southwest now rose straight into the still air, forming a dense black cloud whose shape almost exactly mirrored that of the burned area on the ground below.

Throughout the city, the exhausted soldiers, militia, and citizens dragged themselves out again and fell to the task of extinguishing the flames, damping down and beating out the fires that still blazed and those that sprang up again among the smoldering timbers.

The will to fight the blazes and construct firebreaks, so lacking when the fire was raging at its height, was now everywhere to be found. "The rest of the gentlemen took their several posts some at one part, some at another, for now they began to bestir themselves, and not till now, who hitherto had stood as men intoxicated, with their hands across."[4]

Thousands of those who had fled in panic began flooding back into the city to help with the task of beating down and stamping out the embers. Right around the perimeter of the fire there was the sound of explosions as houses were demolished and the debris dragged away, broadening the cordon of cleared ground around the burned areas.

Robbed of the wind that had driven them on and with it the oxygen that had fed them, the flames were everywhere in retreat, already extinguished in many areas and contained in a few isolated pockets in the rest. The fires in Shoe Lane were put out during the morning, and at Holborn Bridge Lord Craven "gave a check to the fire there and by noon quenched it." When a fresh blaze erupted in Cow Lane, Smithfield, that afternoon, Lord Craven and a party of the Trained Bands went to assist Alderman Sir Richard Browne, "but a weak man in this business,"[5] in extinguishing it.

A strong fire still raged in and around Cripplegate and continued to burn throughout the day and well into the evening. The church of St. Giles just outside the gate escaped undamaged, but the flames burned right up to the walls, destroying the halls of the curriers, plasterers, and brewers, and Sion College.

Barber Surgeons' Hall in Monkwell Street nearby was also burned, though the Surgeons' Theatre in a separate building survived. Fire lodged in the wooden roof, but a seaman climbed up to it and beat the flames out. Among the items saved from the flames were two mummified human figures, "Adam and Eve," and the skeletons of criminals handed over for dissection after being executed at Tyburn.

The Countess of Thanet fled as Barber Surgeons' Hall was engulfed:

> I thank God I came well to Stamford last night, and we are all very well; and I hear it confirmed that Thanet House is safe from the fire and likewise Aldersgate Street. The nearest that it came to my house was Surgeons' Hall on the backside of my garden which is burnt to the ground. Whether I have a bed left at Thanet House or no, I do not know. . . . I have sent a man up to London to Fotherby, that if my beds be carried out of the house, to get some of them in again, for it is dangerous lodging for the plague and smallpox, and scarcely any lodging to be had.[6]

The Duke of York and the King both went to Cripplegate and spent several hours directing operations. "His Majesty Charles II, being then and there present, did in his own person take great pains—in no less, as was told, than if he had been a poor laborer—to promote the extinction of it."[7]

"Had not the King and the Duke of York, even to admiration adventured themselves in the midst of the flames, pulling down and blowing up houses before the fire to deaden the force of it, much more had been destroyed, for which kindness and care the people, as in duty they ought, pay great reverence and thanks."[8]

The Lord Mayor, Sir Thomas Bludworth, notable by his absence since the early hours of the fire, also reappeared in Cripplegate. As if in compensation for his earlier lapses, he supervised the demolition of a "great store of houses there to stop it being grown to a great head."

Kegs of powder were brought upriver and then borne round by Chancery Lane and High Holborn to blast apart houses in the path of the fires, and streets were dug up and pipes opened to utilize whatever water supply remained.

The fires burning through Aldersgate and at London Wall east of Moorgate made little further progress outside the wall, and just before dusk the last remnants of the blazes in the east around the edge of the Tower Ditch and in Mark Lane were beaten out, but the Great Fire still refused to yield completely. In the west, an evening breeze springing up was enough to fan the embers of Shoe Lane back into flame. There was also a fresh and ferocious outbreak at Cripplegate, throwing the familiar terrifying red glare into the sky.

The breeze was also strong enough to cast sparks from the smoldering ruins of King's Bench Walk onto the Temple, igniting some timber buildings close to the walls of the great hall of the Inner Temple, built by the Knights Templars.

The Duke of York, himself a bencher of the inn, hurried from Whitehall when word of the outbreak "occasioned by the carelessness of the Templars" was passed to him. When he arrived he found a crowd gathered around the locked gates and the lawyers refusing to admit anyone to extinguish the fires for fear that it would be the pretext for an orgy of looting.

Four engineers were recruited at a fee of a sovereign each to help the seamen in the demolition of the buildings before the fire, but when the Duke ordered the Paper House to be blown up to save the Temple chapel and the hall, one of the Templars "came to the Duke and told him it was against the rules and charter of the Temple that any should blow that House with gunpowder, upon which Mr Germaine, the Duke's Master of the Horse, took a good cudgel and beat the young lawyer to the purpose."[9]

Little of the Inner Temple had not already been destroyed by fire, and much of what remained, including Tanfield Court and Parsons Court, was then blasted apart by gunpowder, but the hall was still besieged by flames and one end of the roof caught fire. Once more a seaman, Richard Rowe, well used to scaling the masts and ropes of square-riggers, swarmed up the roof, and squatting astride the ridge, beat out the flames and saved the building. The benchers rewarded him with a gift of ten pounds, and a poet commemorated his exploits.

The fire burned up to the walls of the ancient Templars' church, but as the flames approached, the small shops that clustered round its south and west walls were blown up and the debris removed, saving the church. The great timber gatehouse was the only other building of the Inner Temple to survive, but the Middle Temple escaped almost unscathed, losing only a single building to the flames. The Duke remained there until one in the morning, when "by his care, diligence, great labor and seasonable commands for the blowing up with gunpowder some of the said buildings" the fires were again extinguished.

Barnard's Inn, Furnival's Inn, Gray's Inn, and Lincoln's Inn were untouched by the flames. Only one fire now remained, a blaze in Bishopsgate bursting out in a previously unburned area. Samuel Pepys was called to lead a group of seamen to the site. As they went to work with gunpowder and firehooks, others formed bucket chains to feed the squirts throwing water onto the flames.

Groups of women worked to sweep the water from the kennels, but "then they would scold for drink and be as drunk as devils. I saw good butts of sugar broken open in the street and people give and take handfuls out and put in the beer and drink it."[10] The blaze was finally doused just before dawn.

Just as all seemed calm that Wednesday night, an alarm was raised that "fifty thousand French and Dutch"[11] were coming "armed against them to cut their throats and spoil them of what they saved out of the fire. . . . Yet many citizens having lost their houses and almost all they had, are fired with rage and fury and they begin to stir themselves like lions or bears bereaved of their whelps and now 'Arm! Arm! Arm!' does resound the fields and suburbs with a dreadful voice."[12]

The rumor spread like the wildfire that preceded it, and grabbing whatever arms and improvised weapons were to hand, thousands of the refugees spilled from the fields into the city. "They could not be stopped from falling on some of those nations whom they casually met without sense or reason. The clamor and peril grew so excessive that it made the whole Court amazed and they did with infinite pains and great difficulty reduce and appease the people, sending troops of soldiers and guards to cause them to retire into the fields again, where they were watched all this night, when I left them pretty quiet, and came home to my house sufficiently weary and broken."[13]

Chapter 10

Firestorm

L anthorne and Candle light

The greatest fire that ever happened upon the earth since the
burning of Sadom and Gomorrah.
Rege Sincera, *Observations both Historical and*
Moral upon the Burning of London

I
N A CONTROLLED ENVIRONMENT SUCH AS A FURNACE, FUEL, OXYGEN,
and the means of ignition are combined in a predictable and consistent
manner. In the wild, however, fire is unpredictable, capricious, and often
lethal. It may burn itself out by becoming starved of sufficient air or fuel,
be extinguished by a downpour of rain, or be driven back across already
burned ground by a change in the wind. But if the many variables combine
to allow a blaze to build toward its full potential, it can produce a holocaust.
It is worth considering the events of 1666 through the lens of a twenty-
first century knowledge of the physics and chemistry of fire.

The development of a blaze is a complex process, but it is underpinned
by a few basic chemical reactions and physical processes that remain constant whether the fire is in a domestic grate or is a firestorm destroying a

city. A fire requires combustible fuel, oxygen, and some means of ignition. Once ignited, the fuel and oxygen must interact in a self-sustaining chain reaction. Remove any of the three elements of this "fire triangle" and the fire will be extinguished, but if uncontained, it can rapidly become an inferno devouring everything in its path. Human intervention is then almost irrelevant; only as its supplies of fuel and oxygen come close to exhaustion can the fire be contained and extinguished.

Most common fuels combust through the oxidization—the combination of the substance with oxygen—of carbon, hydrogen, sulfur, and nitrogen. Slow oxidization, such as rust forming on iron or paint curing, produces no discernible heat, but fast oxidization of combustibles generates heat, and at ignition point, fire.

A naked flame is not an essential element in the ignition process. If the other requirements are met, heat alone can produce spontaneous combustion, raising the temperature until the ignition point of at least part of the fuel is reached. Explosive combustion occurs when heated vapor, dusts, or gases premixed with air ignite. A previously sealed room or building full of material heated to or beyond its ignition point will not burn without sufficient oxygen. Smoldering, superheated material will instantly combust, however, if it comes into contact with sufficient oxygen; for instance, when a draft of air is admitted by breaking a window or opening a door, as Thomas Farriner did when he tried to enter his servant's chamber in Pudding Lane.

Heat causes damage to structures, intensifies the fire, spreads and enlarges it, and is the greatest barrier to extinguishing it. The greater the heat, the faster the chemical reaction. The rate of combustion roughly doubles with every rise of ten degrees Celsius, leading to a chain reaction: fire generates heat, raising the temperature of the ingredients and the rate of reaction, generating more heat, which again increases the rate of reaction. The nature and availability of fuel and the availability of oxygen, coupled with the loss of heat to the surrounding environment, are all that prevents every fire from becoming an inferno.

Once established, the continuity of the fire is maintained by the transfer of heat through conduction, convection, and radiation. The effects of conduction are limited to localized action, transferring heat from hot to cold areas of solids, and to a much lesser extent, liquids and gases. If heat is being conducted faster than the combustible material can dissipate it, it will eventually reach ignition temperature. Wood is a poor conductor and may burn for some time without heat spreading through it; one side of a board or timber may show deep charring, for example, while the other is unmarked.

Convection—the circulation of heat within liquids or gases—is crucial in the spread of fires. The gaseous products of combustion and the heated air surrounding them expand, become lighter, and move upward rapidly. In large unconfined fires, the upward movement of gases is often so great that it creates firestorms by causing winds of gale or even hurricane force, containing the oxygen necessary to sustain the conflagration, to move in from all available directions, replacing the gases in the upward-moving fire plume.

Fires radiate heat in all directions. Dark-colored objects absorb and radiate heat better than light-colored ones, but the temperatures of all surfaces facing a fire will be raised by its radiant heat in the same way that the radiant heat from the sun warms the earth. When the temperature of the facing material reaches ignition point, it will burst into flame. Superheated gases confined within a room can radiate sufficient heat to ignite combustibles far from the original seat of the fire. Flashover is the almost simultaneous ignition of all the surfaces of combustible materials subject to heat radiated down from the hot gas layer beneath the ceiling.

The speed of spread of the fire depends on the geometry of the building and the nature of the combustible materials. A dramatic example of very rapid fire spread occurred in the timber stand during the disastrous blaze at Bradford City Football Club, in Northern England, in May 1985. In very large unconfined fires it is common for nearby buildings to ignite at a distance from the main blaze, solely through the effects of radiant heat.

Direct flame impingement, combining the effects of conduction and radiation, operates as flames extend upward, raising combustibles to their ignition point by direct contact with the flaming hot gases. As they ignite, the heat produced increases the rate of oxidization of other fuels, spreading the fire at a faster and faster rate.

Almost all fuels are organic in origin, formed of complex compounds based on carbon. The decomposition of such materials under heat provides the simpler, more volatile, and flammable compounds on which fires feed. It is called *pyrolysis,* deriving from the Greek words for fire and decay.

A flaming fire requires a burning gas—a pyrolysate—already formed, evaporated from a liquid or driven off from a solid. At normal temperatures there are very few gaseous fuels, hydrogen, methane, propane, and acetylene being the most common, but many materials emit pyrolysates in a fire and virtually all of them can be converted to a gas when a sufficient temperature is reached.

Convection is the reason that fires spread upward; damage to ceilings is characteristically much more severe than that to floors. The convection heats the fuel above the flames, causing it to emit pyrolysates that ignite and expand the blaze, but the fuel below the fire may remain unburned, as it is not heated enough for pyrolysis to take place.

Strictly speaking, wood does not burn, but it decomposes readily under heat, and this pyrolysis of the wood produces flammable gases and volatile oils and resins, together with large amounts of water vapor. The oxidization of the resultant gases produces an exothermic reaction, generating great heat.

When flames surround a piece of wood, it is the gases that burn, not the wood. A single match generates the equivalent of one BTU—British Thermal Unit—and a pound of resinous wood contains 8,500 to 10,000 BTUs. Resinous woods such as pine, fir, and spruce, all of which were widely used in Restoration London, are more flammable than nonresinous ones, since the heat produced by the volatile vapors given off enhances the ability of cellulose and lignin—the other primary components of wood—to pyrolyze and ignite. Applying a coat of pitch to resinous boards further increases their flammability when heated. Once lit, however, hardwoods such as oak sustain a hotter and longer fire.

Only when the decomposition of the wood has effectively ceased will glowing fire spread across the charred residue—charcoal—as it interacts with oxygen. Pound for pound, it burns with far greater intensity and output of heat than the original wood. There are few, if any, fuels with a higher carbon content than charcoal, and once burning, it gives an intensely hot fire, like the hearth of a blacksmith's forge.

Glowing fire is characterized by an absence of flame and by the presence of very hot materials on the surface. The color of the incandescent glow is directly related to its temperature. When the glow is dull red, the temperature is between 500 and 600 degrees Celsius. When dark red, 600–800; bright red, 800–1,000; yellowish red, 1,000–1,200; bright yellow,

1,200–1,400; and white, 1,400–1,600 degrees. The hammerbeam roof of the Guildhall, blazing in a "bright shining coal as if had been a palace of gold or a great building of brass," must have been burning at a temperature in excess of 1,200 degrees Celsius to produce that gold or brass-colored flame.

The yellow or orange flame of most organic fuels is produced by hot carbon or soot that has yet to react with oxygen to give complete combustion. It is the radiation from the carbon that gives the color, a function of flame temperature. Carbon monoxide burns with a vivid blue flame, the lower alcohols burn with a blue or purple flame, and copper halides with an intense green flame.

There is little or no visible smoke when complete combustion occurs. In such conditions carbon is burned to carbon dioxide, but whenever the supply of oxygen is insufficient or imperfectly mixed with the fuel, a yellow sooty flame will form and great quantities of extremely flammable carbon monoxide and elemental carbon—soot—will remain unburned.

When a fire is ignited inside a building, it is localized at first and burns with an open flame. Water vapor, soot, carbon dioxide, and unburned pyrolysates are produced as by-products of the blaze. Convection raises heat to the ceiling and draws in oxygen at the fire base, and direct flame impingement spreads the fire upward and outward, while the effects of conduction and radiation raise the temperature of nearby materials toward their ignition point, until they too begin to burn.

The soot, smoke, and partially burned products of pyrolysis are generated in increasing concentrations as the oxygen content of the room begins to drop. Thick clouds of toxic gases spread across the ceiling. As the temperature climbs beyond 600 degrees, one or more of the constituent gases reaches its ignition point, either through direct impingement of the flames or the radiant heat of the fire. The outward spread of the burning gases can reach speeds of ten or fifteen feet per second.

The room temperature is now close to its maximum, and these hotter flames radiate sufficient heat to ignite any other combustibles in the room, including wall hangings, furniture, carpets, or floorboards distant from the original site of the blaze. The fire continues until little further fuel remains to be consumed or the oxygen supply is depleted. If the oxygen content of the air falls to around 16 percent, flaming combustion will die back, but the remaining fuels will continue to pyrolyze and smolder. If the ventilation is increased, the combustible gases may reignite into a second blaze.

Compared to the huge temperatures generated by fires, the ambient temperature has little significance, except in the very early stages of a blaze, but dry material obviously combusts faster than wet, and the higher the initial temperature, the faster the combustible material will reach its ignition point.

Most new wood will spontaneously combust at temperatures ranging from 200 to 260 degrees, but the thinner, flakier surface of decayed, old wood ignites at a significantly reduced temperature. Experiments have shown that the ignition point of southern pine is 205 degrees when new, but only 150 when decayed. Wood used in building naturally contains some moisture, but over time it dries out. A drought combined with the baking heat of high summer makes old wooden boards and structural timbers like those in the buildings of pre-fire London so dry that a fire is easy to ignite and very hard to extinguish.

Plaster is noncombustible, but the wooden laths within it burn very readily. The horsehair and straw with which plaster or daub was mixed are also combustible. In the intense heat of a fire, plaster cracks and crumbles, allowing the flames access to the laths within and speeding the destruction of the wall. Ramshackle weatherboard or timber-framed houses with party walls constructed of lath and plaster or lath and daub give flames an easy pathway to travel from house to house along a row. Falling timbers also pierce such flimsy walls with ease, opening fresh vents and avenues for the fires.

As if the structure of the buildings of Restoration London was not combustible enough, the interiors were usually paneled or draped with hangings. Bare, whitewashed plaster was a symbol of poverty, and no one with the means to pay for wall hangings would tolerate it. The rich hung tapestries of wool—the finest were Flemish—while the less wealthy had hangings of buckram (linen) or say (serge), often in vivid colors.

Fire can insinuate itself into the voids behind hangings and wood paneling and spread undetected throughout a building. Fueled by the wainscoting, paneling, paintings, curtains, furniture, and hangings, a fire inside a single timber-framed Elizabethan house, such as occurred at Tangley House in England in 2000, can generate temperatures in excess of 1,000 degrees Celsius—enough to melt lead, glass, brass, bronze, and silver.

Structural timber chars—converts to charcoal as its volatile elements are pyrolyzed—at a very slow rate of roughly one inch every forty-five minutes. That rate is only a crude rule of thumb, however, and the surface charring both insulates the interior of the wood to some extent and reduces its interaction with air, slowing the rate of pyrolysis still further. Roof timbers may remain glowing—just like those of the Guildhall—long after everything beneath them has been consumed. Some of the larger timbers may be charred rather than burned through and remain unconsumed though all else around them is destroyed.

If wood has been preheated by convection or radiant heat before the flames reach it, its speed of burning increases dramatically. The fire at the King's Cross Underground station in London in November 1987 was caused when paper and other debris ignited by a discarded match or cigarette set fire to wooden escalators. Aided by the "trench effect," causing hot gases to flow close to the escalator rather than the ceiling, the heat traveling up the slope raised the temperature of the wood ahead of the flames so much that the fire, which had taken eight or nine minutes to develop beneath the escalator, then took less than half a minute to travel the entire length of it. Temperatures in the booking hall above rose by twenty or thirty degrees a second.

Paper ignites at a temperature of around 230 degrees Celsius and burns well in individual sheets because it is thin, providing a broad surface to heat and access to ample air, relative to its volume. When it is bound in books or stacked in piles, as it was in St. Faith's in the crypt of St. Paul's, its surface area is dramatically reduced compared to its volume and it becomes difficult—almost impossible—to burn.

If the heat is sufficiently intense, however, paper will spontaneously combust when exposed to sufficient air, and falling masonry and timbers and molten metals dripping from above, like the lead from the roof of the cathedral, can carve fresh openings for oxygen to enter. A raging firestorm also produces such a strong updraft that burning papers are simply whirled up into the maelstrom, giving the flames access to the unburned paper below.

Coal is made up of approximately 80 percent carbon and hydrocarbon and 5 percent hydrogen, with most of the remainder oxygen, nitrogen, and sulfur. It does not pyrolyze as easily as other fuels and for this reason requires considerable external heat before it will ignite, but once alight it burns with ferocious intensity, and cellars and stores full of coal will remain on fire for days or weeks on end.

The combustibility of fabrics can depend on their condition and makeup. Wool has such a high moisture and nitrogen content that though it can and does burn, especially in its natural, lanolin-laden "greasy" state, it will sometimes extinguish rather than sustain a fire. Cotton and linen can be far more flammable, having a larger surface-to-volume ratio. Silk is not easily fired when stored in bulk, but when woven it burns with lightning speed.

Glass crazes under a very rapid buildup of heat and shatters into narrow slivers or shards when subjected to an explosion, but when the buildup of heat is slower, glass first starts to buckle when the temperature reaches around 660 degrees Celsius—a temperature reached in many wood-fueled fires—and sags toward the heat source as it loses its structural strength. The piece of stained glass that Samuel Pepys collected as a souvenir from the Mercers' chapel had been melted out of shape in this way.

Flammable liquids such as oils, pitch, tar, and brandy do not burn. They give off a vapor that will ignite once the flash point of the liquid is reached, just as the vapor from the brandy on a Christmas pudding will light once it has been warmed. All such vapors are heavier than air and accumulate near floor levels, acting like liquids as they flow down stairs or under doors to collect in dense concentrations in the lowest parts of a building.

Most liquids reach their boiling point before pyrolysis affects their chemical constituents. When heated by a fire, the liquid at the surface boils off into vapor, but the evaporation allows the rest of the liquid to remain just below its boiling point, as convection continually circulates the hotter and cooler areas of the liquid.

The boiling point of liquids rises in line with increases in pressure, however, and if the liquid is packed into a sealed container such as a barrel, evaporation increases the pressure in the head-space. As the heat rises, so do the pressure and the boiling point of the liquid.

The temperature rises inside the barrel until it reaches the point at which pyrolysis can begin. The barrel is then packed with an explosive mixture of pressurized liquid, vapor, and gases, and when it reaches a sufficient temperature or the barrel is breached by an external fire, it can detonate with the force of a bomb, piercing walls, collapsing buildings, and blasting blazing materials considerable distances. The tar barrels stored in the cellar of the ships' chandler in Pudding Lane exploded in this way.

Soft coal and oils such as linseed, cottonseed, and cod liver oil are particularly dangerous because they are self-heating and can spontaneously combust when the oil reacts with air. Linseed oil is often applied with cloths or rags, and the residual oil in the fabric creates an oxidizing process whereby it generates its own heat and oxygen. If it is allowed to continue without the heat being dissipated, it can generate temperatures high enough to ignite the rags.

When disturbed, fine, dry, powdery substances such as flour, sulfur, and grain can also form explosive dust suspensions hanging in the air above bulk material kept in stores and warehouses. Indeed, dust from almost any combustible material will burn or explode when mixed with the right proportion of air.

The ignition of the suspended dust or vapor and air mixture can be explosive and very violent, possibly demolishing the building in which it occurs, but it will generate less fire than the more common rolling explosion of a "rich" mixture containing insufficient air to burn all the vapor or dust, which then continues to burn as it expands outward, constantly drawing in more air to fuel the combustion.

Black powder—gunpowder—is an even more explosive material. It is black or dark gray in color, and composed of 75 percent saltpeter—potassium nitrate—15 percent charcoal, and 10 percent sulfur. In Restoration London, five to six hundred tons of it were stored in the magazine in the White Tower, but armorers, firework makers, and ships' chandlers also held large stocks of it, stored in wooden barrels. There were also the magazines and armories of the soldiers and Trained Bands, and many former members of the New Model Army, and private citizens held muskets and the powder with which to load them.

Black powder is rated only as a low explosive compared to more modern high-explosive compounds like nitroglycerine, but it is the most volatile and dangerous of all of them. The energy required to ignite it is so low that even a spark of static electricity can detonate it. If unconfined, it burns with an intensity that can generate temperatures approaching 2,000 degrees Celsius. If contained, it explodes with savage force.

Fire tends to flow through and between buildings like a liquid, spreading upward and outward, and even changing course to circumvent obstacles in its path, almost as if it were sentient. Flames also may seem actively to pursue people attempting to flee them, a phenomenon well known to workers in furnaces and foundries. A flame licks out of the mouth of the furnace toward them. They run to escape it, but by blocking the roaring draft into the fire, their body creates a pathway for the flame, and it pursues them, replicating every movement they make.

The chimney effect increases the velocity of fire as it passes upward through small spaces. Any constriction, such as a cramped alley or foot passage, or jettied upper stories of buildings coming together over a narrow street, mimics the effect of the throat of a chimney and increases the speed of the updraft. The narrower the gap, the faster the smoke and flames rise, sucking in air to feed the fires below at a corresponding rate.

Sparks—pieces of glowing or burning paper, wood, and other light materials—are carried upward by the updraft from a fire and can travel considerable distances. The Venturi effect, in which wind blowing across the mouth of a chimney or the narrow gap between two facing jetties lowers the air pressure, also allows larger sparks to be carried aloft, into the stronger winds above the rooftops.

In extremely intense fires, a fireball may also be created, formed from burning clouds of gases and pyrolysis products that far exceed the supply of oxygen locally available to consume them. The powerful updraft created by the fire drives the fireball upward, and fed by the unburned gases at its heart, it continues to burn independent of the original fuel.

Without an ambient wind, sparks will travel outward only a short distance from the source fire before falling back again. In most cases, burning papers will be fully consumed before they fall back to earth, but wood fragments may still be glowing or burning when they land. At the height of forest fires, the ignition rate can be as high as 90 percent; of every hundred flying sparks, ninety will start another fire.

A wind increases not only the distance these fragments can travel but also the rate at which they burn. In theory this limits the distance that sparks can travel without being consumed, but the wind also increases the size and weight of burning objects that can be carried aloft. Firefighters are frequently trapped by the secondary blazes caused by airborne firebrands as well as the undetected spread of fires within buildings, and deaths are a common occurrence.

A small fire burning at level ground on a still day generates a rising column of hot gases at its center. Air is drawn in all around the edge of the fire, and in whatever horizontal direction the fire spreads, it is burning back against the draught, which limits its rate of expansion.

If the same fire is sited on a hill, convection draws air and heat up the hill, and the fire-spread is correspondingly faster on the uphill side, generating a fan-shaped spread; but as the fire grows in size, it also burns back downhill, even against the wind, helped by burning timbers and debris as they fall or roll down the slope.

When a gale-force wind is added to the equation, the spread and intensity of the fire increase dramatically, but independently of the wind, the fire-draft also increases in step with the size of the blaze. A gale provides a constant supply of fresh oxygen, but a single large fire or several fires spread by the wind can also create "convection currents soaring above such a fire . . . violent enough to suck in replacement air towards the center and cause winds far greater than normal."[1] In such conditions, a wall of flame can rise more than forty feet into the air and advance at one hundred to two hundred feet per second. A large bush fire or a blaze raging through an urban area generates a very powerful wind irrespective of the atmospheric conditions.

In meteorology, a difference of a few degrees Celsius between one area and another is enough to produce a wind blowing from the cooler to the hotter area. At the height of a raging firestorm, the temperature difference between the fire cores and the unheated air beyond the perimeter of the blaze will be at least 1,000 degrees Celsius, enough to generate violent winds rushing into the base of the flames from all points of the compass, to replace the ferocious updraft carrying superheated smoke and gases aloft. The resulting inferno of flames and superheated gases will instantly devour everything in its path.

After the incendiary bombing of Hamburg and Dresden during the Second World War, the firestorm winds developed into "tornadoes that uprooted trees and hurled people fleeing from the fire backwards into the very center of it." Ferocious firestorms also accompanied the fire that ravaged Chicago in 1871.

When the Tartars burned Moscow on May 15, 1570,

> then did arise so fierce and violent a wind, that it drove the rafters and long trees from the suburbs into the city. The conflagration was so sudden that nobody had time to save himself. . . . The houses were all of wood and the streets paved with great fir trees, set close together, which, being oily and resinous made the incendy inexpressible. . . . While this fire lasted, we thought that a million of cannons had been thundering together, and our thoughts were upon nothing but death.[2]

Firestorms create updrafts with the power of small tornadoes, sucking debris and even large timbers into the fires and carrying brands and sparks far aloft for the gales to disperse downwind. Eyewitness accounts speak of sparks and flaming brands carried "several furlongs" before landing, still alight, to ignite fresh blazes.[3]

In these conditions, falling sparks and embers fire the roofs of houses, as happened constantly during the Great Fire. The lower stories burn only as falling debris from above pierces the floors below and ignites them. In the meantime wind-driven flames and sparks jump from roof to roof, igniting fresh rooftop blazes while the houses below remain unburned.

The occupants of such properties often remain unaware of their peril until blazing debris begins to crash down around them. The same phenomenon—"crowning"—is often visible in bush and forest fires, where the tops of plants and trees are consumed by a fast-moving firefront, leaving the lower portions untouched.

A pitch coating applied to wooden, weatherboarded houses has the same effect as the volatile oils of desert plants and gum trees. The natural oils give the trees protection from their hot, dry environment, but in a bush fire they volatilize and burn with ferocious intensity. The pitch protecting wood houses from the weather also volatilizes in the heat of fires and spreads the flames like wildfire.

Chapter 11

A Dismal Desert

Thursday, September 6, 1666

Bye my quartern a Smelts

London was, but is no more.
John Evelyn, *Diary*

A T DAYBREAK ON THURSDAY THE GREAT FIRE OF LONDON WAS
at last over, though cellars full of combustibles continued to burn,
and wells still seethed and boiled from the residual heat.

Gray fogs of smoke, dust, fine ash, and steam hung over the city.
Untroubled by any breeze, they rose straight into the air, merging into a
great column of dirty yellowish gray, stretching up into the cloudless sky as
far as the eye could see.

The great mass of the citizens camped beyond the wall in Moorfields
woke from their fitful sleep to see the city again revealed, but transformed
beyond all recognition. As they squinted into the rising sun, for a moment it
seemed unharmed, as if the events of the preceding days had been some terrible dream. Beyond the gray city wall, tall buildings still stood and the towers and spires of the churches still reached toward the heavens. But the walls
enclosed only empty air, and the towers and buildings were blackened stumps.

The rays of the sun were touching ground that had been shaded since before the Conquest. Medieval London had ceased to exist. In its place was a wasteland of shattered stone, melted metal, dust, and ashes. The whole city and the country for miles around seemed rendered into dust thick as the ash that engulfed Pompeii. Masonry had become as white and fragile as chalk, mounds of red, yellow, orange, and brown ash were all that remained of brick houses, and great oak beams had become black charcoal that crumbled at the touch.

London was so empty of buildings that "you may see from one end of the city almost to the other" and "stand where Cheapside was and see the Thames," and so transformed, so bleak and featureless, that to one stupefied onlooker it seemed like the Cumbrian fells, "for there is nothing to be seen but heaps of stones."[1] "You can compare London, were it not for the rubbish, to nothing more than an open field."[2] "Truly it is such a sight to behold that a man can hardly forbear weeping."[3]

"Thus fell great London, that ancient city, that populous city. London, which was the queen city of the land . . . and yet how is London departed like smoke and her glory laid in the dust. . . . How does the whole nation tremble at the sound of her fall. How is the pride of London stained and beauty spoiled, her arm broken and strength departed, her riches almost gone . . . since the firing and fall of this city which had the strength and treasure of the nation in it. The glory of London is now fled away like a bird, the trade of London is shattered and broken to pieces, her delights also are vanished and pleasant things laid to waste."[4]

Not a living thing stirred from one end of the city to the other. The exhausted firefighters had retired to sleep where they could, and like the human inhabitants, every insect, bird, and animal had either fled or perished in the flames.

The distant suburbs and the great buildings in the west survived. The Earl of Clarendon's mansion in Piccadilly, the Duke of York's residence, St. James's Palace, Westminster and Whitehall, Somerset House, the residence of the Queen Mother, and the other great houses and residences of the ambassadors lining the Strand still stood, but all was changed at Temple Bar. From there onward only thirty houses remained in the whole of Fleet Street, "two brief rows of houses ending in desolation, and beyond them nothing but ruins."[5]

As the day wore on, more and more disbelieving citizens began to make their way through the debris as dust devils whirled among the ashes. The stones and rubble underfoot were still so hot that the citizens' shoes were scorched and their hair singed, and the piles of jagged rocks were so treacherous and unstable that they slid and collapsed underfoot as the people moved among them. The fine dust hanging in the air cloaked their features and their clothes, and they moved, barely visible, like ghosts among the ruins.

All cast their heads about from side to side, searching, often in vain, for some familiar landmark to guide them to the wreckage of their homes. If they found them, all that remained were broken stones, rubble and ash, and solidified pools of molten metal, the remnants of their plate, candlesticks, pots and pans. They saw "bells and iron wares melted, glass and earthen pots melted together, as it had been by a fire of fusion; the most big and solid stones (as those of the cathedral) slit, scaled and in some parts calcined to powder by the violence of the flames."[6]

The sound of explosions as more houses were demolished, and the rumble and crash as buildings weakened by the fire collapsed, added to the horror of the scene. The smell of burned, decomposing flesh hung in the air, and everywhere there were strange and terrible sights.

Pepys walked through the burned parts of the city later that day and "did see a poor cat taken out of a hole in a chimney joining to the wall of the Exchange with the hair all burned off the body and yet alive."[7]

William Taswell was one of the first to tread the ruins of St. Paul's:

The ground was so hot as almost to scorch my shoes and the air so intensely warm that unless I had stopped some time upon Fleet Bridge to rest myself, I must have fainted under the extreme languor of my spirits. [So hot were the filthy waters of the Fleet River that gouts of steam surrounded him as he stood there.]

After giving myself a little time to breathe, I made the best of my way to St Paul's. And now let any person judge of the violent emotion I was in when I could see the metal belonging to the bells melted, the ruinous condition of the walls, whole heaps of stone in a large circumference tumbling down with a great noise just upon my feet, ready to crush me to death.

I prepared myself for returning back again having first loaded my pockets with several pieces of bell metal. At last accoutred with my sword and helmet which I picked up among many others in the ruins, I traversed this torrid zone back again. . . .

Near the east walls of St Paul's a human body presented itself to me parched up, as it were, with the flames. Whole as to skin, meagre as to flesh, yellow as to color; this was an old decrepit woman who fled here for safety, imagining the flames would not have reached her there. Her clothes were burned and every limb reduced to a coal.[8]

Several dogs were also "found burned among the goods in the churchyard."[9] Inside the broken tomb of Robert de Braybroke, Bishop of London and Lord Chancellor of England laid to rest in 1404, was found a body: "teeth in the head, red hair on the head and beard etc., skin and nails on the toes and fingers, without circcloth embalming spices or any other condite." It was "so dried up, the flesh, sinews, and skin cleaving fast to the bones that, being set upon the feet, it stood stiff as a plank, the skin being tough like leather and not at all inclined to putrefaction, which some attributed to the sanctity of the person."[10] Two other mummified bodies were also found when the north aisle was cleared of debris.

An even more gruesome relic was discovered in the broken tomb of Dean Colet. "After the conflagration, his monument being broken, his coffin which was lead, was full of a liquor which conserved the body. Mr Wyld and Ralph Greatorex tasted it and it was of a kind of insipid taste, something of an ironish taste. The body felt, to the probe of a stick which they thrust into a chink, like brawn."[11]

Flames were still bursting from the roof and battlements of St. Paul's that Thursday night. So utterly destroyed was the cathedral that people lost, homeless, and seeking shelter could find nowhere better than to join the dead in the crypts beneath. Above ground, all was open to the sky, "only a huge heap of stones cemented together by the lead with which the church was covered."[12]

John Evelyn entered the city on Friday morning, walking across the whole of London from Whitehall by Fleet Street and Ludgate Hill to St. Paul's, along Cheapside and past the Exchange, up Bishopsgate and Aldersgate, out into Moorfields and then through Cornhill and down the hill to the bridge.

He made his way

with extraordinary difficulty, clambering over heaps of yet smoking rubbish and frequently mistaking where I was, the ground under my feet so hot that it even burned the soles of my shoes, and put me all over in sweat. . . . I was infinitely concerned to find that goodly church St Paul's now a sad ruin and that beautiful portico, the structure comparable to any in Europe and not long before repaired by the late King, now rent in pieces. The ruins of the vaulted roof, falling, broke into St Faith's.

Thus lay in ashes that most venerable church, one of the most ancient pieces of early piety in the Christian world, besides near one hundred more. The lead, ironwork, bells, plates, et cetera melted, the exquisitely wrought Mercers' Chapel, the sumptuous Exchange, the august fabric of Christchurch, all the rest of the companies' halls, splendid buildings, arches, entries all in dust.

The fountains dried up and ruined whilst the very waters remained boiling, the voragos [chasms] of subterranean cellars, wells and dungeons, formerly warehouses, still burning in stench and dark clouds of smoke, so that in five or six miles traversing about it, I did not see one load of timber unconsumed nor many stones but what were calcined white as snow. . . . The people who now walked about the ruins appeared like men in some dismal desert or rather in some great city laid waste by a cruel enemy, to which was added the stench that came from some other creatures' bodies. . . .

Vast iron chains of the City streets, vast hinges, bars and gates of prisons were many of them melted and reduced to cinders by the vehement heat. Nor was I yet able to pass through any of the narrow streets but kept the widest. The ground and air, smoke and fiery vapor continued so intense that my hair was almost singed and my feet insufferably surbated [sore]. The by-lanes and narrow streets were quite filled up with rubbish nor could one have possibly known where he was but by the ruins of some church or hall that had some remarkable tower or pinnacle remaining.

I then went towards Islington and Highgate where one might have seen 200,000 people of all ranks and degrees dispersed and lying along by their heaps of what they could save from the fire, deploring their loss, and though ready to perish for hunger and destitution, yet not asking one penny for relief, which to me appeared a stranger sight than any I had yet beheld.[13]

Francisco de Rapicani was also traversing the devastated city:

When the fire had died down, my friend Baumann came to me and offered to walk with me through the burnt-out city, so that we could see and contemplate the distress. We walked and walked and found nothing but heaps of stones and cellars still full of planks and smoldering beams. There was great distress among the people and countless poor persons with nothing but a stick in their hands, who had formerly been prosperous and well-placed, were scattered here and there in the fields where they had built huts for themselves.[14]

Few had time to contemplate for long the ruins of their homes and city. The need to find food, water, and shelter was paramount. The butchers and bakers and brewers and fishmongers had fled with the rest, almost the entire stocks of food in the city had perished in the conflagration, and virtually every market had been destroyed. Even at Court, food was scarce. Dr. Denton, physician to the King, wrote that "Nothing almost is to be got that we have not in possession, bread, beer, meat, all in scarcity and many want it."[15] If action was not taken at once, the people of London would have been saved from the flames only to perish from starvation.

The dwellers in Moorfields and the other open spaces, "some under tents, others under miserable huts and hovels,"[16] and others lying out under the stars, had already been without food for many hours and in some cases for days. On the Wednesday morning, before the fires had even been extinguished, the King made haste to issue two royal proclamations.

The magistrates and Deputy Lieutenants of the surrounding counties were ordered to ensure that all the provisions that could be spared, especially bread, should be sent immediately to London. Temporary markets were set up just outside the burned areas, at Smithfield, Bishopsgate, and Tower Hill and farther from the city at Clerkenwell, Islington, Finsbury Fields, Mile End Green, and Ratcliffe. The King's men for their part would "prevent all disturbances by the refusal of payment for goods or otherwise."[17]

The fields of Lincoln's Inn and Gray's Inn and the piazza of Covent Garden had been designated as storage places for goods watched over by companies of the Trained Bands. The King now ordered that all churches, chapels, schools, and other public places should be thrown open as communal storehouses for the safekeeping of the goods.

All cities and towns throughout the kingdom were required to accept any refugees from London who came their way and to permit them to practice their trades. In return the King pledged that when the emergency was over, he would take care to ensure that no such persons would be a burden on the towns and parishes where they had settled.

To ensure that there was no famine after the fire, the King also ordered the naval storehouses opened and the great stores of ships' biscuit accumulated there sent out into Moorfields. But by that time, most of the people there were already supplied with bread or other food sent in from the country.

Crouching like a vagrant in Moorfields, Thomas Farriner found himself being offered the hardtack that he himself had baked. Most of his fellows turned it down, unused to such fare as the weevil-ridden "warlike provisions" on which seamen were forced to subsist. But feeling that his honor was in some way at stake, Thomas took some and shared it with his reluctant daughter.

On Thursday the King rode out into Moorfields. No great entourage accompanied him, only a few nobles. As the vast crowds of homeless people pressed around him, he spoke from horseback, first trying to lay to rest the rumors of plots:

> The judgement that has fallen upon London is immediately from the hand of God and no plots by Frenchmen or Dutchmen or Papists have any part in bringing upon you so much misery. Many of those who have been detained upon suspicion I myself have examined. I found no reason to suspect connivance in burning the City. I desire you all to take no more alarm. I have strength enough to defend you from any enemy and be assured that I, your King, will by the grace of God, live and die with you and take a particular care of you all.

In his actions at this moment and in the terrible days that had preceded it, this weak, dissolute and intemperate King achieved the only genuine rapport with his subjects of his entire reign. "During the whole continuance of this unparalleled calamity, the King himself, roused from His Pleasures, commiserated the care of the distressed and acted like a true father of his people."[18]

In their hour of greatest need he had shown the leadership—the kingship—he had never displayed before and was never to show again. Whether his intention was truly to serve his people or merely to save his palace and his throne is impossible to ascertain. But by his actions he helped to spare the citizens of London from an even greater ordeal by fire and famine, and for that he received their acclaim.

For those nobles, soldiers, militiamen, and citizens who labored so long and hard to extinguish the fires, there was little reward save the golden guineas pressed into their hand or scattered among them to keep them to the work. For the rest of the citizens, the only reward was the rubble, dust, and ashes where their homes had once stood.

Although a dead calm still prevailed, fires continued to burst out among the still-smoldering ruins over the following days, each one causing fresh alarms and panics. The King was forced to issue another proclamation to calm the "groundless fears and apprehensions . . . and prevent all tumults and disorders." Whatever the alarm, no man was to "stir or disquiet himself by reason thereof, but only attend the business of quenching the fire. We having in our princely care taken order to draw together such a sufficient force both of horse and foot in and about our said City as may abundantly secure the peace and safety thereof."[19]

In place of the exhausted soldiers and militia, hundreds of soldiers from Kent, Surrey, Middlesex, and Hertfordshire had been brought into the city, their carts laden with spades, axes, and buckets. The King, warned by the aldermen that much combustible matter still lay about the city, "faggots, bavins, coal and timber, all still smoldering,"[20] required them to order the owners to remove the material within forty-eight hours. If they did not, the aldermen were to move it themselves. Meanwhile a good watch was to be kept over the whole of the city.

There was little left to watch. Five-sixths of the entire area within the walls, approaching 400 acres, and a further 60 acres outside the walls had been destroyed. Over thirteen thousand houses, eighty-seven churches, and the halls of fifty-two livery companies had been burned to the ground.

The courts and jails had been burned down, and many of the prisoners had escaped. The Royal Exchange was utterly destroyed. The Guildhall and the surrounding buildings housing the civil administration of London were also in ruins. Few of the wharves and boat-stairs on the river were undamaged by the fires. The mail had stopped, the printing presses were destroyed, and every market except Leadenhall had been razed to the ground.

Food there was, for supplies came in from the country to the temporary markets in sufficient quantity to allay the fear of starvation, but of potable small beer or water there was almost none. Wells were dry, full of rubble or still boiling from the stored heat of the blazes. The waterwheels and pumping engines under the bridge were destroyed, and the supplies from springs and the New River, feeble in any event after the drought, ran to waste through the shattered pipes.

Eighty percent of the population of the city was now homeless. Where walls were still standing, a remaining fragment of carbonized door frame sometimes had pinned to it a scrap of parchment for those who could read, or a fragment of cloth, or some keepsake too valueless to be stolen, to show that at least one member of the household had survived the holocaust.

When the survivors flocked into the city on Sunday morning to give thanks for their deliverance, barely a score of churches remained, and each one was jammed to the doors with people. As they emerged, the first rain in months began to fall. It did little to damp down the still-smoldering ruins and the fires that continued to burn in cellars, warehouses, and stores.

On several occasions when the owners dug down into cellars sealed by rubble and debris, hoping to salvage something from the wreck, the smoldering contents burst into flame on contact with the air, destroying everything. When workmen opened a cellar as late as November 30, "there were burning coals which burned ever since the Great Fire, but being pent so close for air there was very little waste."[21]

The great drought was finally ended by a downpour that began on October 15 and continued almost uninterrupted for ten days, turning the city of dust and ashes into a sea of mud. But even this rain was not enough to extinguish some of the still-smoldering fires, and new ones were constantly breaking out among the ruins. Every wind brought fresh blazes and the thunder of collapsing walls.

The fear engendered by the fire spread far beyond London:

The fire did so much affrighten the nation that all towns stood upon their own defense day and night, and particularly Oxon, everyone being so suspicious that no sorry fellow or woman could pass but they examined him, no gun or squib could go off but they thought it the fatal blow.

On 5 September, which was three days after the fire began, a butcher driving certain oxen over Carfax, cried to his beasts "Hiup, hiup" which some taking for "Fire" ran out from the church and all the rest after with the semblance of death in their faces, some saying they smelled smoke, pitch, et cetera, and could not be reconciled to their error a great while.[22]

There was also a fresh alarm at Whitehall when "between seven and eight at night happened a fire in the Horse Guard house in the Tiltyard over against Whitehall which at first arising, as is supposed, from some snuff of a candle falling among the straw, broke out with so sudden a flame that at once it seized the north-west part of the building." The fire "gave a great alarm to the town but . . . by the King's great care and painful endeavor and by blowing up some part of the stables, it pleased God that the fire was mastered and only a part of the stables was burned."

Remnants of the Great Fire still continued to burn. Pepys saw "much fire still being in" on September 17, and though the following "sad, rainy and tempestuous night" further damped down the ruins, throughout that winter he continued to record fresh outbreaks. On December 1 he noted "a cellar in Tower Street in a very fresh fire, the late great winds having blown it up. It seemed to be only of logwood that has kept the fire all this while in it."

On December 14 he traveled "by coach to Whitehall, seeing many smokes of the fire by the way yet." On January 17, 1667, he "observed still in many places the smoking remains of the late fire, the ways mighty bad and dirty." Smoke "of the late fire in the City" was still rising on February 28, and even on March 16 he remarked that "the weather is now grown warm again after much cold and it is observable that within these eight days I did see smoke remaining, coming out of some cellars from the late great fire now above six months since."[23]

The sleep of thousands of Londoners was also constantly broken. "My dear is well, but was very much affrighted, and truly we both are much troubled with sad dreams of fire in the night."[24] Pepys also suffered from such nightmares. "Much terrified in the nights nowadays, with dreams of fire and falling down of houses." Six months after the fire, he was "still mightily troubled the most of the night with fears of fire, which I cannot get out of my head to this day since the last great fire." The fears were fanned by "real fires . . . in one place or another almost ever since the late great fire, as if there was a fate over the people. . . . It is plain that there is a combination of rogues in the town that do make it their business to set houses on fire."[25]

Barely a roof remained within the city walls, yet by the Monday following the fire, only four days after it was extinguished, all the vast armies of refugees camped in the open fields to the north and east of the city had disappeared. "In all the fields about the town, which had seemed covered with those whose habitations were burned, and with the goods which they had saved, there was scarce a man to be seen."[26]

The surviving churches and company halls, inns, taverns, and private houses were thrown open, and the army erected tents and wooden shacks and lean-tos in Moorfields, Southwark, Smithfield, and the Artillery Ground at Finsbury. Pregnant women and the sick were the first to be accommodated.

London Bridge was cleared of rubble and fire debris by an army of men working without cease by day and by night under the light of blazing torches. Much of the debris was dumped over the parapet onto the muddy banks of the Thames, and people were permitted to camp in the burned area at the side of the bridge causeway, separated from the passing traffic by a wooden rail.

Shantytowns of shacks, sheds, and tents sprang up inside and outside the walls. Some salvaged what timber they could and built rude shelters on the ruins of their former homes, while others burrowed into cellars and church vaults.

"There is not a single house complete, only small huts or cabins of the beer sellers which are open for the refreshment of laborers who walk from the suburbs into the City."[27] Such "poor huts and booths built with deal boards" were swiftly erected all over the city to slake the thirst of the men laboring among the ruins.

Over the following weeks, new pathways were created over the wastes of ash and dust by people's shuffling feet. Columns of smoke and steam continued to rise from the still-smoldering cellars and stores, but after dark the wilderness was also speckled with fires lit by those living among the mounds of rubble and debris, or dwelling like troglodytes in cellars and crypts.

They lived in fear, for at night the devastated city was infested with robbers. The watchmen and parish constables had fled with the rest, and in their absence thieves and vagrants from all over the southeast flocked to London, preying on the citizens living and moving among the ruins, and raiding the cellars and crypts that had survived the blaze in search of valuables:

> The only persons who derived benefit from the calamity were those who had nothing to lose. Beggars, the cut-purses, the predatory

tramps, the nocturnal prowlers, availed themselves to the full of the opportunities which the darkness and desolation around now offered them. They pilfered such goods as they could conveniently carry away with them. They made raids upon the poor who were feebly endeavoring to protect the little they had saved from the flames. Under cover of the smoke, they entered burning houses and seized upon any valuables that came within reach. Nor did they scruple to stab and rob those who crossed their path in the purlieus of Thames Street and whose dress and appearance betokened them to be prizes worth securing.

Though constables, the trained bands and militiamen patrolled the streets, the ruin was so great and the confusion so bewildering that it became no difficult task for the robber and the assassin to escape undetected to his haunts in safe possession of his booty.[28]

A fortnight after the fire had been extinguished, the King issued a proclamation

> for restoring goods embezzled during the late fire and since. . . . Many persons were surprised and overtaken by the flames before they could get time or opportunity to remove their goods. . . . Great quantities of plate, money, jewels, householders' stuff, goods and merchandise besides many valuable materials for building are daily found amongst the ruins. All who are in unlawful possession of such are required to bring them to Armory House within eight days or suffer the penalty, even to the loss of life.[29]

The Lord Mayor, Thomas Bludworth, having recovered some of his authority and his nerve, issued his own proclamation for the punishment of "vagrants and sturdy beggars, loose and idle persons, who greatly abound wandering in and about the streets of London and amongst the ruins of this City,"[30] and stocks and whipping posts were set up in every ward, but crime remained rife.

It was Pepys's "common practice, going over the ruins in the night, [to] ride with my sword drawn in the coach."

> There are many people found murdered and carried into the vaults among the ruins . . . three last night, as I hear, and it is supposed

by hasty fellows that cry "Do you want light?" and carry links, and that when they catch a man single, whip into a vault with him, knock him down, strip him from top to toe, blow out their links and leave the person for dead.

And an apothecary's man in Southwark coming into Fenchurch Street being so served and being left for dead when these villains had done, struck fire with a tinder box which they took out of their pockets, lighted their links and away, and by glimpse of their lights . . . the man perceived a dead body lying by him in the said vault.

When the murderers were gone the young man had made shift to get out . . . and a woman dead in the vault is found. For want of good watches, no persons dare, after the close of the evening, pass the streets amongst the ruins.[31]

There were suggestions from other parts of the kingdom, including York, that the capital might be transferred elsewhere. The citizens of London had no intention of allowing that. In only one part of the walled city, the northeastern quarter, could any semblance of normality be restored, but there the city's rulers and merchants flocked to begin anew.

Sir Thomas Gresham's house in Bishopsgate Street, a substantial mansion on extensive grounds, with colonnades and covered walks surrounding an open courtyard, became a temporary home for the Court of Aldermen. Lord Mayor Bludworth, who had been burned out of his house, and the Sheriffs, Sir Robert Hanson and Sir William Hooker, also found lodgings there, along with the City Chamberlain and the Town Clerk.

A bourse was established in the courtyard for the three thousand merchants displaced from the Royal Exchange. Great financiers such as Alderman Backwell and Sir Robert Vyner also found temporary accommodation in the northeast of the city, and much of the latter's great wealth was stored for safety in Windsor Castle. Over four hundred thousand pounds of it found a permanent home there when the King defaulted on his debts to Vyner.

It was poor reward for the financier, whose devotion had even extended to the purchase of a statue of the King on horseback for the new Stocks Market. The statue had a curious provenance, having been commissioned originally by the Polish ambassador in London to commemorate the King of Poland's victory over the Turks. He failed to pay for it, and it languished on Tower Wharf until Vyner purchased it. He had the Polish king's head recarved into a likeness of Charles, and the features of the prostrate Turk beneath his horse's hooves was refashioned into Oliver Cromwell, albeit still wearing Turkish costume and headdress.

The King's Council had filled the void in authority during the fire. It now met with the aldermen, magistrates, and "citizens of quality" on Monday, September 10, at Gresham House. Its first order required the inhabitants of the city to clear all the streets, lanes, and public passages of debris. Everyone was to clear the area before his own ground, and until this work was finished no labor would be permitted upon the ruins themselves. In each ward of the city a booth was set up where former occupiers of burned houses were required to bring details of the sites and the areas of ground covered, so that records could be made, and a register was opened of those willing to buy or sell land.

A committee was appointed, meeting for the first time the next day, with powers to apportion temporary sites among the empty spaces in the city where traders and craftsmen whose dwellings had been burned could resume their occupations. The Post Office, still under the control of James Hickes, was temporarily set up in Covent Garden and then moved to Bishopsgate Street, and the Custom House found a temporary home in Mark Lane.

The Guildhall was cleared of the rubble, and within its perimeter a wooden building was erected to serve as a court for the city. The judges sat for the first time in the first week of November. Part of the ruins of Newgate were repaired enough for a number of felons to be incarcerated there, but the jail remained without water, and in November the sheriffs were ordered to supply it. The following March the walls of the common sewer were breached and it began to leak into the prison, and much of it was not rebuilt.

A wooden building was also erected among the ruins of the Sessions House in Old Bailey for the jail delivery, when prisoners were brought to trial. Former dwellings in the city gates were fitted with bolts and bars to serve as temporary jails. Prisoners from the Poultry Compter were sent to Aldersgate and those from the Wood Street Compter to Bishopsgate.

In a proclamation issued by the Mayor the day after the fire was extinguished, Leadenhall was appointed as a market for flesh brought in by country butchers and for supplies from city butchers whose shops had been destroyed, and also for fish meal, hides, and leathers. Stalls for herbs, roots, and other similar commodities were set in "the usual place" in Aldersgate Street and about the Pump in Bishopsgate Street. They were also sold at the outlying markets already established by the royal proclamation.

Plans for rebuilding the city were set in motion almost at once. On September 13, when a house owner was already rebuilding at Blackfriars,[32] a royal proclamation prohibited any rebuilding until general regulations had been issued. "This our native City" should "appear to the world as purged with fire (in how lamentable a manner soever) to a wonderful beauty and comeliness when consumed by it."[33]

An exact survey was to be taken of the ruins and a model made for the rebuilding of the devastated areas:

> The woeful experience in this late visitation has sufficiently convinced all men of the pernicious consequences which have attended the building with timber and even with stone itself, and the notable benefit of brick which in so many places has resisted and even extinguished the fire. . . . We do hereby declare our express will and pleasure that no man whatsoever shall presume to erect any house or building great or small, but of brick or stone. And if any man shall do the contrary, the next magistrate shall forthwith cause it to be pulled down and such further course shall be taken for his punishment as he deserves.
>
> That man who willfully pulled up a stake or boundary stone should have three months' imprisonment, or a fine of £10, or if a man of mean condition, should be taken to the place of his offence and there whipped till the body be bloody.[34]

A shop tenant in Duck Lane was among the first to feel the impact of this newfound determination to enforce building standards. He built "a shop of deal boards under Captain Clarke's house, dangerous for fire and an encroachment on the waste, therefore ordered to be demolished."[35]

Fleet Street, Cheapside, Cornhill, and "all other eminent and notorious streets" were to be of sufficient width "as with God's blessing would prevent the mischief that one side might suffer if the other be on fire. No street should be so narrow as to make the passage uneasy or inconvenient especially towards the waterside, nor should any alleys or lanes be tolerated but where upon mature deliberations the same be found absolutely necessary."

The riverside was to be kept clear by a quay or wharf extending the length of the city and "all noisome trades such as brewers, dyers, sugar bakers and the likes, which by their continuous smoke made adjacent localities unhealthy" were to be removed and grouped in "a place thereafter to be selected."

Meanwhile, if any persons careless of the royal command presumed to "erect buildings as they might think fit upon pretence that the ground was their own," the Lord Mayor and magistrates were charged to pull down such buildings "and the refractory persons would be punished." On October 9 the council ordered the owners of houses to clear their foundations of rubbish and pile up the bricks and stones within fourteen days so that every man's property might be exactly measured and certified.

The King, "in a religious sense of God's heavy hand upon this Kingdom in the late dreadful fire happened in the City of London . . . a visitation so dreadful that scarce any age or nation has ever seen or felt the like," had ordered that October 10 be observed as a "day of fasting and humiliation . . . to implore the mercies of God that it would please him to pardon the crying sins of this nation, those especially which had drawn down this last and heavy judgement upon us, and to remove from us all other his judgements which our sins have deserved."[36]

The churches were packed to hear the sermons preached on that day, and the special form of prayer used was continued in St. Paul's Cathedral every September 2 until 1859. Collections for the aid of sufferers in London were taken that day in every church and chapel throughout England and Wales, but with many regions still ravaged by the plague, the amount collected was small.

Part of even these modest sums was misappropriated. Sir William Bolton, Lord Mayor in succession to Sir Thomas Bludworth, claimed that twenty thousand pounds collected for relief after the fire had not been paid in, but Bolton was himself accused of withholding money subscribed for the relief of distressed Londoners. He was forbidden to attend the Court of Aldermen and duly convicted of embezzlement.[37]

Others, remembering the extortion of carters, watermen, and porters during the fire, and the plentiful work for laborers clearing the ruins after it, considered the poor had already profited enough from the disaster and needed no further help. The Pewterers' Company rejected a request for donations to the poor: "in consideration of the late calamities by fire in which the Company has been very great sufferers and the generality of the poorer sort of people have been in some measure gainers, it was concluded nothing should be given."[38]

An Act for the Rebuilding of the City of London was passed on February 5, 1667, imposing strict controls on new buildings. All were to be constructed of brick or stone, "not only more comely and durable, but also more safe against future perils of fire." Only four rigidly defined types of houses were permitted, and minimum standards for thickness of walls, depth of cellars, scantlings of timber and other specifications were also imposed. Jetties were prohibited, and the maximum number of stories was fixed at four in the "high and principal streets," three in "streets and lanes of note," and only two in by-lanes.

To speed the rebuilding work, another relic of the medieval city—the ancient privileges of the guilds, and with them much of their wealth and power—was demolished. For as long as it would take to reconstruct the city, "all carpenters, bricklayers, masons, plasterers, joiners and other artificers, workmen and laborers . . . shall have and enjoy the same liberty of working . . . as the freemen of the City."

That liberty included having their wages fixed by any two judges of the King's Bench and being imprisoned for a month if they left any work unfinished. The judges also had powers to fix the price of building materials. Meanwhile the Fire Courts, consisting of twenty-two of the chief judges of England, sat in near-permanent session at Clifford's Inn, devoting themselves "exclusively to the task of evolving order out of the chaos of vanished landmarks . . . and lost boundaries,"[39] and adjudicating on the competing claims of landlords and tenants seeking, or seeking relief from, unpaid rents.

A tax on every chaldron of coal entering the city was imposed, making a modest contribution to the costs of rebuilding and compensating owners where land was compulsorily acquired to widen thoroughfares. The King also remitted the Hearth Tax for seven years on any new house built in the city, but public funds were sorely pinched and much of the reconstruction of London depended on the goodwill, or the avarice, of private citizens.

The grander, more ambitious schemes to remodel the city proposed by Sir Christopher Wren and John Evelyn among others foundered on grounds of cost and practicality. But if the new London that began to emerge after "the highest calamity this nation has ever felt" was less romantic and characterful than the medieval city it replaced, its streets were also cleaner, less congested, and more airy and elegant.

The capital, when finally restored, was "more secure from future contagion, more generally wholesome for the inhabitants, more safe from fires and more beautiful. . . . Such has been the result of that temporary disaster, whether accidental or not, and if intended, a more pardonable instance of doing evil that good may come of it cannot perhaps be produced."

It was assumed and it is still often claimed that the city was safer from infection partly because the Great Fire had not only destroyed the old city but also cauterized the ground on which it stood, ridding London of the menace of the plague forever. It is true that bubonic plague never returned to threaten the city again, but the cause of that was not the fire, since the disease also disappeared from almost every other European city at the same time.

Various explanations have been put forward. One argues that the change from overland caravans bringing trade goods along the Silk Route to seaborne shipments broke the link with the plague's main breeding grounds in India and Asia. Others claimed that improvements in hygiene, combined with the gradual displacement of the black rat, which lived cheek by jowl with its human hosts, by the brown rat, which usually lived away from human habitations, were the crucial factors.

Perhaps the most persuasive argument is that—just like the flea-borne myxomatosis virus that destroyed rabbit populations in Britain during the 1950s and 1960s—the more virulent strains of the disease were simply too effective to survive. If a virus kills all its hosts, it will itself perish, whereas other, weaker strains survive. Humans also develop resistance and immunity. There is some evidence that this was happening in London during 1666, when many more people caught the plague and recovered than had been the case in the previous fateful year.

For whatever reasons, plague had disappeared from London and most of the Western world by the end of the seventeenth century, but the last great pandemic was as recent as the 1890s and the disease still survives, notably in Asia, where it claims many lives to this day. With a rat population that is rapidly growing and becoming progressively immune to the poisons used to control it, it would be unwise to assume that the plague will never again return to menace Britain.

Chapter 12

The Fatal Contrivance

Ripe yeoung Beanes

Great calamities naturally produce various conjectures and prodigious imaginations; men seldom considering that the most stupendous effects often proceed from the most minute causes or most remote accidents. At first the people naturally and generally looked upon this as the judgement of heaven upon a wicked city and nation, not sufficiently humbled by the preceding pestilences. But time soon produced abundance of suspicions.
Archdeacon Laurence Echard, *The History of England*

A FIRE STARTING IN A BAKERY, WHERE AN UNTENDED OVEN would offer a ready explanation, in the dead hours of the night, on the quietest day of the week, when a gale was blowing to fan the flames and no water was available to extinguish them; many citizens found these too many coincidences to accept. Thomas Farriner might indeed have simply gone to bed "leaving his providence with his slippers"[1] and a fire still burning in a hearth stacked with kindling and brushwood, but there was no shortage of more sinister explanations.

After any suspicious fire, the first thing that arson investigators look for is motive. Few citizens believed that the Great Fire of London had been nothing more than a terrible accident, and suspicions hardened over the following weeks in the wake of arson attacks in other English cities, two causing severe damage in Oxford. There were many individuals, factions, and nations with a potential motive for arson.

England was at war with the Netherlands and France. The war had been a disaster; the naval "victory" in the Four Days Battle in early June, proclaimed with the ringing of church bells and bonfires—"a horrid mocking of God and a lying to the world"[2]—had seen the Dutch lose five ships and suffer 2,800 casualties, compared to English losses of ten ships and 6,000 men killed or captured. Some of the English corpses floating in the water were still dressed in their best Sunday clothes, for the press gangs had seized them as they made their way to church.[3]

English morale was only partly restored by putting the Dutch to flight at the St. James's Day battle on July 25, and on August 8 the fleet had come upon a huge number of Dutch merchantmen sheltering in the channel between the islands of Vlie and Terschelling. Fourteen had been captured and 138 burnt after fireships were set adrift among them. The following day, raiding parties went ashore and put the settlement of Westerschelling to the torch. The Dutch were rabid for revenge and might have seen the firing of London as just retribution. It had certainly been mooted in Holland, for "some came to [the Dutch leader] de Witt and offered a revenge, that they would set London on fire if they might be well furnished and well rewarded for it. He rejected the proposition; for he said he would not make the breach wider, nor the quarrel irreconcilable. . . . He made no further reflections on the matter until the city was burnt. Then he began to suspect there had been a design and that they had intended to draw him into it and to lay the odium of it upon the Dutch."[4]

Although France was also at war with England, Louis XIV was quick to send messages of sympathy to Charles II. He forbade any triumphalism in his court at the crippling of France's traditional rival; but the Sun King was the most wily ruler of his age, and many, including the Duke of Buckingham, saw the hand of England's enemies behind the Great Fire. He reported that "about three score French and Dutch are taken, that were firing of houses."[5] Others claimed that a group of captured Frenchmen had an armory of "ten baskets of fireballs and grenades."[6]

There was even a financial incentive for finding that England's enemies had caused the blaze. Tenants' liabilities in cases of fire were relieved if their houses were destroyed by an act of war.[7]

In the absence of the mails, ever wilder rumors of impending invasions from France or the Netherlands and plots by papists or presbyterians, "anabaptists and other disaffected persons" continued to sweep the country.

On September 7, 1666, Bulstrode Whitelocke,

> going to Littlecote to inquire what news Colonel Popham had of the fire, was met in the way by Sir Seymour Pyle; who told him that . . . in the time of the fire in London there were 60,000 presbyterians with French and Dutch up in arms and that the King's forces had fought with them and killed 30,000 of them and taken many prisoners and among them eleven ousted ministers and French. . . .
>
> All this proved only the fiction of Sir Seymour, who had too much wine and too little grace and in the midst of this sad judgement this godly magistrate was drunk and swearing and lying at almost every word. Whitelocke kept close within doors but heard no more of plots or securing, yet his wife was full of fears that all places would be fired.[8]

The Mayor of Bristol "committed some Dutchmen who in their drink spoke of a design of firing the ships at the quay and said it would be a lost day for Bristol and a bloody one for England." "Since the fire at London, both seamen and landmen are rampant and outrageous for revenge upon the enemy."[9]

The Governor of Hull "ejected all disaffected persons from the town and set a strong guard on the harbor and the streets." In Norwich, where the plague was still raging, a proclamation warned that "none should lodge strangers" before the mayor had examined them. Lacking any other suitable foreigners, the Governor of Falmouth detained all ships from Hamburg in the harbor.[10]

Reports poured in from as far off as Carlisle that the Trained Bands were in the streets and brutal reprisals were being exacted against Catholics, foreigners, and strangers. Hundreds were arrested, interrogated, and thrown into prison on the faintest suspicion. Many others were beaten by the mobs, and some were lynched.[11]

In this fevered atmosphere the search for scapegoats showed no sign of abating, and even those willing to accept the fire as an act of God still insisted on attributing the cause of the divine intervention to his hatred of one faction or another. "It is well known that the Papists are generally charged with being the Contrivers and Managers of that direful Calamity; while on the other hand, the Papists retort it back again upon the Fanatics." "The Presbyterians and Fanatics will look a little starched and will have it that the judgement of the Fire of London is for the sins of others not so holy as themselves."

Royalists talked of "the destruction of the wicked city of London, which all but the ignorant conclude to be just for the murder of the King"[12]—God's punishment because the city had been "polluted with the sacred blood [of] King Charles the Martyr." The Quakers "intimate no sorrow for the late burning down of so many 'steeple houses' as they call them, in the city,"[13] and blamed it on the persecution of their faith, and nonconformists cited the sin and debauchery of the Court.

Catholics declared it God's vengeance for London's heresy, the Spanish ambassador citing the survival of the Catholic church in which Henrietta Maria, the Queen Mother, worshiped as evidence of divine intervention:

> At this very point the onrush of the flames was arrested and it is clear and certain that in this way the Almighty wished to rebuke the blindness of those heretics and to show in what respect he held the Sovereign Sacrament of the altar. A hundred and forty of the churches of the heretics, including St Paul's . . . were destroyed by the flames but at the sight of a Catholic Temple, the fire acknowledged itself to be conquered. Five and fifty thousand houses were left in ruins, it was only at the sight of one of them, one that contained within its walls memories and the worship of our holy faith, that the flaming tempest which involved so many in a disaster, allowed itself to be subdued.[14]

Others looked to human, not divine, hands for the cause of the blaze, and few shared the sentiments expressed in the *French Gazette:* "To tell the truth, nobody knows whom legitimately to blame, nor can it be believed that there are citizens so vile or enemies so malignant as to resort to an action of that nature."

Those certain of the existence of such vile and malign enemies found strong circumstantial evidence to support their beliefs. The pumping engine in the Water House at the bridge was out of order before being destroyed in the fire. The failure of the New River supply soon afterward, and the fact that the tide was also at its ebb when the fire began, making water to fight the blaze even harder to obtain, seemed to offer further confirmation.

The location of the outbreak of the fire was also highly suspicious. "If all the engineers of mischief would have compacted the irredeemable burning of

London, they could not have laid the scene of their fatal contrivance more desperately to a probable success than where it was, where narrow streets, old buildings all of timber, all contiguous each to other, all stuffed with aliment for the fire, all in the very heart of the trade and wealth of the city."[15]

Papists were immediately suspect. "The hand of man was made use of in the beginning and carrying on of this fire. The beginning of it in such a place where there were so many timber houses and the shops filled with so much combustible matter, and . . . when the wind did blow so fiercely upon that corner toward the rest of the city, which then was like tinder to the sparks; this does smell of a popish design."

Quakers and nonconformists had motive enough in the suppression of their religions, and the lechery and debauchery of the King and his Court were also the subject of constant common gossip. Pepys remarked on "an ill condition of discontent against the height and vanity of the Court."[16] The King had "abandoned himself to his lust," a lady-in-waiting had given birth to a bastard during a royal ball, and a shocked observer in Oxford saw the Horse Guards wearing face paint, perfume, and long wigs.

The courtiers, whose conversation was "so base and sordid that it makes the ears of the very gentlemen of the backstairs to tingle,"[17] were disparaged as "rude, rough whoremongers, vain, empty, careless, high, proud, insolent. Though they were very neat and gay in their apparel, yet they were very nasty and beastly, leaving at their departure their excrements in every corner, in chimneys, studies, coal houses, cellars."[18]

Many groups were still loyal to the memory of Cromwell and the ideals of the Commonwealth. The timing of the fire, on the eve of the anniversary of Cromwell's death and the battles of Dunbar and Worcester, made opponents of the Restoration and veterans of the New Model Army in particular equally suspect.

Fears of attempts to overthrow the King were fanned by Venner's rising in 1661, when a score of plotters against the Crown were executed for high treason, and the Derwentdale plot of 1663, when twenty-four men were executed. Their heads were impaled on poles around York, Appleby, and Leeds, and some remained there for thirteen years.

Far from suppressing dissenters, the Conventicle Act and the Five Mile Act established "a class which had apparently nothing to hope for from the existing regime and which was therefore constantly suspected of wishing to overthrow it."[19] There was a further Parliamentarian plot in April 1666, when eight former "officers or soldiers in the late rebellion, were indicted for conspiring the death of His Majesty and the overthrow of the government.... The better to effect this hellish design, the City was to have been fired and the portcullis to have been let down to keep out all assistance; the Horse Guards to have been surprised in the inns where they were quartered." After consulting Lilly's almanac for the year, the conspirators had settled on September 3 for the coup, "a day of luck . . . a planet then ruling which prognosticated the downfall of monarchy."[20]

Confessions were exacted from the men, who were found guilty of high treason and hung, drawn, and quartered; but not all the conspirators had been found, and the leader, Robert Danvers, managed to escape when a number of his fellow sectaries overpowered his guards as they rested at a tavern on the way to the Tower.

It was claimed that "a Council of the Great Ones" in London had controlled the plot, receiving "their directions from another in Holland. . . . Though the hand of justice laid hold of these last criminals, yet the city was burned at the very time thus projected and prognosticated which gave a strong suspicion, though not a full proof, of the authors and promoters of it."[21]

There was also "a whisper that the government itself was not without some ground of suspicion of having been the secret cause of the conflagration."[22] Although the citizens of London now preferred to carry on their daily lives without thought for the plague, the disease was still in their midst. Fresh "Rules and Orders to be observed by all Justices of the Peace, Mayors, Bailiffs and other Officers for prevention of the spreading of the infection of the plague" had been introduced on May 11, 1666. They reimposed the sealing of infected houses, restrictions on travel and public gatherings, and ordered that fires must be kept burning in all houses.

In Greenwich and Deptford—where Pepys heard that "this poor town does bury still of the plague seven or eight in a day"[23]—it was far worse than in the previous year. The population of Stepney was so depleted that it became difficult to find men enough for the navy, and the press gangs roamed farther and farther inland in search of able-bodied men.

If fire and smoke were believed to drive off the plague, might not burning out the foul tenements of the inner-city parishes and the liberties that harbored it extirpate the menace forever? One man declared "it to be my full and decided opinion that London was burnt by Government to annihilate the Plague, which was grafted in every crevice of the hateful old houses consumed in the Fire."[24]

There were those who thought the Duke of York "a little too gay and negligent for such an occasion, [and] it is known that the gaiety of his look and air discovered the pleasure he took in that dreadful spectacle." "A jealousy of his being concerned in it was spread about with great industry."[25]

Some "endeavored to charge at least the connivance of the Guard, the Earl of Craven, the Duke of York and even the King himself" with having a hand in it, and drew "an odious parallel between his Majesty and Nero," even though the King suffered financially as a result of the fire.

Between 1662 and 1665, the Crown's permanent ordinary revenue had averaged £824,000. In 1666 to 1667, it fell to £647,000. "The two great branches of the revenue, the customs and excise, which were the great and almost inexhaustible security to borrow money upon, were now bankrupt and would neither bring in money, nor supply credit."[26]

Yet despite Charles's protestations that "no particular man has sustained any loss or damage by the late terrible and deplorable fire in his fortune or estate in any degree to be compared to the loss and damage we our self have sustained, so it is not possible for any man to take the same more to heart,"[27] rumors were circulating that His Majesty was not wholly displeased with the destruction of the city.

The King lived "in greater fear of the poor than the plague,"[28] and the slighting of the city walls in areas where Dissenters were believed to be numerous showed the Crown's anxiety that unless snuffed out at once, a rising in the country might spread to the capital. The walls and defenses of the City of London were no longer completely impregnable, but they still stood, thirty-five feet from foundation to ramparts and ten feet thick. They were not only a mighty barrier enclosing and protecting the city, but the physical embodiment of the political divide that had pitched the country into bloody civil war.

Restored to the throne only in 1660 and far from secure in his tenure of it, Charles II and his capital existed in close but uneasy proximity. The city had been at the heart of the revolution against Charles I, the fount and the scene of the regicide, and it had played a decisive part in the Civil War. In the early stages the military advantage had lain with the Royalists, but the wealth generated by the City of London enabled Cromwell to raise, train, equip, and pay the New Model Army that tipped the balance of the war decisively against the cash-starved King.

Charles II had no love for those who had colluded in the defeat and execution of his father. He was reminded of it every day, for he could never look upon the Banqueting Hall in Whitehall without recalling the events of the afternoon of January 30, 1649. When Charles, in exile, heard that his father was to be executed, he sent a signed, otherwise blank, piece of paper to Westminster inviting the country's new rulers to write any terms they chose above his signature if they would only reprieve his father. His appeal was unsuccessful.

After a weeklong show trial, the King was led from the first-floor window of the Banqueting House onto a wooden scaffold erected outside its windows. The executioner, Charles Brandon, and his assistants awaited him, disguised with wigs and false beards to protect them from reprisals. Charles I was forced to kneel and lay his neck on the block ready for the headsman's ax.

Moments later the ax fell and his bloody head was raised. Many cheered, but from others in the crowd there arose "such a groan as I never heard before and desire I may never hear again." An element of black farce attended this moment, for the executioner, grasping the wig rather than the King's own hair, saw the head fall from his grasp and roll across the platform.

Nor had the Restoration extinguished the republican temper of London. By ancient tradition the sovereign could not even enter the city without the permission of the Lord Mayor and the Corporation of London, and it remained a focus of opposition to the King. It was the financial, commercial, and manufacturing heart of the kingdom, and the members returned by the city wards, though few in number, were an influential force in Parliament.

Much as the King hated them, he also needed them, but he "had reason to believe that Parliament would not so soon be in good humor enough to give more money, which was the principal end of calling them together."[29] Their refusals forced him to borrow crippling sums from rich merchants such as Sir Robert Vyner. Members of Parliament had already set themselves on a collision course with the King by making clear their extreme reluctance to grant any further money without an inspection and audit of the Crown accounts.

In the wake of the fire the merchants, bankers, and rentiers sitting as members of Parliament now had other, more immediate priorities than seeking to call the King to account for his expenditure. Fueled by war fever, the Parliament had voted almost four million pounds in 1664 and 1665 to fund the war against the Dutch. A discrepancy in the accounts for His

Majesty's Navy left well over two million pounds unaccounted for. As Pepys himself noted, "What then is become of this sum?"

Pepys had previously commented on "how the King has lost his power by submitting himself" to a parliamentary examination of his accounts, but it was unlikely to be pursued with quite the same vigor as it would have been before the fire. "The King must, if they do not agree presently, make them a courageous speech; which he says he may do, the City of London being now burned, and himself master of an army, better than any prince before him."[30]

Charles "loved money only to spend it and would privately accept of a small sum paid to himself in lieu of a far greater to be paid to the Exchequer." His profligacy was as legendary as his capricious and often cruel nature. "One day lavish to his servants, the next leaving them to starve . . . glad to win a little money at play and impatient to lose but the thousandth part of what, within an hour after, he would throw away in gross."[31]

Charles could not govern without the revenues that Parliament grudgingly granted him, but the courtiers and nobles at Whitehall and Westminster had little contact with and less time for London's dour merchants and traders, and there were some who privately urged His Majesty to break the power of the city and cast down its great walls.

He had so far held back from too open a confrontation, but his tenuous hold on his crown was further threatened by social unrest. The Restoration in 1660 had brought for many a welcome release from the joyless, puritanical rule of the saints, and the return of prosperity to the capital; but in its wake had come a growing weight of taxation, partly to fund the war against the Dutch, but much more, in the public perception at least, to pay for the excesses of the King. Even without the extremes advocated by the Levelers and Fifth Monarchy Men, countless republicans, former soldiers of the Commonwealth, Puritans, and other dissenters felt themselves betrayed, and rancor, bitterness, and hostility still seethed just below the surface.

When Parliament would not meet the cost of his excesses, Charles imposed taxes that were widely reviled. Far from abolishing the excise, as many had hoped, the King increased the number of goods on which it was levied. The poll tax of 1660 was "generally accepted since it was calculated to relieve the people of the hated burden of the army."[32] But "chimney money"—the Hearth Tax, introduced in 1662—was the object of particular hate, provoking even stronger anti-Royalist sentiment.

As early as August 1662, only two years after the Restoration, a saying was circulating in London, complaining that "the Bishops get all, the Courtiers spend all, the Citizens pay for all, the King neglects all, and the devils take all." By the following year courtiers were writing in anxious terms about the hostility of the citizens toward the King.

The royal arms were torn down in Southwark, and Samuel Lewis, a merchant tailor, was charged with treason after saying, "We were made to believe when the King came in that we should never pay any more taxes. If we had thought that he would have taxed us thus, he should never have come in. But he will never leave till he come to the same end as his father did."[33] During the plague year, many shared the belief that the King had "provoked God to send this judgement upon us by taking and assessing the poor. If this King had been hanged when the other was beheaded we should have had none of these taxes; but I think we must all rise."[34]

There was also a widespread suspicion that, for all his avowed Protestantism, Charles might be a secret supporter or adherent of the old faith. It was suggested that the King's words to the homeless in Moorfields had not been entirely disinterested. His mother was a papist, he had married a Catholic, Catherine of Braganza, and his mistress, Lady Castlemaine, had converted to Catholicism in 1663. His brother, James, Duke of York, was also rumored—correctly—to be one. Might Charles not also be a covert papist? Samuel Pepys also expressed fear that the Duke of York might one day "come to the Crown, he being a professed friend to the Catholics."[35]

Although the resourcefulness that he and his brother had displayed in the face of the fire had brought him some respite from his previous unpopularity, the King knew how quickly discontent could spill over into rebellion, especially when fueled by such inflammatory rumors.

While the fire was still burning, Charles had summoned General Monck, Duke of Albemarle, then in charge of the fleet seeking battle with the Dutch, to return to London. The fact that it was phrased as a request rather than an order showed the tact Charles felt was necessary in dealing with a man who commanded far greater public confidence and respect than himself.

Monck, a stolid, phlegmatic character, had fought for the Commonwealth during the Civil War, but he became disillusioned by events during the Protectorate and the disastrous two-year rule of Oliver Cromwell's son, Richard—"Tumbledown Dick"—following the death of his father. While the Rump Parliament and the ragged remnants of the New Model Army wrangled over power, Monck marched his battle-hardened and well-disciplined army south to London and used the threat of its presence to secure the restoration of Charles II to the throne. As reward, the King had showered Monck with titles and granted him a pension of seven thousand pounds a year.

When the plague had ravaged London, Monck, the man who "hated a coward as ill as a toad," chose to remain in the city. He became something of a talisman to many citizens; as long as he was at hand, the worst might yet be avoided. Whatever the public felt about the excesses of the King and his Court, Monck remained hugely popular, the one public figure with support from both the Royalist and Parliamentarian sides.

The letter bearing instructions from Lord Arlington to Sir Thomas Clifford, who was to approach Monck on the King's behalf, read:

> I leave you to judge what a distraction this misfortune puts us to whereof the consequences are yet more terrible to us by the disorders that are likely to follow. . . . If my Lord General could see the condition we are in, I am confident, and so is everybody else, he would think it more honor to be called to this occasion than to be stayed in the fleet where it is possible he may not have an opportunity of fighting the enemy. But here it is certain he will have it in his hands to give the King his kingdoms a second time, and the world see therein the value the King makes of him.
>
> [Charles added a private note to the bearer of the letter.] If His Grace admits you to discourse the point with him you must take pains to enforce it all you can but still with this reserve and conclusion that His Majesty leaves him to make his choice himself.[36]

Monck responded to the summons at once and by Friday was "riding through the rubbish in Fleet Street,"[37] but his presence did little to allay the discontent in some quarters.

A man so obsessed by fire that he toured the river in his barge seeking blazes to view and extinguish, Charles II would have turned to no other weapon if he felt moved to wage war on London. The city was the source of much of the nation's wealth, but if its old order was swept away, a newer, more amenable London might arise from the ashes, less eager to confront and deny its sovereign, and more willing to pay him his due.

Hugh May, Paymaster of the King's Works, was one of the few at Court willing to give public expression to these sentiments. He declared that

> This was the greatest blessing that God had ever conferred on him [the King], his Restoration only excepted, for the walls and gates being now burned and thrown down of that rebellious city, which was always an enemy to the Crown, His Majesty would never suffer them to repair and build them up again to be a bit in his mouth and a bridle upon his neck, but would keep all open, that his troops might enter upon them whenever he thought necessary for his service, there being no other way to govern that rude multitude but by force.[38]

In his determination to stop the rumors, given fresh fuel by remarks such as May's, the King sent for the Lord Chief Justice, Sir John Kelyng, and gave him immediate charge of the "severe inquisition"[39] of witnesses to the burning of the city.

The Lord Chief Justice and the Privy Council sat day after day examining witnesses brought from the prisons of Southwark and Westminster, the only ones still standing where miscreants could be lodged. But the examinations taken proved inconclusive. "Many who were produced as if their testimony would remove all doubts, made such senseless relations of what they had been told, without knowing the condition of the persons who told them, or where to find them, that it was a hard matter to forbear smiling at their evidence."[40]

By appointing Kelyng, the King had hoped that none would be able to say that the allegations of a plot and willful firing of the city had not been fully investigated. In this he was signally disappointed. Rumors began to circulate at once that any evidence pointing to a papist plot was being discounted. Many of those seized in the streets and handed over to the Guards after allegedly being seen firing houses were never examined or brought to trial.

Parliament was not sitting when the fire broke out. The King summoned it only when his extreme financial hardship required him to seek parliamentary assent for increases in the Civil List. Prorogued since April, it was finally recalled to Westminster on September 18 to be addressed by the King: "My lords and gentlemen, I am very glad to meet so many of you together again and God be thanked for our meeting in this place. Little time has passed since we were almost in despair of having this place left us to meet in; you see the dismal ruins the fire has made and nothing but a

The Great Fire from Hieroglyphicks.

miracle of God's mercy could have preserved what is left from the same destruction."[41]

A Commons motion requested that the "humble thanks of this House be given to His Majesty for his great care and endeavor to prevent the burning of London," but dissatisfied with the King's explanations for the causes of the fire, the Commons at once appointed their own investigating committee.

The temper of the House can be judged from another parliamentary committee set up at the same time to investigate "the insolence of Popish priests and Jesuits and the increase of Popery." It authorized a general search for arms in the houses of papists, and Sir Richard Browne produced "some ugly knives, like poignards to stab people."[42] Two hundred of these "desperate daggers fit for massacres" had been found "in the rubbish of a house in London wherein before the fire two French persons lodged."[43] Such actions further fueled the xenophobia ruling in the streets.

The committee took a wealth of testimony showing little more than the suspicion and paranoia about foreigners and papists, but it led to a petition to His Majesty requiring the banishment of all popish priests and Jesuits, the enforcement of the laws against papist recusants and the disarming of all who refused the oaths of allegiance and supremacy. The King gave his assent with what good grace he could muster, well knowing "the springs upon which the animosity to the Roman Catholics rises and how hard it is for His Majesty to forbear declaring against them when the complaint arises from both Houses of Parliament."[44]

The committee investigating the causes of the fire had also been busy. It had powers to examine all records and papers and summon witnesses, and it met for the first time on September 26 under the chairmanship of Sir Robert Brook. It received "many considerable informations from divers creditable persons about the matter wherewith they were instructed,"[45] but many were as fatuous as that of the boy gathering blackberries near Warwick who saw "a man doing something in a ditch, he then put something into a bag and went away."

The boy found "a blackish brown ball" in the ditch and took it to the Deputy Lieutenant. There was no appearance of anything combustible in it, but the Mayor of Warwick declared it to be a fireball. His opinion was shared by all save an "ingenious gentleman" who said it was no such thing. A hue and cry was raised round the town, every man standing to arms and the militia keeping guard at night.[46]

At Coventry a "strange robbery" was committed, "many sheep having been killed in the field, and only their tallow taken away; this was thought to be intended for making of fireballs and one malefactor was apprehended, who said he did it through poverty and sold the tallow."[47]

There was also much gossip and hearsay foretelling unspecified dire events for London during 1666:

> Mrs Elizabeth Styles informed that in April last a French servant of Sir Vere Fen told her "the English maids will like the French men better when there is not a house between Temple Bar and London Bridge. . . . It will come to pass between June and October." . . . Mr Light of Ratcliff informed that Mr Longhorn of the Middle Temple did say, "You expect great things in '66 and think that Rome will be destroyed, but what if it be London?" . . . William Ducket MP informed that John Woodman of Kelloway said to Henry Baker of Chippenham, "Since you delight in bonfires you shall have your bellies full of them ere it be long, if you live one week longer you shall see London as sad as ever it was since the world began."[48]

The committee even summoned Will Lilly, the author of one of the numerous almanacs purporting to foretell the future, to explain why his book *Hieroglyphicks* included "in one of the plates, a large city, understood to denote London . . . enveloped in flames; and another rude woodcut, containing a large amount of graves and corpses, was afterwards interpreted to bear reference to the plague."[49]

Not all the evidence laid before the committee was so feeble, however, and on the face of it, some was proof absolute of fire-raising and criminal conspiracy. "John Powell informs that on the Wednesday of the fire he learned from a crowd in Fetter Lane that a man in woman's apparel had been taken in the act of firing a house there. He questioned this person who admitted to having fired the house and to being a Roman Catholic, whereupon the people fell upon him and were ready to pull him to pieces had he not been rescued by some foot soldiers."

"True Bill that . . . Elizabeth Shaw, spinster, had in her possession divers fire-balls compounded of gunpowder, brimstone and other combustible matter with the intention of placing and firing the said balls so as to set on fire and destroy the city."[50]

At Hurley Manor Court in Berkshire, Edward Taylor confessed that on the night the Great Fire broke out, he went to Pudding Lane with his father and his uncle, Joseph Taylor, "a Dutchman and baker" in Covent Garden. They found a glass window open, and threw in "two fireballs made of gunpowder and brimstone."

From Pudding Lane, joined by two or three other men, they went on to fire houses in Thames Street and Fleet Street and set the Royal Exchange alight, "and so went on doing such mischiefs two or three nights and days" while "divers Frenchmen, Dutchmen, women and boys did go about the City with fire balls." He claimed his uncle had hired his father to do the work and "gave him £7 to undertake this firing." A note appended to the statement suggested that Taylor's age—he was ten years old—"renders the whole suspect, but it is to be put into my Lord Chief Justice's hand."[51]

Many eyewitnesses alleged that they had seen the throwing of fireballs. "Dr John Packer informs that he saw a person in the time of the fire throw some combustible matter into a shop in the Old Bailey which he thinks was the shop of an apothecary, and that immediately thereupon he saw a great smoke and smelt a smell of brimstone. The person that did this immediately ran away, but upon the outcry of the people he was taken by the Guards."

"Mr Freeman of Southwark, brewer, whose house was lately fired, informed that . . . a paper with a ball of wildfire containing near a pound weight wrapped in it was found in the nave of a wheel in a wheelers yard where they had a great quantity of timber."[52]

On Tuesday about noon during the burning of the City of London, three men broke into the counting house at Holborn Bridge. I first finding them there asked what they did there. They answered that they were sent by the Lord Craven . . . to advise us to get away what we could, for the fire would be quickly upon us. One of them was a Frenchman in a livery suit.

I went down the yard to see if those men whom I had hired to cast the hay in the Rose Inn, which was uncovered, into the Ditch, were at work. On seeing some men on the hay, I bid them go to cast it down but they gave me no answer but went down. Immediately after their descent, a small light burning like sulfur appeared and presently flashed over the hay like brimstone, whereupon I heard them in the inn cry "Fire! Fire in the hay!"

It was not two of the clock I think that Tuesday when the said hay was fired and no house on fire by a great way as is known to many. I did diligently observe and I verily believe that the Rose Inn was fired by instruments and shall be of that judgement as long as I think of what I saw.[53]

A Frenchman, Belland, King Charles's firework maker, "employed by the office of ordnance for making grenades of all kinds, as well for the hand as for mortarpieces,"[54] had bought large quantities of pasteboard and stored "twenty gross" in his shop before the fire. Asked what he did with all this, he replied that he made fireworks for the King's pleasure. The stationer who had supplied the pasteboard expressed wonder at the thousands of fireworks piled up around his premises.

"Sir," Belland said, "do you wonder at this? If you should see the quantity that I have made elsewhere by other men you would wonder indeed."

The day before the fire, Belland came again to the stationer's in great concern because four more gross of pasteboards had not been delivered.

"Mr Belland, what is the reason of your haste?" he was asked. "Have you any shows suddenly before the King?" At which he blushed and would give no answer.

"What kind of fire do you make, only such as will crack and run?"

"I make all sorts," Belland said. "Some that will burn and make no crack at all, but will fly up in a pure body of flame higher than the top of Paul's and waver in the air."

"Mr Belland, when you make your show shall I see it?"

"Yes," Belland said. "I promise you," and gave him his hand upon it.

Within a week the stationer was fleeing from the fire in a boat on the Thames and saw, just as Belland had described, flames as high as St. Paul's wavering in the air.

When the fire was extinguished, the stationer and a neighbor went in search of Belland. They found two maids and his boy, who said they knew nothing of their master's whereabouts, but seeing that they carried food, the stationer and his neighbor concluded that the servants were going to him in hiding.

They followed them to Whitehall, to the King's palace, where the firework maker had taken refuge. The servants attempted to lose them in the maze of passages, but they stuck to their heels, and at last one of the maids knocked at a door, crying out that they were dogged by two men whom they could not be rid of. Belland's son then appeared and wished them good day.

"I and many thousand families more are the worse for you," the stationer said. "For you, under pretence of making fireworks for the King, have destroyed a famous city and ruined a noble people."

At this Belland senior appeared. "Sir, I hear you charge my son with suspicion of burning the city. I pray you speak lower." He cast his eyes about, fearing the ladies passing by might hear, and said, "My son does nothing but what he has a patent from the King for, and shall have an order to sue any man that shall accuse him. My son is no prisoner, but lodged here to protect him from the rage of the common people."

"Well," the stationer said, "he must give an account for what you have done."[55]

None was ever offered, and Belland was never interrogated or charged. In all, "above forty informations upon oath proving that London was burnt by the Papists" were made, but many more witnesses remained unheard and many suspects apprehended in the act of firing houses, according to their accusers, were neither interrogated nor charged, nor heard of again. Lord Russell and Sir Henry Capel observed to the House of Commons in 1680 that "those that were taken in carrying on that wicked act were generally discharged without trial."

"Near West Smithfield in Cheek Lane there was a man taken in the very act of firing a house by the inhabitants and neighbors . . . the King's Life-guard . . . told them that he was one of the King's servants and said 'We will have him' and thereupon they drew out their swords and pistols and rescued him out of the people's hands by force of arms. A Bill of Indictment was brought against him and two or three witnesses did swear upon it and the bill was found by the Grand Jury who . . . presented it to the Lord Chief Justice but it came to no further trial nor was ever seen after at the Old Bailey."[56]

"A Bill was likewise found" against a housekeeper at Soho, but "the petty-jury, being too much influenced and overawed by the Lord Chief Justice Kelyng, did not find him guilty."[57]

"A constable took a Frenchman firing a house and going to a magistrate with him, met the Duke of York, who . . . spoke to him in French. . . . The Duke took him into his custody and said 'I will secure him' but he was heard of no more."[58]

Another witness reported that a Frenchman had been seized "in the act of firing a house in Shoe Lane on the morning of 4 September. He took him to Fleet Street where he was met by the Commander of the Guard. . . . Asked if he would go with him to give his evidence, [the witness was told that] he had done enough and might go home. What became of the Frenchman he knows nothing."[59]

"Several evidences were given to the committee that men were seen in several parts of the city casting fire-balls into houses; some that were brought to the guard of soldiers and to the Duke of York, but were never heard of afterwards. Some weeks later, Sir Robert Brook, chairman of the committee, went to France and, as he was ferried over a river, was drowned with a kinsman of his, and the business drowned with him."[60]

For some, the information that was recorded was evidence enough of arson. "At the committee concerning the firing of London, many strange discoveries have been made about it so that it is strongly presumed it was done by villainy. It is proved that during the fire several persons were taken who had about them composition of wildfire but would not give any account of themselves and strangely escaped in the tumult."[61]

Not all subscribed to a conspiracy theory. "The examinations of divers persons were read and there appeared to be many wicked and desperate expressions in them, but yet there are none of them that can be laid hold on to extend to the punishment of death of them that uttered them or to prove it to be a general design of wicked agents, Papists or Frenchmen to burn the city."[62]

Some were less easily persuaded by the testimony to the committee. "I should have acquainted you if anything had been made out of a design in firing the City, but that cannot be found . . . all the allegations are very frivolous and people are generally satisfied that the fire was accidental . . . although many are still of opinion there were some actors in the mischief."[63] A few dismissed the report in even more emphatic terms. "Troop, troop then away your informations, they are not worth a fart."

The King's Council was equally unimpressed. "Notwithstanding that many examinations have been taken with great care by the Lords of the Council and His Majesty's ministers, yet nothing has yet been found to argue it could have been other than the hand of God upon us, a great wind and the season so very dry."[64]

The belief that a chain of unfortunate coincidences was the sole cause of the conflagration was summarized by Edward Chamberlayne in *The Present State of England:*

Of this dreadful fire there were many concurrent occasions. First the drunkenness or supine negligence of the Baker in whose house it began. Or of his men.

Next, the dead time of night wherein it began, viz between one and two of the clock after midnight when some were wearied with working, others filled with drink, all in a dead sleep.

Thirdly the dead time of the week, being Saturday night when traders were retired to their country houses and none but children or young servants left behind.

Fourthly the dead time of all the year being the long vacation on 2 September when tradesmen were generally abroad in the country, some in the remotest parts of England, to fetch in their debts.

Fifthly the closeness of the buildings in that place facilitating the progress of the fire and hindering the usual remedy which was by engines to shoot water.

Sixthly the matter of the buildings thereabouts which was generally wooden and of old timber.

Seventhly the long continued drought of the preceding summer even to that day.

Eighthly the matter of wares in those parts, where were the greatest magazines and storehouses of oils, pitch, tar, rosin, wax, butter, brimstone, hemp, cordage, cheese, wine, etc.

Ninthly an easterly wind, the driest of all other, that had continued long before.

Ten the Thames water tower then out of order and burnt down immediately after the beginning of the fire, so that most water pipes were soon dry.

Lastly an unusual negligence at first and a confidence of easily quenching the fire, on a sudden changed into a general consternation and despondency, all people choosing to save their goods than by a vigorous opposition to save their houses and the city.

These causes thus strangely concurring, (to say nothing of God's just anger for the notorious impenitency of the citizens for their abetting and instigating the shedding of the innocent blood of God's anointed . . . and of their still going on in their own heinous sins) . . . by a general prodigious conflagration did make a greater spoil of the place in three days . . . than three or four armies unresisted could probably have done in twice the time.

Those who believed that the city had been deliberately fired were not so easily dissuaded from their opinions. However, despite the scores of allegations of willful firing, only a single case was sent for trial at the Old Bailey, that of Robert Hubert, against whom the only evidence was his own confession.

Chapter 13

The Duke
of Exeter's Daughter

Hot Codlings Hot Hot

*Many persons are gifted with such a patience or power of enduring tor-
ments that the truth cannot by this means be pressed out of them; while in
others there is such faintness of heart that they will tell any kind of
falsehood rather than undergo the torture . . . it often happens that the latter kind of persons will from dread of pain, tell all manner of fables not
only falsely accusing themselves, but bringing other innocent people into
suspicion and danger.*
Quoted in David Jardine, *A Reading on the Use of Torture
in the Criminal Law of England*

A WEEK AFTER MAKING HIS ESCAPE FROM THE *MAID OF STOCK-
holm*, Hubert was arrested at Romford. How he came to be there,
twelve miles northeast of London, after being seized by the mob at St.
Katharine's Dock, and what had happened to him in the intervening period
have never been explained. In the first of the many, often contradictory
statements he was to give, Hubert merely said that he "came this way to go
towards the sea coasts," in the hope of finding a vessel on which to get a
passage home.

Captain Petersen had already sailed from London in the *Maid of Stockholm* in the days immediately following the fire. He was on the high seas, bound for Rouen, when Hubert was arrested.

After "examination" by his captors, Hubert made a confession. He spoke in French, since despite his former years in England he understood almost no English, and his words were translated by a gentleman who, like most nobles and courtiers, spoke passable French. In the statement, taken at Romford on September 11, 1666, "before Cary Harvie, alias Mildmay Esquire," one of the justices of the peace for the county, Hubert claimed that "about mid-Lent" he came out of France with one Stephen Piedloe, a Frenchman. They stayed in Sweden for four months, and then sailed for England "in a Swedish ship called the *Skipper*, which was laden with iron, steel and copper plates." According to the statement, the name of the ship's master was also Skipper.[1]

The ship "lay at St Katharine's brewhouse" in London, and while keeping Hubert on board, "Piedloe himself went several times into the City and came on board again and had often private discourse with the master of the ship."

Hubert said that "when the City was on fire," Piedloe handed him a fireball and told him to "fire a house near the King's Palace" for which Piedloe "gave him a shilling and promised him a greater reward when he came into France." Hubert threw the fireball through the window of the house and "stayed there and saw it burn two or three hours." Piedloe himself and "divers other Frenchmen" also used fireballs. In all, Hubert said, twenty-three men were involved in the fire-raising.[2]

The Romford magistrates wasted no time in making arrangements to transfer Hubert to London. Chained and manacled and escorted by a score of guards, Hubert rode in a farm cart, jolting over the dusty, rutted tracks. Word spread fast that one of the authors of London's misfortunes was being taken to the city to answer for his crimes, and crowds lined the route, booing, jeering, and throwing rotten vegetables, stones, and clods of earth and manure. No one, not even the King of France, was more hated and reviled than the man who had confessed his part in firing London.

With Newgate in ruins, he was taken to His Majesty's Jail for the County of Surrey, the White Lion prison, better known as the Southwark Clink and as notorious as Newgate for its disgusting conditions. The stench was noxious in the extreme, and his ears were battered by the noise of hundreds of other inmates, quarreling, pleading their innocence, calling for alms, or fighting for scraps, all set against the grim scraping sound of their fetters dragging over the cold stone floors. As the bruised and bleeding Hubert was first stripped of any items of value he still possessed and then thrown into a dark, dank cell, he can have had little doubt about what lay in store for him.

Torture had always been against the common law of England—it was contrary to the Magna Carta—but it was lawful as an act of Royal Prerogative and was hallowed by precedent down the centuries. The principal instrument, the rack, had been installed in the Tower by the Duke of Exeter in the reign of Henry VI, and became known in the gallows humor of the warders as "the Duke of Exeter's daughter."

Sometimes the sight of the rack was enough to break a prisoner's nerve. "Deliver him to the Lieutenant of the Tower whereby he may be brought to the place of torture and put in fear thereof." If the sight of the terrible instrument was not sufficient, the rack-keepers were "to spare not to lay him upon it to the end he may feel such smart and pains thereof as to their discretions shall be thought convenient."[3]

When the Protestant martyr Anne Askew was put to the rack in 1546, "the Lord Chancellor, finding the rack-keeper falter in his operations, threw off his gown, drew the rack himself so severely that he almost tore her body asunder."[4]

Torture reached its peak of refinement under Elizabeth, and though its use was publicly disowned in the seventeenth century, both physical and psychological torture remained widespread. The last recorded instance of the use of the rack was on May 21, 1640,[5] but the Duke of Exeter's daughter remained in her chamber and prisoners continued to be brought to it as a way of terrorizing them into confessions. Sixteen years later a leading judge justified the practice, claiming "to bring men to the rack in such cases (where there was only one witness) for trial's sake is not to be censured for cruelty."[6] It was thought that the terror it engendered would be guaranteed to produce honest testimony.

At the Newgate Sessions in 1663, "George Thorely, being indicted for Robbery, refused to plead and his two thumbs were tied together with whipcord." He was hung up by his thumbs and "an hour after, he was brought again and pleaded. And this was said to be the constant practice at Newgate."[7]

Prisoners were also placed in the "dungeon among the rats," an unlit cell below the high-water mark. As the tide rose, "innumerable rats which infest the muddy banks of the Thames were driven through the gaps in the walls into the dungeon. The alarm excited by the irruption of these loath-some creatures in the dark was the least part of the torture which the unfor-tunate captives had to undergo; instances are related which humanity would gladly believe to be the exaggerations of Catholic partisans, where the flesh had been torn from the arms and legs of prisoners during sleep by the well known voracity of these animals."[8]

What torments Robert Hubert was forced to endure were never revealed, but in the four weeks he was incarcerated before being brought to trial he was undoubtedly subjected to repeated interrogations and the most brutal treatment. He had already confessed to igniting a fire, but his inter-rogators were not looking for evidence of fire-raising once London was already in flames. What they wanted was a confession from the man who had set the city ablaze in the first place.

The examination of any accused man was intended to be a vigorous pursuit of the evidence that would lead to a conviction, not an evenhanded attempt to discover the truth. It was not a magistrate's duty to discharge prisoners. All suspects were to go to trial, accompanied by the most unequivocal evidence of their guilt the magistrate could produce. "He was not actually forbidden to report information that was in the prisoner's favor but nor was he expected to search for such evidence as 'maketh against the King.'"[9]

The prisoner was not told what evidence had been gathered, or allowed to hear the deposition against him. It was believed that the truth would be most clearly revealed if the prisoner was confronted with the case against him only in the courtroom, so that the jury could judge his unprepared response.

Far from denying his guilt, however, the "mopish, besotted"[10] Hubert showed an almost pathological determination to confess to everything that was put before him. Having at first claimed only to have fired a house near Whitehall on Tuesday, September 4, when London was already well ablaze, by the time he appeared in court he was ready to confess that he had begun the Great Fire itself by firing Thomas Farriner's house in the early hours of the previous Sunday. Whether this new confession was the truth or a falsehood inspired by fear, torture, brainwashing, or Hubert's mental insta-bility was impossible to determine.

A second charge was also laid against Hubert at the Middlesex Ses-sions, where a True Bill was found that "at St Martin's, in the county of

Middlesex on the said day, Robert Hubert, late of the said parish, laborer, set fire to a certain fire-ball compounded of gun powder, brimstone and other combustible matter, and with it fired and destroyed the dwelling house of a certain man to the jurors unknown. Robert Hubert 'Not Guilty' to this indictment, process on which ceased," pending the outcome of the other proceedings.[11]

On October 11, 1666, Hubert appeared at a jail delivery session of the Old Bailey before Lord Chief Justice Kelyng, the Recorder of London Sir William Wild, and the Lord Mayor, Sir Thomas Bludworth. The session was held in a temporary courtroom hastily erected on the site of the Old Bailey.

The presence of the irascible Kelyng on the bench was enough to snuff out any chance that the jury would acquit Hubert, not that it was ever likely, given the temper of the city since the fire. "His bearing on the bench, both before and still more after his advancement to the chief justiceship, was haughty and brutal, and he did not scruple to browbeat, fine and even imprison the jury. This scandalous practice being brought to the notice of the House of Commons, Kelyng was summoned before a committee appointed to investigate the charge, which reported . . . that he has used an arbitrary and illegal power."[12]

Hubert was charged that, "led away by the instigation of the Devil," he had committed the felony of setting on fire "with a fire ball compounded and made with gunpowder, brimstone and other combustible material" the house of Thomas Farriner senior, baker, of Pudding Lane on September 2, 1666.

Once more he altered his story, testifying that he had been suborned to set London on fire when staying in Paris a year before. "When asked who it was that suborned him to this action, he answered that he did not know, having never seen him before." In this latest version of Hubert's story, Piedloe was still the chief instigator, but the number of accomplices had now dwindled from twenty-three to three. They had come to England at the time of the plague to put the plan into effect, but he and two of his companions then went to Sweden, returning at the end of August to carry it out.

Hubert now claimed that Piedloe took him ashore early on the morning of September 2. They walked along the wharves and then across Thames Street into Pudding Lane, arriving at the baker's house. Piedloe told him he had brought three fireballs and gave him one of them to throw into the house. Hubert said he protested but Piedloe ignored him, and at his insistence, Hubert placed the fireball on the end of a long pole and put it in through a window, staying there until the house was in flames.

He claimed his two companions had escaped to France. When Kelyng asked him, "What money did you receive to perform a service of so much hazard?" Hubert said his sole reward was a pistole—a gold coin worth a little less than a sovereign—but he had been promised five pistoles more when he had accomplished his work. It seemed a trifling reward for such an enterprise.

Called to give evidence next, Thomas Farriner swore on his oath that his building could only have been maliciously fired. "He had after twelve o'clock that night gone through every room thereof and found no fire but in one chimney, where the room was paved with bricks, which fire he diligently raked up in embers.... Having occasion to light a candle about midnight there was not enough fire in the bakehouse to kindle the match and he had to go into another place for that purpose."

Asked if there was no window or door that might have let in wind to fan the embers, he swore it was impossible. "It was absolutely set on fire on purpose." Nor was there any such window as Hubert had described, nor did the fire start in that part of the building.

Between one and two o'clock "his man waked with the choke of the smoke" and roused the family. When Farriner looked out, he claimed, the stack of bavins (brushwood) for the ovens in his yard was not then alight and the crackling of the fire he could hear was remote from the oven and the chimney. As further proof of this, he claimed that the pile of faggots for relighting the fire and "several pots of baked meat as is usual for Lord's day dinner were not touched by the fire and so found entire several days after the city was in ashes. His maid was burned in the house not adventuring to escape," as Farriner, his daughter, who was "much scorched, and his man did out of the window and gutter."[13] Hannah Farriner's testimony echoed her father's in every detail.

A French merchant called Graves living in St. Mary Axe gave the first corroboration of any part of Hubert's story. He claimed that he knew Piedloe well, "a most debased man apt to any wicked design." He also said he had known Hubert since he was four years old and believed him to be "a person of mischievous inclination fit for any villainous enterprise."

Graves had visited him in prison in Southwark, and endeavoring to discover the truth, had pretended that he disbelieved his confession. Hubert, he said, replied, "Yes Sir, I am guilty and have been brought to this pass by the instigation of Monsieur Piedloe, but not out of any malice to the English nation but from desire of a reward which he promised me on my return to France."[14]

The testimony of the mysterious Monsieur Graves, about whom nothing is known apart from his court testimony, was a powerful counter to those who were already saying that Hubert's continual reinvention of his story and his willingness to confess to almost any charge put before him laid his credibility and his sanity open to very serious question. Whether Monsieur Piedloe even existed is far from certain; he was never identified by anyone else and no attempt seems to have been made to trace him.

Hubert made no plea in mitigation and was "without the least show of compunction or sorrow for what he said he had done, nor yet seeming to justify or take delight in it; but being asked whether he was not sorry for the wickedness and whether he intended to do so much he gave no answer at all."[15]

Several people who had had the chance to observe or converse with Hubert were willing to testify that he was insane. "My Lord Hollis gave evidence that he was lunatic, so did Dr Durell, the late Dean of Windsor, the French church of Stockholm gave the same testimony." In his direction to the jury, even the judge "delivered himself frankly that the man said he did not know what. Yet all the aforesaid testimonies . . . signified not one button."[16]

The jury, solid citizens of good Protestant stock, lost no time in returning a verdict against the self-confessed, French, Catholic arsonist before them:

> The jury for our Lord the King present upon their oath that Robert Hubert, late of London, laborer, not having the fear of God before his eyes but moved and led away by the instigation of the devil, on 2 September about the second hour of the night with force and arms . . . voluntarily, maliciously and feloniously did throw a fireball made with gunpowder, brimstone and other combustible materials into the mansion house of one Thomas Farriner the elder, baker, in Pudding Lane. . . .
>
> There devilishly, feloniously, voluntarily and of his malice aforethought [he] set on fire, burned and wholly destroyed not only

the said mansion house but also a great number of churches, and other mansion houses and buildings of thousands of lieges and subjects of our Lord the King, contrary to the peace of our Lord the King, his crown and dignity.

[The True Bill recording the verdict and sentence against Robert Hubert was terse and brutal.] He puts himself on the country [pleads not guilty and asks to be tried by jury]. Found guilty. Let him be hanged by the neck until etc.[17]

The House of Commons Committee, good Protestants too, were less easily convinced than the jury at the Old Bailey Sessions. They interviewed Hubert, and in the face of his contradictory testimony and the doubts about his sanity, they ordered John Lowman, the keeper of the White Lion Prison, to take Hubert to the ruins of Pudding Lane. There they hoped that he would prove his guilt by his ability to identify the scene of his alleged crime, or in failure, show his innocence.

On Thursday, October 24, accompanied by the Recorder of London and several guards, Lowman carried Robert Hubert "by water to St Katharine's Tower, to show me where the Swedish ship lay that brought him and other Frenchmen from Stockholm. He brought me to the dock over against Mr Corsellis's brewhouse, and did certify to me and Mr Corsellis that the ship lay there."

The dock laborers denied any knowledge of the ship—"with all the enquiry and diligence I could make or use, I could neither find nor hear of any such ship or vessel," which was scarcely surprising, since the ship was not named *Skipper* but *Maid of Stockholm*.

Lowman then took Hubert up to Tower Hill and "desired him to show me the house they did fire." Hubert said that it was near the bridge and that he "knew it well and would show the house to anybody." They then went along Thames Street toward London Bridge, their pace hindered by Hubert's limp.

The area surrounding Pudding Lane was a tangled mass of rubble and debris from the fire, with even the lines of the streets invisible. "The lane not being but ten feet over at most and the ruins were buried in the rubbish." Yet

before we came to the bridge, Robert Hubert said that the house was up there, pointing with his hand up Pudding Lane. So I bid him go to the place and he went among the bricks and rubbish and made a stand.

Then I did ask one Robert Penny, a wine porter, which was the baker's house and he told me that was the house where Robert Hubert stood. So I stood by Hubert and turned my back towards the baker's house and demanded of him which house it was that he fired. But he, turning himself about, said "This was the house," pointing to the baker's house, "that was first fired."

Then by reason of his lameness I set him on a horse and carried him to several other places but no other place he would acknowledge but rode back again to the baker's house and said again "That was the house," pointing to the baker's house.[18]

London had been so transformed by the fire that "inhabitants of thirty or forty years standing were at a loss to find their own houses in the fairest streets of the town." In Pudding Lane, "the house and all which were near it were so covered and buried in ruins that the owners themselves, without some infallible mark, could very hardly have said where their own houses stood; but this man led them directly to the place, described how it stood, the shape of the little yard, the fashion of the doors and windows and where he first put the fire; and all this with such exactness that they who had dwelt long near it could not so perfectly have described all particulars."[19] Again varying his story, Hubert also claimed that after he had sent one fireball into Farriner's house, Piedloe put two others through the same window.

Hubert was led back to prison while the Tyburn gallows were readied for him. His performance at the scene of the fire seemed to offer utterly damning confirmation of his guilt. Yet the starting point of the fire that had destroyed London—and whatever else was in dispute, the site of the fire's ignition was confirmed by every witness—was the focus of much interest and curiosity. A regular stream of people moved over the rubble toward the wreckage of Pudding Lane and stood in the ruins of Thomas Farriner's bakery staring at the ground, as if their gaze, by its very intensity, could penetrate the still-smoking ruins and decipher the mystery of the fire's ignition.

Word had also traveled ahead of Lowman's little procession that the man who fired the city was being brought to the seat of his crime and London's misery, and when Lowman and the weary and bemused Hubert reached the area, they were greeted by expectant crowds who had arranged themselves in an arc around the fire site. "Hundreds of people went directly that way before him and they all stopped in a ring around about the place where the house stood so that his finding the house was no more than his gaping the same way that the rest did."[20]

Lowman chose to ignore these people so effectively that his statement to the House contained no reference to them. Instead he related only Hubert's apparently extraordinary ability to rediscover a place he had seen only once before, in the dead of night, and which was now so altered and destroyed that even lifelong residents struggled to identify their former houses.

The Recorder of London who accompanied Hubert and Lowman to Pudding Lane "had much discourse with him" and also concluded that it was impossible that Hubert's confession "could be a melancholy dream."[21] But there were some who saw the pathetic and unreliable figure that Hubert cut as a witness, uttering "extravagant things that savored of a distempered mind," and in private some people "shammed away this confession and said he was non compos mentis and had a mind, it seems, to assume the glory of being hanged for the greatest villain."

Hubert "could not be the person that fired Farriner's house, he being very lame for he had a dead palsy on one side—one arm useless and much ado to throw one leg after him." Could such a man really have been strong enough to put a fireball through a window on the end of a long pole?

"It was suggested that the alehouse in Botolph Lane joining to Mr Farriner's house was the place to which Piedloe brought Hubert and put in the fireball through a hole broken in the wall which he mistook for a window. This is an ornament which we call in English helping a lame dog over the style. How this lame man should manage the long pole with one hand is a question . . . another how Hubert, that was never here before, came hither in the night when it was so dark that he could not know a window from a hole in the wall."[22]

Whatever their private reservations, in public few were ready to risk the wrath of the outraged citizenry and the danger of being accused of papist sympathies themselves by speaking out on Hubert's behalf. The members of the parliamentary committee, "touching the debate of the House and what report they should make," were equally reluctant to attract opprobrium. "Some person of honor and a member of the committee of Parliament which examined Hubert" said that "it being generally concluded that the man was not right in his wits and that he talked he knew not what, they resolved barely to report the matter of fact as it appeared to them without interposing any opinion of their own."

The chairman, Robert Brook, was more forthright but, once more, only in private. "Being asked his opinion touching this Hubert by a gentleman of his acquaintance, he frankly confessed that he was a mad man and said that he was no more guilty of burning the City of London than he was."

The Lord Chief Justice, "who was not looked upon as a man who wanted rigor," had also told the King that he "did not believe a word of Hubert's discourse, so disjointed was it," but His Majesty forbore to interfere. Hubert was a convenient scapegoat. When he was hanged, the talk of plots and conspiracies might die with him.

Hubert made no attempt to save his own life. "No man could imagine any reason why a man should so desperately throw away his life which he might have saved though he had been guilty, since he was only accused upon his own confession. Yet neither the judges nor any present at the trial did believe him guilty. . . . He was a poor distracted wretch, weary of his life, and chose to part with it in this way."[23]

One man could still have cleared Hubert, but the testimony of Lawrence Petersen, the master of the *Maid of Stockholm*, was to remain unheard for a further fifteen years.

There was never the slightest doubt about what punishment Robert Hubert would face once convicted. Not guilty by reason of insanity was not a defense ever likely to find favor in a seventeenth-century courtroom. Justice was exemplary and punishment brutal.

Except for political offenses, prison was used as a last resort. Debtors were incarcerated only when there was no alternative. Providing they had money, friends and family could visit prisoners in jail and bring in food, or the jailers themselves were willing to provide extra comforts in return for bribes. Minor crimes were punished by fines, flogging, or fettering in the stocks or pillory, and misdemeanors in the home and workplace were so routinely met with flogging that street hawkers toured the city selling rods and wands for the purpose.

Hanging and gibbeting remained the staple punishments for all other crimes. Those sentenced to hang could sometimes escape their fate by pleading benefit of clergy, the proof of which was taken to be the ability to read the fifty-first Psalm, also known as the "Neck Verse." The judge would ask in Latin, "Does he read?" and if the response of the chaplain was, "Like a cleric," the court would impose a lesser punishment.

Few escaped the sentence of death, however, and the approaches to London and the banks of the Thames were lined with the rotting bodies of highwaymen and other criminals. They were hung in chains, from the gallows or on the gibbet—an iron cage—and left to rot as a warning to others.

If left untreated, the bodies were opened by kites, crows, and ravens, devoured by a wriggling mass of maggots, and soon reduced to a crumbling heap of bones. To prolong the gibbeting, bodies were parboiled and preserved with a coat of pitch. Newgate had its "kitchen" where this was done. "Their bodies are then covered with tallow and fat substances, over this is placed a tarred shift fastened down with iron bands and the bodies are hung with chains to the gibbet." They might be left dangling for an indefinite time—weeks, months, or even years—until the gibbet was needed for a fresher occupant.

To Englishmen, such treatment of criminals was the mark of a civilized nation. A lookout on a sixteenth-century ship rounding Cape Horn spotted a gibbet on the coast of Patagonia. "They were much comforted by finding a gibbet standing, proof that Christian people had been there before."

This attitude was mocked by a contemporary satirist: "After having walked eleven hours without having traced the print of a human foot, to my great comfort and delight I saw a man hanging upon a gibbet; my pleasure at the cheering prospect was inexpressible, for it convinced me that I was in a civilized country."[24]

Those guilty of treason suffered further refinements of cruelty, being hung, drawn, and quartered. Drawing originally required the victim to be bound and dragged behind a horse to the foot of the gallows. The distance from Newgate to Tyburn Tree was three miles, and not all condemned men survived the journey. Later they were drawn on a wooden hurdle or ox hide, and subsequently a cart, less to spare their sufferings than to ensure they reached the gallows alive.

The sentence of death required the victim, having endured the drawing, to be "hanged by the neck and being alive (after around six minutes) shall be cut down and your privy members be cut off, your entrails to be taken out of your body and you living, the same to be burned before your eyes and your head to be cut off, and your body to be divided into four quarters, and head and quarters to be disposed of to the pleasure of the King's Majesty." The King's pleasure generally required the heads and quarters to be displayed at vantage points, particularly the entrance to London Bridge but also at Westminster Hall and over the city gates.

Even after the ending of quartering, judges retained the power to vent their own displeasure by ordering the bodies of hanged men to be dissected and anatomized. Crowds flocked to the "theater" in Newgate to watch anatomizations carried out by barber surgeons from Surgeons' Hall.

Part of Newgate had been sufficiently repaired for Robert Hubert to spend his last night on earth there. He was led in through the stone arch and taken to the press room. Although the prison had been roofless since the fire, the tradition of centuries dictated that here the condemned man would be ironed—fettered with chains of heavy iron.

He was led past the rubble-choked wreckage of the drinking cellar, where inmates with money had been accustomed to pursue oblivion, and was lowered through a hatch into the condemned hold of the jail. It was "a place of calamity . . . full of horrors, without light and swarming with vermin and creeping things."

Hubert explored his cell by the dim light seeping from the hatch above him, where a succession of curious faces peered down, eager for a glimpse of the man who had fired London. Thick, rusting chains and shackles "to bring those to a due submission that are stubborn and unruly" lay across the stone floor, which had been carved out of the rock on which the prison stood.

By tradition the condemned man shared his final supper with the chaplain, the Ordinary of Newgate, who augmented his meager stipend by passing deathbed confessions and orations to printers who would often have them on sale before the victim had even been hanged. One chaplain was sufficiently brazen to petition for copyright in dying speeches and confessions in the shadow of the gallows.

Hubert was hauled out of the condemned hold for his last meal on this earth. He dined in the ruins of the chapel with the chaplain, watched by spectators who had paid for the privilege. There was little entertainment for them, and no further profit for the chaplain, for Hubert had no deathbed speech or confession to make. The chaplain preached a final admonition to him and departed as soon as he had eaten. Hubert was returned at once to the condemned hold.

In the dark hours of the night, the silence of the ruined city was broken by the ring of a handbell. It had been left to the parish church of St. Sepulchre in Elizabethan times, so that the parson could go "in the night-time

and likewise in the early morning to the prison where they lie and there ringing certain tolls with a handbell, he does afterwards (in most Christian manner) put them in mind of their present condition and ensuing execution."

Over time the parson's duty had passed to his bellman, who now stood
outside the walls of the jail intoning:

> All you that in the condemned hold do lie,
> Prepare you for tomorrow you shall die.
> Watch all and pray; the hour is drawing near,
> That you before th'Almighty must appear.
> Examine well yourselves, in time repent,
> That you may not to eternal flames be sent.
> When St Sepulchre's bell tomorrow tolls,
> The Lord above have mercy on your souls.
> Past twelve o'clock.[25]

He gave a final toll of the bell, and then Hubert heard the scuffle of his
feet in the dust as he moved away down the hill.

Chapter 14

The Triple Tree

Monday, October 29, 1666

The Night Man

*It was soon after complained of that Hubert was not sufficiently exam-
ined who set him to work or who joined with him . . . the Commons resolving
to examine Hubert upon that Matter, next day, Hubert was hanged
before the House sat so could tell no further tales.*
Sir John Hawles, *Remarks upon the Tryals of E. Fitzharris*

T HE SUN WAS WELL RISEN THE NEXT MORNING WHEN THE
trapdoor of the hold was raised and a ladder lowered. Hubert
climbed out with difficulty, the heavy iron chains dragging at his legs. He
was led out through the yard. The expectant crowd packing the street outside erupted as he came in sight, his slight, stooped, limping figure dwarfed
by the men around him.

The hangman, Jack Ketch, stood waiting for him just outside the gate of
the jail. The most famous of all executioners, he trod the boards at Tyburn for
twenty-three years and regarded himself as the master of his art. "A man may
be capable, as Jack Ketch's wife said of his servant, of a plain piece of work, a
bare hanging; but to make a malefactor die sweetly, was only belonging to her
husband."[1] Ketch became so notorious that centuries after his death, the public hangman was still popularly given that name.

He was well paid for his work. He would earn £11 for the hanging of Hubert, which, though far less than the £30 Charles Brandon received for beheading Charles I, compared more than favorably with the 2s 2d daily rate that sextons digging, filling, and covering at the plague pits had been paid.

Ketch could also draw on a number of additional sources of income. A hanged man might take an hour to die, and victims were routinely left for that time on the gallows. In return for a tip, Ketch would add his weight to the man's legs in order to hasten the end. If there was no tip, the executioner was "not bothered to pull his victim's legs"[2] and left the victim's friends, if there were any, to do it.

It was the hangman's privilege to keep the rope used in the hanging. Cut into one-foot lengths, it was sold by auction at a tavern near Tyburn, and there was spirited bidding for the rope used on notorious victims. He also sold the clothes and shoes of the victims, though some deliberately kicked their shoes into the crowd to show their contempt and rob him of his extra money. After their death Ketch would have his revenge, for he had the right to sell the bodies to surgeons for dissection or to charge the relatives of the dead man a similar fee to prevent this.

Hangmen were believed to have healing powers, and just as people queued at Whitehall for Charles II to lay hands on them, "touching for the King's evil"—scrofula, or tuberculosis of the lymph glands—while retainers held their arms, "lest they should do the King a damage," so Ketch received fees for rubbing warts and blains. He could also sell the hands of hanged men, which fetched as much as ten guineas from those who believed these grisly tokens carrying the "death sweat" of the executed man also had the power to cure ills at a touch. Women even held their children up to be stroked by the severed hands.

Ketch also received payment from innkeepers for appearing after the execution as a public attraction. Few would approach him, but many paid to stare at this bringer of death, while mothers warned their children that if they did not mind their manners, Jack Ketch would be waiting for them.

The public hangman was a hated figure, often rough-handled by the mob, but he was also greatly feared. So despised and ostracized were the man and his profession that he was not even permitted to enter the jail to pinion his victim or receive his payment. Ketch had to stand in the shadow of the gate to do the work of lashing Hubert's arms tightly with the rope that would hang him. Then the leg irons were struck from the condemned man.

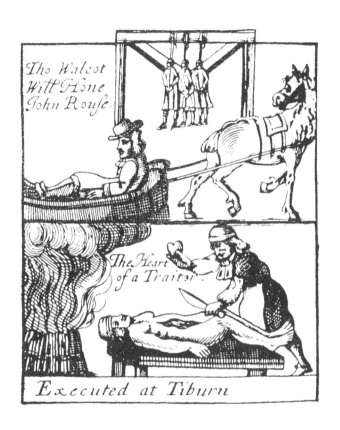

The crowds shrank back from Ketch as he led Hubert to the cart that was to take him to Tyburn. He pushed him into the cart and then climbed in and squatted at the other side. As custom required, Hubert was to travel to meet his maker facing the man who would be his executioner. The noose of hemp rope, "an herb which light fellows merrily will call gallowgrass or neckweed,"[3] was tied around his neck and the rest of the rope wound around his body.

Many men went to the gallows in fine clothes, some even wearing the garb of "bridegrooms going to espouse old Mrs Tyburn." Hubert had nothing but the stinking, drab, crow-black garments he had worn since leaving Sweden.

The procession formed up outside the jail, led by the chief warder and his men. Next came the cart containing the victim and hangman, while the governor and sheriff and the jail surgeon and his attendant brought up the rear. A company of Guards traveled with them.

There was a roar from the crowd as the warder gave the signal to move off. The cart rumbled through the fire-blackened arch of Newgate and down Snow Hill to Holborn Bridge. As they breasted the hill on the far side, Hubert looked back across the wasteland of ash and rubble and took his last sight of the city. The enclosing walls hid much of it from his view, but the broken tower of St. Paul's rose high above them, its calcined stones white against the vivid blue sky.

Some people ran ahead of the procession through the streets; others stood jeering, cursing, and spitting at him as he passed. Children ran alongside the cart pulling faces, and the first brickbats began to fly. Hubert's ride to the gallows was to be a physical as well as a mental ordeal, and stones, mud, rotten vegetables, and lumps of horse shit were soon splattering around him.

There was cruel laughter as a stone split his eyebrow and sent blood trickling down his face. He crouched as low as he could in the cart, but with his arms bound there was little he could do to protect himself. Ketch received his share of brickbats too, but few dared to throw them when his piercing gaze was directed toward them.

The procession, now swollen to several hundred strong, paused at Resurrection Gate at St. Giles in the Fields where the bellman from St. Sepulchre's rang another toll twelve times, asking for prayers for "this sinner now going to his death for whom this bell does toll." Tradition required that Hubert also be presented with a posy of sprigs of rosemary—associated with remembrance— and "a great bowl of ale ... the last refreshment in this life."[4] He took a few sips of the ale, then the cart lumbered on, accompanied by an ever-swelling throng.

A wax effigy of the Pope, containing a number of trussed live cats, was paraded through the streets ahead of the slow procession and then set alight. The terrible screaming of the animals as they perished in the flames served only to delight the mob further. Shaking with terror, Hubert slumped deeper into the bottom of the cart as it rumbled toward Tyburn.

First used as a place for hanging in 1196, Tyburn had become the prime execution site by virtue of its remoteness from the city. In former times heretics were burned in Smithfield, and executions had long been carried out at Newgate. Three years previously, eight of the regicides were hung, drawn, and quartered at Charing Cross within sight of the Banqueting House where Charles I had been executed. Major General Harrison was first to die. "He was presently cut down and his head and his heart shown to the people at which there was [sic] great shouts of joy."[5] By the time the mass execution was over, "the stench of their burnt bowels had so putrified the air"[6] that the local inhabitants petitioned that executions should be held elsewhere, and the five other regicides who were subsequently convicted were all hung, drawn and quartered at Tyburn.

Early afternoon was the favored time for hangings, long enough after the winter sunrise to give the crowds time to assemble and with enough time afterward for them to disperse again before nightfall. Executions were a huge popular attraction, and on "hanging days"—always Mondays—crowds besieged the triangular gallows at Tyburn to watch the victims "ride the three-legged mare." Grandstands were erected, with prices rising or falling depending on the interest in the execution. Pepys paid a shilling for a place on a cartwheel to watch the hanging of Colonel Turner in 1662.[7]

The condemned man was expected to contribute more than his death for the mob's entertainment. The Tyburn rituals first required him to make a speech from the back of the cart. Contrition and repentance or curses and defiance were equally well received. The gallows etiquette had to be strictly observed, however. When Lord Capel began his farewell address from the gallows he was told to remove his hat, "such being the custom of the scaffold."

Having concluded his speech, the condemned man then had to kneel in prayer with the minister and then help to adjust the noose around his neck, before the cart was driven away, leaving him jerking in the air. The Triple Tree at Tyburn could accommodate two dozen victims at once, and sometimes it was full.

The body was left hanging for an hour before being cut down. While the sated crowd dispersed, the jail surgeon would ensure that life was extinct, and the hangman would deliver the corpse, stripped of its clothes, to be anatomized or preserved in the Newgate "kitchen" for gibbeting. Bodies unwanted for these purposes were simply thrown into a crude unmarked grave at the foot of the gallows, for normal burial was denied to hanged men.

The cart rumbled on along High Holborn and out beyond the suburbs, heading west over the dusty Oxford Road leading to Tyburn. The brickbats and missiles came even more frequently now, and Hubert remained hunched on the boards of the cart.

At length, Ketch leaned forward and prodded Hubert's leg. When he raised his unwilling gaze, he saw Ketch gesturing ahead of them. He already knew what he would see but still could not stop his head turning in that direction. In the distance, the stark outline of the gallows was etched against the winter sky. To either side of it were banked grandstands erected only that morning. They were packed with figures, and as the cart came into view Hubert heard a distant baying noise.

The cart slowed, struggling to find a way through the press of people hurrying before them to Tyburn. There were more angry shouts, boos, and jeers, and he was jabbed with sticks and canes, pelted with stones, and soaked in spittle. The Guards forced a way through the throng and the cart rumbled on, but a few minutes later it came to a dead stop.

Waves of noise broke over Hubert as he sat, head bowed. He kept his eyes downcast, but he could feel the cold shadow cast by the gallows upon his skin. There was the scrape of boots on the rough wood of the cart floor, and Ketch's hand was on his arm, hauling him to his feet. The hangman invited him to acknowledge the crowd with a bow, miming the action to take, but Hubert shook his head. There were even more jeers and boos at this breach of Tyburn etiquette.

He felt every eye upon him and heard the noise of the mob change with each movement he made. Beads of sweat began to trickle down his brow. The day was warm but the packed, expectant arena also seemed to generate its own heat. He risked a glance at the crowd. It was a mistake. He stumbled and almost fell as the noise redoubled. Row upon row of faces reddened with drink and hatred stared back at him, their mouths agape, showing their blackened teeth as they howled and catcalled, spit flecking their chins. Cheapjacks, peddlers, and mountebanks added to the cacophony as they shouted their wares among the fringes of the crowds, and painted whores lurked by the beer sellers and in the shadows beneath the grandstands.

Unseen and unknown by Hubert, Thomas Farriner also moved among the crowd, drawn almost against his will to watch the last act in the drama that had begun in his own house. He watched, silent and motionless, as all around him shouted and jeered, full of hatred for the man who had fired London and irate at being denied the customary pleasure of an oration from the condemned prisoner. Even if Hubert had had a mind to oblige them, he spoke almost no English.

The noise of the crowd began to die down as the priest mounted the cart and spoke to Hubert. The murmur of his replies did not even carry as far as Ketch, and what passed between them has never been revealed. Some said Hubert died insisting on his guilt, "and though at first he said he was a Protestant, at his death he professed himself a Papist and was confessed and absolved by the Queen's confessor."

Others insisted he was a Protestant, a French Huguenot, "a person falsely said to be a papist but really a sort of lunatic." Still others claimed that he "denied the fact at the gallows, though before he had stood obstinately to it."[8] Since the conversation was in French, most witnesses almost certainly filled the gap in their knowledge with the details that their own prejudices required.

The priest knelt and motioned Hubert to do the same, but he stared at him slack-jawed and remained standing until Ketch took his shoulders and forced him to his knees. The priest muttered a prayer, then stood up and stepped down from the cart. He waited at the foot of the gallows intoning a final invocation.

Hubert was now alone with his executioner. He stood mute and white-faced as Ketch positioned him in the center of the cart and unwound the rope from around his body. One of the hangman's assistants had swarmed up a support of the Triple Tree and secured the end of the rope taut about the cross-beam.

As Ketch finished checking and adjusting the noose and stepped back, silence fell, broken only by the drone of the priest still reciting his prayers. Hubert stood rigid, his mouth gaping and his eyes following Ketch's every movement as he walked to the back of the cart, his footsteps echoing on the wooden boards.

Letting the tension build, Ketch jumped down and walked around the cart with a measured tread, inspecting his handiwork from every angle. Then he stood motionless alongside the flank of the horse. Impatient to be gone, it took a step forward but was then restrained by an assistant holding its harness. The movement shifted the cart, and as Hubert half stumbled, his palsied leg bent beneath him and the rope tightened around his neck.

He regained his balance, but what was left of his composure was now gone. He tried to cry out but the rope constricting his neck prevented him. His gaze shifted from face to face in the ranks before him, seeking some sign of hope, even now, at the brink. There was none to be seen.

Ketch nodded to the assistant holding the horse's head. He released the harness and stepped back. A murmur ran through the crowd as Ketch the showman, every movement slow and deliberate, pulled a coiled leather whip from the pocket of his coat and raised it high above his head.

Ketch exulted in this moment. He was hated and despised, but for these few seconds he had a power that only judges, kings, and gods could know, holding a man's life in the palm of his hand. He paused motionless, savoring the hush, the fear in Hubert's eyes, and the almost palpable excitement of the mob. Then he brought the whip down. The tip traced an accelerating black arc across the sky, then hit the flank of the horse with a crack that echoed in the silence.

The horse started forward and the cart lurched, its wheels bumping and rumbling over the uneven ground. Hubert fell sideways, his feet still scrabbling at the edge of the cart against the inexorable pull of the rope. Then it jerked taut as his toes lost their hold and his body was hauled upright, answering the tug of the rope like a marionette.

The pent breath of the mob was exhaled in one great exultant roar. There were shouts and laughter as Hubert's body twisted and his legs kicked wildly. Children capered in front of the crowd, matching their steps to those of the man dancing the Tyburn jig above their heads.

It took Hubert many long minutes to die. His frail body had not the weight to give him a quick end, and without a tip Ketch would not add his bulk to the dying man's legs. None of Hubert's family was there to do it and no member of the crowd would risk depriving the mob of its due.

Shaken by spasms, his body still jerked and twisted, but its movements slowed as the minutes passed until at last it hung there, turning slowly in the wind. The contorted, blackened face, bulging eyes, and protruding tongue were mimicked by the crowd.

As was the custom, Ketch left the body hanging for an hour to ensure that all life was extinguished before it was cut down. While he waited, he sat within the triangular shadow cast by the gallows, smoking his clay pipe and staring out past the dangling heels of Hubert at the sea of faces confronting him. Once the body hung lifeless before them, some of the mob grew bored with their sport and began to move away, making for the Tyburn taverns or the dusty road leading back to the city.

Many still remained, however, among them those determined to exact a final vengeance on the man who had fired their city. By the time the mortal remains of Robert Hubert were cut down from the gallows, four or five hundred people still waited, implacable. Among them was Thomas Farriner, unable to leave, it seemed, until the last act had been played out.

Ketch laid the body on the ground. The jail surgeon examined it and then pronounced Hubert dead. A number of braver souls pressed close around the cordon of Guards, while the remainder watched in sullen silence from a few yards' distance as Ketch retrieved the rope, jerking it free from the torn and swollen flesh of Hubert's neck.

He next removed the shoes and stripped the soiled clothes from the body. It looked even more frail and pitiful without its garments, the palsied leg and arm as thin as a child's. Ketch made a rough bundle of the clothes. They were worn and reeking but of good cloth and would bring him a few extra coins from the dealers at the Rag Fair.

He stood up, coiling the rope, and looked around the circle of faces. No family or friends of Hubert stepped forward from the crowd to treat with him about the disposal of the body. He shrugged and nodded to a hunched, black-coated figure, the beadle of the Worshipful Company of Barber Surgeons who stood waiting by the cart that had brought them to the gallows. He walked over to Ketch, and there was the chink of coins.

Ketch leaned down and closed Hubert's staring eyes with his callused thumb. It was less an act of Christian charity than of calculation. The barber surgeons were wont to complain if the bodies to be anatomized arrived with the eyes pecked out by ravens.

Ketch and the beadle began half carrying and half dragging the body toward the cart. The movement broke the spell of silence holding back the crowd. There was a terrifying roar, embodying all the anguish and loss, all the bile and hatred engendered by the firing of London. Then the mob hurled itself, as one, against the cordon of Guards. They yielded ground, then turned and fled, leaving the mob to do its will.

Ketch had already dropped his end of the body, leaving Hubert's head trailing in the dust. He could not defend the body against such a horde and was concerned only to save his other booty from their fury. The beadle stood his ground for a second but then was punched, kicked, and thrown aside by the mob.

"Abandoned to the fury of the people,"[9] Hubert's body was raked by nails like talons, bruised and torn, then stabbed and hacked apart by knife-wielding men. The limbs were torn from their sockets, the head severed, and the tongue, eyes, and ears hacked from it. The mutilated head was brandished in the air and then thrown down to be kicked from one man to another. The heart was torn out of the chest, hurled to the ground, and spat and stamped upon.

The mob "tore it to pieces and could not assuage its wrath against the criminal except by extending it to the whole [French] nation. The people shouted that they wanted war against the French to the last limit of their strength."[10] Only when the bones and bloody fragments of Hubert's body had been smashed and scattered beyond recognition as human did the crowd relent. They marched away, still shouting their cries for war, as Ketch advanced once more to stand in the shadow of the Triple Tree.

Hubert's body would not now be serving the barber surgeons, nor would it even be joining the countless others down the years that had been tossed into a pit at the gallows' foot. Ketch turned aside, leaving the bloody remains where they lay.

He gathered up the bundle of shoes and clothing and placed the coil of rope around his own neck, well knowing the frisson it would cause in the Tyburn tavern for which he was now bound. The stares and the scowls that would greet him bothered him not at all. He would collect a fee from the landlord for appearing there, drink his fill, and hold an auction that should bring him further reward. The rope used to hang the man who started the Great Fire of London should fetch a rich price indeed.

He nodded to himself in satisfaction and strode away. The last remnants of the crowd straggled after him. Thomas Farriner watched them go. He rested his hand on the worn, weathered wood of the gallows and looked toward the city, where the mob was still visible in the distance, trailing a cloud of dust behind it.

Beyond the gray city walls rose the jagged, fire-ravaged outline of the ruins of St. Paul's. Cloud like smoke drifted over it on the wind, and as the guttering sun sank lower in the west it bathed the broken, calcined stones with a baleful red light. As Thomas began to walk toward the city, the setting sun at his back cast his long shadow over the ash-strewn ground.

Chapter 15

The Wastelands

bye my sweet straving Yearb.

London rises again, whether with greater speed or greater magnificence
is doubtful, three short years complete that which was considered the
work of an age.
Inscription on the Monument

T HE CLAIM THAT LONDON ROSE COMPLETE FROM THE ASHES
within a handful of years was repeated by historians for at least a
century afterward: "By the beginning of this year [1670] the City of London was rebuilt with more space and splendor than has been before seen in
England." "To the amazement of all Europe, London was in four years'
time rebuilt with so much beauty and magnificence."[1]

In reality, for decades the city lay "marked all over with ruins. About
them the wild flowers grew."[2] The pink spikes of fireweed—willowherb—
were everywhere to be seen and the yellow flowers of wild mustard spread
so rapidly over the wastelands that it was given the nickname "London
rocket" that it has borne ever since.

Some rebuilding had begun almost at once, but in 1668 it was still "an
ill prospect and a ghastly sight, for those that look from the balconies or

tops of their stately new houses, to see ashes and ruinous heaps on every side of them; to see ten private houses—besides churches and public halls—in the dust for one that is raised again."[3]

Even by the end of 1670, not a single one of the eighty-four destroyed churches had been rebuilt, and "the major part of the houses built upon the ruins of London are let to alehouse keepers and victualers to entertain workmen employed about the City." So few houses had been rebuilt in the parish of St. Bartholomew Exchange in the heart of the city that the wardens forbore to list the householders, "being so few inhabited in our time we thought it prudence to leave it to the succeeding churchwardens."[4]

The great public buildings such as the Custom House, the Guildhall, and Blackwell Hall, the halls of the worshipful companies, the city gates, and prisons such as Newgate and Ludgate remained unreconstructed, and the foundations of Wren's new St. Paul's were not even laid out. The cathedral was not completed until 1711.

Enough rebuilding work was going on in London to empty the surrounding counties of craftsmen; the Press Gang had to be used to recruit workmen, joiners, and carpenters for the Royal Dockyards at Chatham and Sheerness.[5] The Lord Mayor in 1670, Sir Richard Ford, complained that work on the new Royal Exchange was being delayed as a result and demanded an end to the pressing of men on public works.

Many London houses and shops had been rebuilt according to the strict requirements of the 1667 Rebuilding Act, but the development was piecemeal and most streets looked as gap-toothed as their occupants, patchworks of isolated new dwellings and empty, weed-strewn wastelands still awaiting the rebuilding of the adjoining properties. Even the completed buildings often stood empty. A survey in 1673 put the number of unoccupied houses in the city at 3,423. There were whole streets of empty houses where "no person so much as asks the price of any."[6]

The gift of the Freedom of the City to the King and the Duke of York, on a parchment roll enclosed in a massive gold casket, made in 1674 when the devoted Sir Robert Vyner was Lord Mayor, aroused fury at the wasteful misuse of public monies when so much of the city remained to be rebuilt:

Whilst their churches unbuilt and their houses undwelt,
And their orphans want bread to feed 'em,

Themselves they've bereft of the little wealth left,
To make an offering of their freedom.[7]

The books of the City Surveyors were still recording the staking out of scores of ground plots ten years after the fire. The last such entry was not made until 1696 when, apart from St. Paul's, five other churches still remained unfinished.

By similar slow degrees the citizens of London also rebuilt their lives. Many people resumed their former trades, many rich merchants rebuilt their fortunes as well as their great houses, and others profited from the misfortunes of their rivals. Rents soared in the unburned portions of the city, and Captain George Cocke complained just after the fire that he "heard a gentleman ask one hundred pounds for what he would have taken fifty eight days ago, because he is almost master of the commodity."[8] Yet others made new fortunes from the redevelopment of the city, but the Great Fire of London also dealt a blow to many, many others from which they never recovered. "This terrible judgement has made such an impression in the souls of every one of us that it will not be effaced while we live."[9]

Tens of thousands found that their homes and their jobs had been consumed by the flames and were forced into a desperate scramble for survival in which many perished. In the cruel winter of that year many were close to starvation, and constant disorders and riots had to be quelled by troops. When the seamen once more found themselves unable to obtain their pay, they too rioted at Wapping. Again the Guards and the Trained Bands were turned out to suppress them.

Even formerly rich merchants and tradesmen found themselves destitute. Thomas Catchmead, a rich fishmonger, lost his fortune of seven thousand pounds to the flames and had to seek a license to erect a hut near the Maypole in the Strand to carry on his trade. Richard Pierce, Master of the Company of Cooks and Yeoman of the King's Kitchen, also lost everything. With his large family reduced to penury, he petitioned the King for permission to use part of Cooks' Hall, still standing outside Aldersgate, as a temporary home and workplace.[10]

Booksellers and stationers suffered grievous losses, and many authors were also ruined or lost their life's work. One celebrated writer, Sir William Dugdale, complained,

The lamentable fire has . . . consumed the whole impression [of *Origines Juridiciales*] which, with the plates, stood me in no less than £400, and all the remaining parts of Sir Henry Speelman's *Glossary and Councils*, of which not many were sold. The paper merchant is not yet wholly paid for the paper taken up to print them.

Nearly three hundred of my books of Paul's and about 500 of *my History of Embanking and Draining* perished also in these flames and—what troubles me not the least—my whole copy, except thirty sheets which were printed, of the third volume of the *Monasticon Anglicanum.* . . . You see here a sad story of my own losses, and somewhat of the public. There can be no thought of printing any of these for three or four years at least.[11]

There was no insurance, no moratorium on debt, and many, unable to resist "the merciless fury of their creditors upon them,"[12] were incarcerated in the debtors' prisons of the Fleet, Ludgate, and the Marshalsea.

The King was deluged with petitions from desperate, destitute citizens, many of whom were owed money by the monarch himself: "John le Roy, jeweler, for speedy payment of £357, balance due for a diamond ring for the Countess of Castlemaine."

"Sarah, widow of Francis Crafts, for grant of aid towards rebuilding houses worth £5,000 burnt down in the late fire, whereby she and her children are reduced from a plentiful condition to turn servants and work hard for a poor livelihood."

"The vicar and churchwardens of St Sepulchre's . . . have lost most of their poor rents; can scarcely keep their poor from starving."

John Gamble, one of His Majesty's wind-instrument concert, petitioned the King "for payment of 221 pounds, ten shillings and fourpence halfpenny, arrears of his salary of four and three-quarter years; lost all he had by the late dreadful fire and contracted a debt of 120 pounds for which one of his securities is now sent prisoner to Newgate, and ruin awaits them and their families without this payment." Twenty-two violinists made similar pleas.[13]

The wife of the King's physician, Dr. Denton, lost all her property and with it her entire income. "Now she has had a little time to recollect herself, she cries all day long. All in my power cannot make it good to her."[14]

The impoverished livery companies also petitioned the King for repayment of outstanding loans to him of over one hundred thousand pounds; His Majesty was unable to oblige them.

By contrast, Thomas Bludworth retained sufficient wealth to replace the house destroyed in Gracechurch Street with a "splendid mansion" in Maiden Lane and continued to serve as MP for Southwark, but he was never to be free of criticism over his role in the Great Fire of London and was forever afterwards regarded as a drunken incompetent. "People do all the world over cry out of the simplicity of my Lord Mayor in general, and more particularly in this business of the fire, laying it all upon him."[15]

He repeatedly sought to vindicate himself, writing to Joseph Williamson, Lord Arlington's secretary, on September 29, the day his successor as mayor was elected. "Some little mention was made in the Gazette as if neglect had caused the flames to increase. I have been prejudiced thereby." He wished to "have the character given" of being Lord Arlington's "friend or servant so as to assure distant friends that I was not out of favor till something is made out against me. I live not by popular applause, yet wish some esteem in the government and need some support, having had the misfortune to serve in the severest year that ever man did."[16]

His plea to Lord Arlington achieved little. When Parliament reconvened he was named to the committee "for providing utensils for the speedy quenching of fire"—a sarcastic reference to his ill-fated remark on the night the blaze broke out. A decade later he was accused by Titus Oates, the notorious conspirator and perjurer, of having had a hand in burning London "at the Duke of York's orders."

He died on May 16, 1682, and his fulsome funeral oration made oblique reference to his critics:

He has indeed, as all of us, to live in an age that is full of uncharitable censures, most unreasonable divisions and animosities . . . and it is no wonder if such men as he who are invariably true and firm to the present government in church and state should have their most innocent actions slanderously reported, their misfortunes reckoned their faults, their little mistakes blown into crimes of the greatest magnitude, and their names loaded with many evil reproaches but . . . it is such dirt as will not stick.[17]

Blame was also attached to Thomas Farriner, and few of his neighbors and fellow citizens accepted at face value his statements about the condition of his hearths on the night the fire broke out.

After digging among the ruins of his house for several weeks, Thomas managed to find some of his gold, which had melted in the heat and then fused with the debris and ashes, but his store of coin had fused into a solid lump and all he could obtain for it was the value of the metal.

He found temporary premises to resume his trade, and his house and bakery in Pudding Lane eventually were rebuilt, though work did not begin until January 20, 1668. Prior to rebuilding, in common with many of the other narrow streets and lanes of the old city, Pudding Lane was widened and fire debris used to lessen its gradient. The householders were given modest compensation for the loss of their land, which in most cases had been won by encroachment, not title.

Thomas and Hannah moved back into Pudding Lane in late summer 1668, but their time there together was to be short. Thomas was a lonely and isolated figure. The conviction and hanging of Robert Hubert had not removed the suspicion that Thomas's drunkenness or negligence might have caused the blaze that had ruined so many of his neighbors. His health grew poor and the burdens of debt and guilt he carried further debilitated him.

His one consolation was that his son Tom had survived the plague and returned to London. The young man was hastily apprenticed to his father in 1670 when it became clear that Thomas was entering his last illness. He died on Christmas Eve of that year. Weakened by the plague and badly burned before she made her escape from the garret in Pudding Lane, Hannah Farriner also fell ill that winter and died the following spring.

It was the custom for the widow or heir to carry on a deceased craftsman's trade, and Tom was admitted to the Worshipful Company of Bakers in his father's place and made a Freeman of the City.[18] He also died young, following his parents and his younger sister to the grave in 1678. After his death, a vitriolic battle for the inheritance was fought out in the courts between his widow Martha and his surviving sister Mary Halford.[19]

The Great Fire that began in Thomas Farriner's bakery was commemorated by the Monument erected on the site of St. Margaret's Church in Fish Street Hill between 1671 and 1677. An inscription on one face recorded the age's certainty that London had been fired by malice, not accident: "This pillar was set up in perpetual remembrance of the most dreadful burning of this protestant city, begun and carried on by the treachery and malice of the popish faction, in the beginning of September in the year of our Lord 1666. In order to the carrying on [of] their horrid plot for extirpating the protestant religion and old English liberty, and introducing popery and slavery."

The inscription was erased in 1683 as the avowedly Catholic Duke of York, later James II, prepared to succeed his brother to the throne. His reign was brief; he fled the kingdom for the last time in 1688, throwing the Great Seal into the Thames. The inscription was restored to the Monument the following year, "reinscribed . . . in such deep characters as are not easily to be blotted out,"[20] and not finally removed until 1830.

At a "distance eastward from this place of 202 feet" a second, more modest monument, a stone plaque, was set up in front of Thomas Farriner's house. "Here by the permission of heaven, hell broke loose on this protestant city, from the malicious hearts of barbarous Papists by the hand of their agent, Hubert, who confessed and on the ruins of this place declared this fact, for which he was hanged, viz: That he here began the dreadful fire, which is described and perpetuated on and by the neighboring pillar. Erected 1680, in the Mayoralty of Sir Patience Ward, knight."[21]

The plaque was also removed in 1830 and thought lost, but in 1877 it was found in the cellars of 23 Pudding Lane, lying facedown "in an arched vault on the old premises," when the building was demolished to construct Monument Street.

The report of the committee appointed by the House of Commons to inquire into the firing of the City of London was formally presented to Parliament on January 22, 1667. It made no recommendation for action but consisted only of a selection of the evidence presented before it. It was tabled for the members' consideration, and to Andrew Marvell, MP for Hull, it was "full of manifest testimonies that it was by a wicked design," containing "things of extraordinary weight which, if they were not true, might have been thought incredible."[22]

On February 7 the House resolved that "the debate of the said report be held tomorrow morning and the report concerning Popery be then also heard." Instead, on that very morning of February 8, 1667, the King again prorogued Parliament. The committee was never again recalled, nor its report debated, despite a petition to the Court of Common Council on November 15, 1667, of "divers citizens believing that the Fire revealed not only the immediate hand and justice of God" but "very much of the malice and practice of men." A further petition delivered in March of the following year requiring the inquiry to be reopened and fresh evidence taken to find "the wicked instruments of the fire"[23] was no more successful.

Unofficial copies of the report, *A True and Faithfull Account of the Several Informations Exhibited to the Honorable Committee appointed by the Parliament to Inquire into the Late Dreadful Burning of the City of London*, were circulating almost at once, including additional evidence taken by the committee but not forming part of its formal report to Parliament.

The King at once took steps to have the *True and Faithfull Account* suppressed, claiming it was likely to "seduce persons against the Government."[24] Copies were impounded throughout the country, and one was ceremonially burned by the common hangman, Jack Ketch, in Westminster Palace Yard.

Rumors about the origin of the fire continued to circulate, and in 1678 Israel Tonge and Titus Oates approached a prominent magistrate, Sir Edmund Berry Godfrey, claiming that a former secretary of James, Duke of York, had maintained a treasonable correspondence with Louis XIV. When the incriminating letters were duly produced, they "made as much noise in and about London . . . as if the very cabinet of Hell had been laid open."[25]

The allegations appeared to be given added credence when Godfrey was found on Primrose Hill run through with his own rapier. There were already strong fears that the autocratic Duke of York, intent on ruling not through Parliament but by the divine right of kings, would use his power to force the reversion of England to Catholicism. Enough Protestants had burned on the bonfires of Smithfield during Mary's bloody reign for that to strike terror in English hearts.

The "papist plot" uncovered by Oates and Tonge seemed to offer proof positive, and prompted by the allegations, a fresh inquiry into the causes of the Great Fire was held in 1681. It reached no more reliable conclusions than its forerunner, despite a unanimous Commons resolution that "it is the opinion of this House that the City of London was burnt in the year one thousand six hundred and sixty-six by the Papists, designing thereby to introduce arbitrary power and Popery into this Kingdom."[26]

A former Sheriff of the City was fined £100,000 the following year for giving public voice to the view privately held by many, that "the Duke of York had burned the city in 1666." Others were less sanguine. "As to the reports concerning the King and the Duke, and Oates' and Bedloe's narratives as to this matter, the suppositions are so monstrous and the evidence so wretchedly mean that they deserve no historian's consideration, but to judge on the charitable and perhaps probable side, we may say that the beginning of this dreadful fire was the judgement and the end of it the mercy of heaven; for neither of them seem to have been the effects of human means or counsels."[27]

The inquiry did produce one significant piece of new evidence about the fire, however. Lawrence Petersen, the master of the *Maid of Stockholm*, was located and persuaded to break his fifteen-year silence. If true, the statement he made on December 17, 1681, utterly demolished the idea that Robert Hubert could have conspired to burn London or been the one who fired Thomas Farriner's house.

Petersen testified that, with his ship "freighted with several commodities to carry to the City of Rouen in France, he was desired by one Mr Haggerstern, a merchant and his neighbor, to carry in his ship Robert Hubert, the son of Mr and Mrs Hubert of Rouen, he being not well in mind and being very poor, so that he was chargeable to them there."

Instead the English fleet under Prince Rupert stopped the *Maid of Stockholm* at sea and ordered Petersen to take his ship to London. He "came to anchor at St Katharine's near Mr Corsellis's brewhouse two days before the City of London was on fire," but Hubert was "never ashore nor out of his ship from his coming into it until the Tuesday after the fire began."

During the fire Hubert "seemed to rejoice and say 'Very well! Very well!' which with the word 'Yes, Yes,' was all the English he could speak." Petersen, "angry and troubled to see him rejoice," shut him into the hold but "he crept out of the private scuttle and got ashore upon Mr Corsellis's quay," where he was "seized by the multitude and presently carried away."

Some days later, Petersen heard that Hubert was in prison but "would not trouble himself about him." He heard no more about him until he docked in Rouen and went to his father to obtain the three pounds ten shillings due to him for Hubert's "passage and diet." Hubert's father then told him that his son had been hanged for firing the City of London. The news left Petersen "much amazed, well knowing to the contrary."

Petersen's extraordinary statement raised as many questions as it answered. He made it clear that only one passenger, Hubert, sailed with him, yet if his fellow conspirators were a product of Hubert's fevered imagination, why had Graves claimed that he knew Piedloe well as "a most debased man apt to any wicked design"? Coupled with his description of

Hubert as "fit for any villainous enterprise,"[28] Graves's testimony seemed to offer the trial jury crucial corroboration of Hubert's criminal intent.

There are many other contradictions and questions that demand answers that can now never be obtained. Why did Petersen wait so long to break his silence? If Hubert was seized by the mob at St. Katharine's Dock, as Petersen claimed, how did he escape, and where was he in the intervening time before he was arrested a week later in Romford, twelve miles northeast of the capital? Were the statements of Graves and Petersen true versions of events, or fabrications designed to serve the differing political ends of the shadowy figures behind them? And what happened to all the other people alleged to have fired houses who were handed over to the Guards or the watchmen, but never subsequently interviewed or charged?

Many witnesses were willing to swear that they had seen fireballs being used, but history is full of incidents where mass false statements have been made. Twenty-six years after the Great Fire, nineteen people in Salem, Massachusetts, were accused of witchcraft and hanged solely on the basis of the allegations of their neighbors and fellow citizens. The stress of a disaster on the scale of the Great Fire of London can unhinge even the most reliable of witnesses, let alone those whose suspicion of outsiders and determination to find scapegoats lead them to imagine events that could not have happened.

It is easy to see how witnesses to the Great Fire might have been deluded into thinking that the blazes erupting on every side were the result of human action, not of embers and brands carried on the wind, particularly when the mass panic and confusion engendered by the fires was coupled with a virulent suspicion and hatred of outsiders, foreigners, and papists. Such xenophobia was no new thing in England. Foreigners and religious minorities were always subject to hostility, intimidation, and persecution, and there are numerous cases down the centuries that suggest parallels to the allegations made in the wake of the Great Fire.

On Good Friday, March 24, 1144, the discovery in Norwich of the body of a dead eleven- or twelve-year-old boy led to allegations—growing by the day in scope and complexity—that he had been killed by Jews as part of some blasphemous ritual. No evidence worthy of the name was ever produced in that case, nor in similar ones in Gloucester in 1168, Bury St. Edmunds in 1181, Bristol in 1183, nor in Lincoln in 1255, when the discovery of a boy's body down a well led to the summary execution of eighteen Jews on the flimsiest of pretexts.[29]

Flemish weavers, invited into England by Edward II to improve cloth manufacture, were also the frequent target of attacks. The most brutal came during the Peasants' Revolt, when "there was a very great massacre of Flemings and in one heap there were lying about forty headless bodies . . . hardly was there a street in the city in which there were not bodies lying of those who had been slain."[30]

False confessions are also a frequent phenomenon throughout history, made both by psychologically damaged notoriety seekers and by those pressured or bullied into admitting their guilt. Even without access to the apparatus of physical and psychological terror available to seventeenth-century inquisitors, the courts in our own time have seen many confessions that were once considered the unshakable basis for a conviction but that have since been demolished as false, often having been obtained from "emotionally vulnerable and suggestible" personalities under duress.[31]

Was Robert Hubert, the enigma of the Great Fire, a similar personality? How could he have described Farriner's house and "the little yard" unless he had been there or had been told what to say? Was he a criminal conspirator, a pyromaniac, or merely a useful scapegoat, "an innocent lunatic person" who through torture or his own mental instability was persuaded to confess to a crime he did not commit?

Modern statistics suggest that out of every ten urban fires, two are caused by defects in buildings, one by products, processes, or materials, and the remaining seven by arson or human error. Even with modern forensic capabilities and investigative techniques, fire chiefs estimate that no more than 15 to 20 percent of arsonists are ever detected and prosecuted.

An American study, interviewing over eighty convicted serial arsonists, showed they had set an average of thirty fires each and begun their firesetting careers at around the age of fifteen. They were overwhelmingly male and white, and almost nine out of ten had other criminal convictions.

Of those who were apprehended, some had delusions, hallucinations, or beliefs that "voices" were telling them to do it, but 40 percent described their motive as a desire for revenge and 30 percent were simply looking for excitement.[32] Such thrill seekers often remain at the scene of the fire and watch it develop. In modern times many have even tried—some successfully—to join a fire service in order to get closer to the action, and when there is none they may create it themselves.

If Lawrence Petersen's statement was true, it is undeniable that Robert Hubert was excited by fire. That is a charge that could equally have been laid at the King's door, and Charles II's constant riverside patrols in search of fires would certainly have caused modern arson investigators to scrutinize him very closely; but Hubert also exhibited strong symptoms of mental instability.

Pyromania is not a term favored by modern psychologists, but they do identify a syndrome featuring an obsessive-compulsive need to set fires. By so doing, these arsonists dissipate the anxieties that drive them. Some are dormant for most of the year, only becoming active around a date significant to them, but they may then set ten to fifteen fires during that period.

Although all fire-setters are arguably mentally disordered, three forms of mental illness are particularly associated with fire-raising: manic depression, paranoid schizophrenia, and psychopathy or sociopathy. A manic depressive is either on a terrific high, when he is belligerent and likely to set fires, or in the depths of the blackest depression, during which he may kill himself. The loneliness and social inadequacy he feels may find their expression in other crimes, even murder. David Berkowitz, the "Son of Sam," the serial killer who terrorized New York, confessed to setting over two thousand fires in a three-year period during the 1970s.

A paranoid schizophrenic develops delusions around one fixed idea. He may hear voices in his head, urging him to set fires. There are three stages of the delusion: retreat, during which he tries to avoid and escape from a nonexistent enemy; a defensive stage, in which he seeks help in combating his imaginary enemies, and finally an attack stage. Since nobody will listen to him or help him, he will attack his enemies himself.

Some believe that psychopathic arsonists become more active during phases of the full moon, but their need to set fires may also be linked to sexual gratification. Some masturbate or ejaculate without any stimulus other than the excitement of seeing the smoke and flames and the panicking crowds. After orgasm they may simply walk away from the scene of the blaze or even be moved to help the victims.

Pathological fire-setters begin early in life with an interest in fire that rapidly develops into an obsession. They may have set as many as seventy-five fires by the age of ten, and though their activity tends to peak between the ages of nineteen and twenty-two, they may well continue to set fires throughout their lifetime. A total of five hundred fires is by no means atypical. Some set fires in adolescence and abandon the habit when they reach maturity, while others continue until they are either caught or cured of their psychosis. Many are never caught at all.

These persistent fire-setters commit arson to release stress and to help them cope with any emotion that is not acceptable to them, and there may be elements of rage and sexual gratification in their fire-setting behavior. They exhibit aggression, and self-destructive behavior is also common. They tend to be socially isolated loners, often with severe specific learning problems, and their verbal skills are usually very poor. Around half of them are estranged or separated from one or both parents. "Family disruption . . . is *the* key factor in the background of many juvenile arsonists."[33]

Their main goal is to set the fire, and they are uninterested in its results, showing no feelings of guilt, no social or moral conscience. Fire-setters also "nearly always clearly remember where their fires have been, even in the case of those who have set hundreds of fires."[34]

Robert Hubert almost perfectly conforms to all these elements, but there is one crucial difference. Hubert confessed to fire-setting, whereas in general "arsonists confess so rarely and keep so many secrets that they usually sail through police interrogations."[35]

Modern fire investigation techniques would enable investigators to identify the seat of the blaze and determine whether flammable liquids or incendiary devices had been used to fuel it by the distinctive burn patterns these materials leave, or by suspicious variations in the way the building itself was burned. The corners of a room are usually the last areas to burn, for example, because the circulation of air is lowest and slowest in those confined areas. If an investigator found severe burning in areas in which such damage would not be expected, it would point strongly to the use of an accelerant.

No such investigative techniques were available to seventeenth-century investigators, and almost all evidence has long disappeared. But archaeologists have produced significant recent evidence, if not of the origin of the fire, at least of the way it spread so rapaciously. In the 1980s, a dig at one site in Pudding Lane, a neighboring property to Thomas Farriner's house, uncovered a cellar in which twenty barrels of Stockholm tar were stored on five racks.

The tar, a by-product and pyrolysate of the production of charcoal from resinous woods such as pine, larch, and fir, was used for waterproofing house timbers and caulking the planking of ships. The carbonized remains of fragments of the barrels and racks were "covered by the tar-like substance once contained in the barrels. It had formed a compacted crust on the upper surface of the blackened brickwork and had percolated between the bricks, the sides of which were also stained."[36]

Fire debris still filled the cellar, "mixed deposits of bricks, tiles, mortar and other material, some of which showed signs of burning and vitrification . . . over 100 whole stock-molded bricks in these dumps suggests that the debris had not been sorted."[37] The fragments of roof tile had been "badly burnt, contorted and warped by the fire and some fragments had exploded with the intensity of the heat. Molten and twisted nails were mixed in with the building debris, as were fragments of window glass."[38]

As the fires spread down the street from Thomas Farriner's house, those tar barrels, heated beyond their combustion point, must have exploded into flames with shattering force, advancing and spreading the fires with terrifying speed.

Chapter 16

Dust to Dust

A Corpes Bearer

Louden thy cry to God, to men,
And now fulfil thy trust;
Here thou must lie, mouth stopped, breath gone,
And silent in the dust.
Thomas Vincent, *God's Terrible Voice in the City*

I N THE 335 YEARS SINCE THE GREAT FIRE, NUMEROUS ACCOUNTS have discounted Thomas Farriner's version of events as the false protestations of a man trying to escape blame for the disaster he had inadvertently ignited, and have treated the confession of Robert Hubert as no more than a curiosity, a footnote to the accidental blaze that destroyed much of London. While Hubert's and the other claims of fire-raising were dismissed as the product of hearsay or the fevered imaginations of unreliable witnesses, the testimony of Graves and that of Petersen, delivered fifteen years after the event, have been treated as gospel truth.

If Farriner's statement was correct, however, and if Hubert's conflicting accounts also contained within them at least a kernel of truth, a very different picture emerges. Every religious and political faction and everyone from papists and "fanatic" nonconformists to the King himself then comes into question.

One observer even found grounds for a belief that those plotting to fire the city might deliberately have sought out a person of Hubert's slow-wittedness and mental instability:

> Tillotson, who believed the city was burnt on design, told me a circumstance that made the papists employing such a creased man in such service more credible. Langhorn, the popish counsellor at law, who for many years passed for a Protestant, was despatching a half-witted man to manage the elections in Kent before the Restoration. Tillotson being present, and observing what a sort of a man he was, asked Langhorn how he could employ him in such service.
>
> Langhorn answered, it was a maxim with him in dangerous services to employ none but half-witted men, if they could but be secret and obey orders; for if they should change their minds and turn informers instead of agents, it would be easy to discredit them and to carry off the weight of any discoveries they could make and show they were madmen, and so not like to be trusted in critical things.[1]

If the Great Fire was not set deliberately by Robert Hubert or people unknown, the most probable cause is a stray spark from the bakehouse hearth igniting the kindling laid in the mouth of the oven, which in turn would have fired the brushwood stacked on the floor. If Thomas Farriner was correct in claiming that the bakehouse was not alight when the house was already burning, then a spark from the domestic hearth, an unextinguished candle, or even the smoldering tobacco from the inebriated Farriner's clay pipe may have been the cause.

There is one other possible explanation of the outbreak of the fire in Pudding Lane, which requires no intent or carelessness by anyone. Prolonged exposure to heat, in poorly ventilated or unventilated conditions, can cause wood to decompose and become charred into a kind of charcoal known as pyrophoric carbon. Temperatures as low as 120 degrees Celsius can be sufficient to initiate the process, and exposure to these conditions has been shown to result in a lowering of the ignition temperature of the wood.

As the wood chars, fissures or cracks open up and the pyrolysis moves into the body of the wood. A change in the heating or the ventilation, for example, by a crack developing enough to open a supply of air, can then be sufficient to cause ignition. This process has been suggested as the cause of many modern fires, particularly in factories and mills where steam pipes pass through wooden beams and walls.

It is possible, but no more than possible, that parts of the timber frame and lath and plaster walls of Thomas Farriner's bakehouse had been subject to such decomposition through prolonged exposure to the heat from the ovens or chimney. If so, they could have spontaneously combusted that night. Such a version of events does not tally with Thomas Farriner's insistence that the fire did not begin in the bakehouse, but he had much to gain by avoiding blame for causing the holocaust that followed, and his statements must be seen in that light.

Whether Hubert or others unknown fired London, or whether it was just an unhappy conjunction of wind, weather, and human error, will now never be known with certainty. But given London's previous fire record, even if fire-raisers were at work that night, in all probability they were only preempting an accidental conflagration that would surely have engulfed the city sooner or later.

Only one fact is indisputable: convicted solely on his own confession, Robert Hubert was hanged on October 29, 1666, leaving unresolved the mystery of whether he was truly the architect of the Great Fire or merely a pawn in a greater game.

The number of people who perished in the Great Fire is equally clouded with doubt. The significant causes of death by fire are asphyxia, burns, falls, internal edema following inhalation of hot gases, or being struck by falling timbers or masonry. Fires within buildings tend to consume the available oxygen faster than it can be replaced, and even where the heat of the fires is insufficient to cause death, asphyxia will result.

The oxygen content of air is normally 21 percent. If the content is higher, a fire will burn faster and generate more heat; if less, it will be slower and cooler, and except in very hot fires, when the oxygen content falls below 16 percent, burning will almost cease. Human life remains sustainable down to an oxygen level of 10 to 6 percent.

Carbon monoxide is by far the most frequent cause of death from fires, and can be fatal even in a concentration in air as low as one part in a thousand. In the Dresden firestorm of 1945, it has been estimated that 70 percent of the victims were killed by carbon monoxide and other toxic gases, rather than by the direct effects of the bombs or the resulting fires.

Like oxygen, carbon monoxide combines with hemoglobin in the blood, but it forms a complex with hemoglobin that is two hundred times more stable than the oxygen/hemoglobin mixture. The result is to displace the oxygen, starving the cells of it and causing internal suffocation. In death it produces a characteristic bright pink or red coloration to the skin. Asphyxia by poisonous fumes under intense heat, combined with the effects of putrefaction, can also result in a range of other colors in the corpses. After the Dresden firestorm of the Second World War, the streets were littered with corpses in vivid hues of blue, green, and orange.[2]

The inhalation of very hot gases causes the larynx to constrict in a reflex action, choking the person until breathing stops altogether. As one fortunate survivor of such an occurrence commented, "It was like acid. . . . It gets into your throat, your stomach, your lungs and you can't breathe. You choke and the more you try to breathe, the more you choke."

The death toll from the Great Fire of London has always been claimed to be minimal. "Merciless to the wealth and estates of the citizens, it was harmless to their lives."[3] Only four, six, or in some versions, eight people are said to have died, but the most casual scrutiny shows this figure to be manifestly absurd.

Four people were known to have died: Thomas Farriner's maidservant, Rose; the old woman whose charred corpse was found by Taswell near St. Paul's Cathedral; Paul Lowell, the Shoe Lane watchmaker; and an old man mentioned by Pepys who "said he would go and save a blanket which he had in the church; and being a weak old man, the fire overcame him and was burned."

The body found inside a broken tomb in the crypt of St. Paul's, "teeth in the head, red hair on the head and beard etc., skin and nails on the toes and fingers," was claimed to be that of Robert de Braybroke, laid to rest in 1404. It was "so dried up, the flesh, sinews, and skin cleaving fast to the bones that . . . it stood stiff as a plank, the skin being tough like leather and not at all inclined to putrefaction."[4]

The finding was hailed as a near miracle of preservation, "which some attributed to the sanctity of the person," but the body was almost certainly not that of de Braybroke but of one of those fleeing the Great Fire who sought sanctuary in St. Paul's. Finding himself cut off as the flames roared through the cathedral, the man could have taken refuge in the broken tomb. There he would have been suffocated as the firestorm drew every breath of oxygen from the air, and then mummified, baked by the heat until the flesh of his body was as dry as bone. A very similar body was found after the firestorm that engulfed Dresden, "a completely shriveled corpse of a man, naked, his skin like brown leather, but with a beard and hair on his head."[5]

Two other mummified bodies were also found in St. Paul's when the north aisle was cleared of debris. There was no way for those finding them to know if they had lain there for centuries or if they too had been suffocated and desiccated by the fire as they sought refuge in the cathedral.

The poor woman suspected of carrying fireballs and murdered in Moorfields by the mob could be counted another victim of the fire; and the church records of St. Botolph, Aldgate, also note the burial of a parishioner who "dropped dead of fright on Tower Hill" during the fire. The records of St. Mary Woolnoth include the death of Richard Yrde, found "stifled in a house of office backside of Deputy Canham's house after the City was burned."

"The mistress of the Bear Tavern at the bridge foot did lately fling herself into the Thames and drowned herself."[6] She was said to have done so because of the destruction of her tavern in the Great Fire.

The poet James Shirley and his wife were driven by the flames from the house they occupied in Fleet Street and forced to take refuge among the crowds in St. Giles in the Fields. The terror they endured and the hardships they suffered living in the open brought on a fatal illness that claimed both of them on the same day. They were buried in one grave in the parish churchyard of St. Giles.[7]

Others, searching the ruins of their houses, perished when walls collapsed upon them or they fell through into the cellars clogged with rubble.[8] "It is presumed the hasty removal to which sick persons and women lying-in [childbirth] were forced, occasioned the death of some."[9] Many more survivors of the holocaust, huddled in shacks or living among the ruins that had once been their homes, perished from hunger and cold or succumbed to disease in the terrible winter that followed.

The mob rule on the streets also must have accounted for a number of other deaths. It stretches credulity to believe that the only papists or foreigners being beaten to death or lynched were the ones rescued by the Duke of York or the men of the King's Guard. Nor is it conceivable that all the citizens managed to rouse themselves from their beds and escape before the flames were upon them during the first night of the fire.

All those deaths must be added to the toll; all common sense, circumstantial evidence, and the experience of every other major urban fire down the centuries also suggests that the number of those lost to the fire itself cannot have been four or six or eight, but must have been far, far greater.

John Evelyn mentioned the stench that came from "some poor creatures' bodies"[10] as he explored the ruins immediately after the fire. Marc Antonio Giustinian, Venetian ambassador to France, wrote of "the terrible sights of persons burned to death and calcined limbs . . . the old, tender children and many sick and helpless persons were all burned in their beds and served as fuel for the flames."[11] Countless other bodies must have lain undiscovered among the ruins of their houses and the churches to which they had fled for shelter.

Such was the disruption to city life that no Bill of Mortality was published for three weeks. The first one after the fire, issued on September 18, recorded 704 deaths—a figure treble that in the week before the fire. It included all those deaths notified since August 28, but inevitably, given the disruption caused by the fire, many deaths went unrecorded. A hundred and four had died from the plague in that period, but the Bill of Mortality included only four "burnt at several places," six "frighted," and seven "killed by several accidents."

Shock, hunger, and exposure must have taken a heavy toll of the survivors of the fire, but those killed while it still raged remained uncounted. The burned-out survivors had priorities in the aftermath of the fire other than inquiring after the whereabouts of neighbors, or even friends and relatives, who had been scattered to the four winds by the blaze. Only one citizen in fifty could read the scraps of parchment sometimes pinned to the ruins of houses appealing for news of missing families, and few had time to devote to searching for lost relatives when the business of survival took all their time and strength.

The struggle to find food, drink, and shelter was all-consuming, and even when some element of normality returned to city life, any attempt to record or count the dead and missing was doomed. Many citizens had moved to different, unburned areas of London or to the suburbs. So many physicians were "flocking westwards . . . they find so many more of their craft bereft of patients that they fear they shall be reduced to bleeding one another."[12]

Many people had fled to other cities, towns, and villages, never to return. Anthony a Wood reported that "several traders set up here in Oxon afterwards," and William Cadman, a stationer, moved to Preston. Many people emigrated to the New World. Thirty "burnt Londoners" even settled on the remote island of St. Helena in the South Atlantic. A census taken in 1673, seven years after the blaze, revealed that a quarter of London's prefire citizens had never returned.[13]

Those who reclaimed their land and rebuilt on it had no time to ponder the fate of their fellows who did not return. And these were the solid, respectable citizens of some means. The propertyless tens of thousands living in poverty in cellars, tenements, rookeries, shacks, and hovels, and those dwelling in the criminal sanctuaries, had none to record their coming and going, or their passing.

Alcohol is all too frequently associated with modern fire deaths, as victims, unconscious from alcohol, are asphyxiated or burned without regaining their senses. The prodigious drinking of citizens on Saturday nights is no modern phenomenon, and many people "in their first dead sleep" may have been overtaken by the rapid progress of the fire through Thames Street on its first night.

The speed with which the flames advanced, the way that sparks and burning brands hurled on the wind hundreds of yards ahead of the main fire created fresh blazes and cut off the retreat of frightened citizens, the streets blocked with rubble, barricaded by soldiers or jammed by overturned carts, the heat so searing that men spoke of being unable to stand within two hundred yards of the flames, the collapsing buildings, the stones exploding like grenades, the molten lead cascading through the streets, the firestorms sucking the very air from the places where people huddled in fright, the poisonous gases and deadly carbon monoxide: all these undoubtedly claimed their victims.

Human skin, tissue, and bones are made brittle by fire. Fire boils the blood, causing hemorrhages, broken bones, and skull fractures. It also causes the muscles to contract, flexing the limbs and making many fire victims adopt a characteristic "pugilistic pose" as if about to fight an adversary. Bodies also shrink. Many corpses recovered from intense fires have shriveled to only three feet or so in length.

In normal domestic fires temperatures are rarely of sufficient intensity or duration to ensure the complete destruction of the body. The skeleton is usually preserved, and even parts of the soft tissues can survive, because of their high water content.

Full cremation of an adult human requires a minimum temperature of 750 degrees Celsius, sustained for between eighty and a hundred minutes, to consume flesh and turn bones to calcium and salts. The body of a child or small person normally takes much less time—around fifty to sixty minutes for a 110-pound body—whereas a 300-pound corpse might require as much as two and a half hours.

The temperatures are higher in the secondary chambers of modern crematorium furnaces, but this is mainly to ensure that emissions conform to modern standards by burning off the carbon monoxide and other gases that otherwise would be vented. The temperature normally peaks at around 1,020 degrees, and even at the end of a day in which a furnace has been in constant use it does not exceed 1,150 degrees.

The flesh of the lower body is consumed first. The midriff, high in water content, and the brain, insulated from the heat by the skull, are usually the last parts of the soft tissue to burn. Once the furnace has been preheated to above 750 degrees, little or no further fuel is required. Fed with sufficient air, the body fats supply all the necessary fuel to cremate the body, except in cases where a wasting disease such as cancer has reduced the victim to little more than skin and bone. This suggests that even when the fast-moving fire-front of an inferno like the Great Fire had moved on, the bodies of the dead would continue to burn, independent of other burning material.

At the end of cremation, the body of an adult is reduced to a couple of pounds of gray dust and a few calcined bone fragments. The smaller bones have disappeared; only portions of the skull and the major bones like the femur are likely to survive. They are barely recognizable as human, with something of the look of fragments of limestone or driftwood, and are so porous and fragile that they crumble to dust in your fingers. The bodies of children and small people are much easier to destroy, and their skeletons are usually completely consumed during cremation. Even in relatively minor blazes, such bodies may be—and often have been—destroyed.

Supplied with sufficient air, a wood or coal fire burning at much lower temperatures over a number of hours can achieve the same effect as cremation, and under some conditions the body can be incinerated even in quite low intensity fires. The fat rendered from the body during burning acts like the tallow in a candle, sustaining the flames for such a long period that the body is almost totally destroyed.

The Great Fire of London was fed not just by timber-framed and weatherboard houses, with all their wood paneling, paintings, curtains, furniture, and hangings, but by oils, coal, tallow, fats, sugar, alcohol, pitch, turpentine, and a host of other combustibles as well. Force-fed oxygen by the ferocity of the gale, the fires swelled into firestorms in which the temperatures far exceeded the heat needed to fully consume bodies.

The temperatures at the heart of those firestorms raging across London were high enough to melt glass, iron, and steel. Steel melts between 1,250 and 1,480 degrees Celsius, and iron has a melting point of between 1,100 and 1,650 degrees. The imported steel lying on the wharves, the great iron chains and locks of the city gates, and the iron bars of Newgate jail, thick as a man's wrist, were all melted and vaporized by the fires.

The infernos during the Great Fire of London burned at well in excess of 1,000 degrees. Such intense heat calcined the bodies of victims. Hair burned in an instant, blood boiled, flesh turned to ashes, bone crumbled into dust. Modern police and firefighters are taught not to train hoses on burning bodies and to use extreme delicacy when moving them, because they can so easily disintegrate.

Some textbooks on arson investigation claim that teeth are more resilient than bone at these temperatures, saying that although the front teeth may be destroyed, the back teeth are almost the only things to survive fires of this intensity. In Restoration London the teeth of the citizenry as a whole and the poor in particular were so decayed and rotten that most people had few or none at all. Teeth were even cited as a cause of death in the Bills of Mortality.

False teeth made from the teeth of animals were expensive and so ill-fitting that eating or speaking became all but impossible while wearing them. Instead "plumpers," wooden forms worn over the gums in the spaces left by extracted, rotten, or broken teeth to plump out hollow cheeks, were to be found in even the most fashionable houses. The bodies of the poor—as in the plague, the providers of the vast majority of the victims—contained few if any teeth.

In any event, although teeth may be found after some blazes, the belief that they will survive intense fires is not borne out by the experience of crematorium technicians. One told me that in his entire career he had never seen a single tooth survive cremation.

If there were any remains at all of the victims of the Great Fire, they would have been no more than a few fragments of calcined skull or bone that would disintegrate at a touch. Any movement or disturbance of the bones or the ash and rubble around them would have caused them to crumble into dust.

Tens of thousands of tons of rubble, ash, and debris had to be cleared, and as streets were widened and street levels raised in the rebuilding of the city, vast quantities were moved and leveled with no concern for what they might contain. Fish Street Hill was widened, and in common with the other precipitous streets and lanes feeding into Thames Street, its gradient was reduced by raising the level of its lower end by several feet, reducing the height of the road surface at Eastcheap at the top by another yard and grading the remainder of the hill.

Thames Street itself was widened to thirty feet and raised by between four and seven feet along its entire length. New quays and wharves were constructed on the riverfront, and still thousands of tons of fire debris had to be dumped on islands in the Thames between Maidenhead and Windsor. Monkey Island at Bray was covered with a layer six feet thick to raise it above flood level.[14]

Who among those hungry men sifting through the ashes in search of abandoned or hidden valuables, or quarrying the ruins for the melted and fused remains of lead, iron, gold and silver plate, or those workmen later clearing the rubble to prepare for rebuilding, would have paused to consider any pathetic fragments of bone, the last mortal traces of burned souls consumed by the fire?

Even if they were identifiable as human rather than animal remains, there was no knowing to whom they had belonged or when they had died. Who would trouble to report a pile of burned and splintered bones that might have been a fire victim or a corpse from centuries before? They would have tossed aside any they found without a second glance.

As in the plague of the previous year, the rich, the gentry, the tradesmen and merchants had time and notice in which to save themselves and their goods, for the fires did not reach the more fashionable districts around Lombard Street, Gracechurch Street, Cornhill, and Cheapside until almost two days after they began raging through the poorer quarters. They may have lost their buildings and some part of their wealth, but most such people—even Thomas Farriner, who escaped with only the nightgown in which he stood up—were able to rebuild their lives and their trades after the fire.

For the poor trapped in their rotting, combustible tenements, the fire was upon them with furious speed. Many escaped, but many others—the old, the very young, the halt, and the lame—were lost, consumed by the fires, their bones buried or reduced to dust and ashes. The faint traces of their passing would have lain where they fell, to be swept away, unrecognized, with the rest of the fire debris, or buried under the rubble of cellars that were never excavated.

The true death toll of the Great Fire of London is not four or six or eight, it is several hundred and quite possibly several thousand times that number. Those who died of hunger and cold in the terrible winter that followed the fire are listed in the parish registers, but those who perished in the flames left no record of their passing. There is no memorial to them, but modern London was built on their bones and ashes.

Notes

It is not the custom in Britain to attribute every single quotation when some are no more than a couple of words long. In a book such as this, drawing heavily on primary sources, it would risk burying the text under an avalanche of contents.

In addition, where two or more consecutive quotes have been taken from the same source, I have cited the source at the end of the last one in the sequence.

The prime sources I have drawn on are credited below and a full list of every primary and secondary source is given in the Bibliography.

Chapter 1: Repent or Burn

1. Churchwardens' Accounts, St. Margaret's, Fish Street Hill (GL).
2. "E.S." "Funeral Garlands."
3. Paul Slack, *The Impact of Plague in Tudor and Stuart England*.
4. Clarendon, *Selections from the History*.
5. J. Hawarde, *Les Reportes del Cases in Camera Stellata, 1593–1609*.
6. Thomas Vincent, *God's Terrible Voice in the City*
7. Nathaniel Hodges, *Loimologia, or an Historical Account of the Plague in London in 1665*.
8. Nathaniel Hodges, op. cit.
9. *Oxford Gazette,* Number 16.
10. Clarendon, op. cit.
11. Nathaniel Hodges, op. cit.
12. Thomas Delaune, *The Present State of London*.
13. Thomas Delaune, op. cit.
14. Thomas Delaune, op. cit.
15. John Evelyn, *Diary*.
16. Tobias Smollett, *Humphrey Clinker*.

17. James Howell, *Londinopolis.*
18. C. Read, *Mr. Secretary Cecil and Queen Elizabeth.*
19. Samuel Pepys, *Diary.*
20. Andrew McCall, *The Medieval Underworld.*
21. John Evelyn, op. cit.
22. Thomas Dekker, *The Seven Deadly Sinnes of London.*
23. John Earle, *Micro-cosmographie, Or, A Peece of the World Discovered.*
24. Edward Waterhouse, *A Short Narrative.*
25. John Stow, *The Survey of London.*
26. Count Cominges, *Relation de l'Angleterre en l'annee 1666.*

Chapter 2: The Hellish Design

1. Daniel Baker, *A Certaine Warning for a Naked Heart Before the Lord.*
2. Walter Gostello, *The Coming of God in Mercy, in Vengeance.*
3. Thomas Ellwood, *Alarm to the Priests.*
4. Samuel Pepys, *Diary.*
5. Dr. George Thomson, *Loimotomia, Or, The Pest Anatomised.*
6. John Allin to Philip Frith (East Sussex RO).
7. John Allin, op. cit.
8. CSPV (BL).
9. John Allin, op. cit.
10. Anthony a Wood, *The Life & Times of Anthony a Wood.*
11. John Evelyn, *Diary.*
12. Churchwardens' Accounts, St. Margaret's, Fish Street Hill (GL).
13. James Howell, *Londinopolis.*
14. John Bate, *The Mysteryes of Nature and Art.*
15. Churchwardens' Accounts, St. Margaret's, Fish Street Hill (GL).
16. John Evelyn, op. cit.
17. Sir William Davenant, quoted in Walter George Bell, *The Great Fire of London in 1666.*
18. CSPV (BL).
19. Fynes Morison, *Unpublished Notes for Itinerary.*
20. H. Misson de Valberg, *Memoires et Observations.*
21. William Maitland, *The History of London.*
22. Rege Sincera, *Observations both Historical and Moral.*
23. John Stow, *The Survey of London.*
24. Macaulay, *History of England.*
25. CSPV (BL).
26. Thomas Delaune, *The Present State of London.*
27. Thomas Delaune, op. cit.

28. Thomas Delaune, op. cit.
29. Thomas Delaune, op. cit.
30. *Death's Masterpeece* (BL).
31. Lord Mayor of London, *Seasonable Advice for Preventing the Mischief of Fire.*
32. CSPV (BL).
33. Samuel Pepys, op. cit.
34. Nathaniel Hodges, *Loimologia, or an Historical Account of the Plague in London in 1665.*
35. Anon, *Plague's Approved Physitian.*
36. John Findlay Drew Shrewsbury, *History of Bubonic Plague in the British Isles.*
37. Lady Martha Giffard, *Her Life and Correspondence, 1664–1722.*
38. Samuel Pepys, op. cit.
39. Andrew Spielman and Michael D'Antonio, *Mosquito.*
40. Quoted in William Maitland, *The History of London.*
41. Journal 46 (CLRO).
42. Rege Sincera, op. cit.

Chapter 3: The Lodge of All Combustibles

1. Samuel Freeman, "The Character of Sir Thomas Bludworth, Knight."
2. Italian account, quoted in Walter George Bell, *The Great Fire of London in 1666.*
3. Gough MSS (Bodl.).
4. Repertory of the Court of Aldermen (CLRO).
5. Samuel Pepys, *Diary.*
6. Gough MSS (Bodl.).
7. Gough MSS (Bodl.).
8. Gideon Harvey, *The City Remembrancer.*
9. John Evelyn, *Diary.*
10. London Bridge is often described as having nineteen or sometimes eighteen arches, but contemporary illustrations show twenty, though those at either end of the bridge were obstructed by waterwheels. The bridge was reduced to nineteen arches only after its rebuilding in 1762, when the pier between the ninth and tenth arches from the south was removed, creating a broad central arch.
11. Francisco de Rapicani, "A Foreign Visitor's Account of the Great Fire."
12. Francisco de Rapicani, op. cit.
13. Edward Waterhouse, *A Short Narrative.*
14. Quoted in Clarendon, *Selections from the History.*
15. Italian account, quoted in Walter George Bell, op. cit.
16. Thomas Vincent, *God's Terrible Voice in the City.*
17. Gough MSS (Bodl.).

18. Spanish account, quoted in Walter George Bell, *The Great Fire of London in 1666.*
19. Walter George Bell, op. cit.

Chapter 4: A Lake of Fire

1. Samuel Pepys, *Diary.*
2. Samuel Pepys, op. cit.
3. Thomas Gainsford, *The Rich Cabinet Furnished with varietie of Excellent discriptions.*
4. John Evelyn, *Diary.*
5. Samuel Pepys, op. cit.
6. Clarendon, *Selections from the History.*
7. James Welwood, "Memoirs of the Most Material Transactions in England."
8. John Oldmixon, *History of England During the Reign of the Royal House of Stuart.*
9. Arthur Onslow, in Gilbert Burnet, *History of My Own Time.*
10. John Evelyn, op. cit.
11. Gilbert Burnet, op. cit.
12. Samuel Pepys, op. cit.
13. Gough MSS (Bodl.).
14. Gough MSS (Bodl.).
15. Sir Edward Atkyns, "Letter."
16. Anne Conway, *The Conway Letters.*
17. Sandys to Scudamore (BL).
18. Sandys, op. cit.
19. John Evelyn, op. cit.
20. Gough MSS (Bodl.).
21. Gough MSS (Bodl.).
22. Samuel Pepys, op. cit.
23. Francisco de Rapicani, "A Foreign Visitor's Account of the Great Fire."
24. William Taswell, *Autobiography and Anecdotes.*
25. Italian account, quoted in Walter George Bell, *The Great Fire of London in 1666.*
26. Gough MSS (Bodl.).
27. Clarendon, op. cit.
28. Gough MSS (Bodl.).
29. Samuel Pepys, op. cit.
30. Francisco de Rapicani, op. cit.
31. Sandys, op. cit.
32. Quoted in John E. N. Hearsey, *London and the Great Fire.*

Chapter 5: A Hideous Storm

1. *Londens Puyn-hoop.*
2. Edward Waterhouse, *A Short Narrative.*
3. Frances Parthenope Verney, *Memoirs of the Verney Family.*
4. Edward Waterhouse, op. cit.
5. Thomas Vincent, *God's Terrible Voice in the City.*
6. Edward Waterhouse, op. cit.
7. William Taswell, *Autobiography and Anecdotes.*
8. Edward Waterhouse, op. cit.
9. Gough MSS (Bodl.).
10. Gough MSS (Bodl.).
11. Thomas Delaune, *The Present State of London.*
12. Gough MSS (Bodl.).
13. Le Fleming MSS (HMC).
14. Le Fleming MSS (HMC).
15. Samuel Pepys, *Diary.*
16. Samuel Pepys, op. cit.
17. Sir William Davenant, quoted in Bell, op. cit.
18. Thomas Vincent, op. cit.
19. Edward Waterhouse, op. cit.
20. Walter George Bell, op. cit.
21. Gough MSS (Bodl.).
22. Samuel Pepys, op. cit.
23. Thomas Vincent, op. cit.
24. Thomas Vincent, op. cit.
25. William D. Robson-Scott, *German Travellers in England 1400–1800.*
26. Samuel Rolle, *The Burning of London in the Year 1666.*
27. Samuel Wiseman, *A Short Description of the Burning of London.*
28. Gough MSS (Bodl.).
29. Thomas Vincent, op. cit.
30. Clarendon, *Selections from the History.*
31. Edward Waterhouse, op. cit.
32. The location of the Post Office, the subject of some uncertainty (cf. Bell, op. cit.), was resolved by Foster Bond in "State Papers Domestic Concerning the Post Office in the Reign of Charles II."
33. James Hickes to Secretary Williamson, Le Fleming MSS (HMC).
34. James Hickes, op. cit.
35. Walter George Bell, op. cit.
36. L. C. Sier, "Experiences in the Great Fire of London."

37. John Rushworth, "A Letter Giving Account of that Stupendious Fire."
38. Rege Sincera, *Observations both Historical and Moral.*
39. John Evelyn, *Diary.*
40. Thomas Vincent, op. cit.
41. Gough MSS (Bodl.).

Chapter 6: Outlandish Men
1. Anon, *A True and Faithfull Account of the Several Informations.*
2. Count Lorenzo Magalotti, *Travels of Cosmo the Third.*
3. Thomas Delaune, *The Present State of London.*
4. Thomas Vincent, *God's Terrible Voice in the City.*
5. William Taswell, op. cit.
6. Henry Care, quoted in J. Miller, *Popery and Politics in England 1660–1688.*
7. Anon, *A True & Faithfull Account of the Several Informations.*
8. Anon, *A True & Faithfull Account,* op. cit.
9. Italian account, quoted in Walter George Bell, op. cit.
10. William Taswell, op. cit.
11. *Londens Puyn-hoop.*
12. Gough MSS (Bodl.).
13. *Londens Puyn-hoop,* op. cit.
14. de Repas to Sir Edward Harley, Portland MSS (HMC).

Chapter 7: A Sign of Wrath
1. Gough MSS (Bodl.).
2. John Locke, quoted in Robert Boyle, *A General History of the Air.*
3. Paul Hentzner, *Travels in England during the Reign of Queen Elizabeth.*
4. James Howell, *Londinopolis.*
5. John Stow, *The Survey of London.*
6. Paul Hentzner, op. cit.
7. John Stow, op. cit.
8. Quoted in Walter George Bell, *The Great Fire of London in 1666.*
9. Walter George Bell, op. cit.
10. John Rushworth, "A Letter Giving Account of that Stupendious Fire."
11. CSPD (BL).
12. Richard Baxter, *Reliquae Baxterianae.*
13. William Taswell, *Autobiography and Anecdotes.*
14. Gough MSS (Bodl.).
15. CSPD (BL).
16. Anon, *A True and Faithfull Account of the Several Informations.*
17. CSPD (BL).

18. Gough MSS (Bodl.).
19. Francisco de Rapicani, "A Foreign Visitor's Account of the Great Fire."

Chapter 8: The Fires of Hell

1. Samuel Pepys, *Diary.*
2. Samuel Pepys, op. cit.
3. Samuel Pepys, op. cit.
4. John Stow, *The Survey of London.*
5. John Stow, op. cit.
6. Thomas Dekker, *The Seven Deadly Sinnes of London.*
7. Gough MSS (Bodl.).
8. John Rushworth, "A Letter Giving Account of that Stupendious Fire."
9. Samuel Pepys, op. cit.
10. Thomas Vincent, *God's Terrible Voice in the City.*
11. Walter George Bell, *The Great Fire of London in 1666.*
12. John Stow, op. cit.
13. *Dictionary of National Biography.*
14. Thomas Vincent, op. cit.
15. Thomas Vincent, op. cit.
16. Gough MSS (Bodl.).
17. Reverend Stillingfleet, *Sermon to the House of Commons.*
18. Italian account, quoted in Bell, op. cit.
19. Walter George Bell, op. cit.
20. Christopher Wren, quoted in John E. N. Hearsey, *London and the Great Fire.*
21. Edward Chamberlayne, *The Present State of England.*
22. Edward Chamberlayne, op. cit.
23. Quoted in Walter George Bell, op.cit.
24. Quoted in Walter George Bell, op. cit.
25. John Rushworth, op. cit.
26. Rugge's Diurnal (BL).
27. CSPD (BL).
28. Gough MSS (Bodl.).
29. Gough MSS (Bodl.).
30. Samuel Pepys, op. cit.
31. Clarendon, *Selections from the History.*
32. Sandys to Scudamore (BL).
33. Clarendon, op. cit.
34. Anne Conway, *The Conway Letters.*
35. Henry Griffith, "The Great Fire."
36. Sandys to Scudamore (BL).

37. Sandys to Scudamore (BL).
38. Sandys to Scudamore (BL).
39. Gough MSS (Bodl.).
40. J. Crouch, *Londinienses Lacrymae.*
41. Walter George Bell, op. cit.
42. Rege Sincera, *Observations both Historical and Moral.*
43. Gough MSS (Bodl.).
44. Vestry Minutes, St. Sepulchre's, quoted in Walter George Bell, op. cit.
45. William Taswell, *Autobiography and Anecdotes.*
46. Spanish account, quoted in Walter George Bell, op. cit.
47. John Evelyn, *Diary.*
48. Gough MSS (Bodl.).
49. Sandys to Scudamore (BL).
50. Clarendon, Finch MSS (HMC).
51. Sandys to Scudamore (BL).
52. John Evelyn, op. cit.
53. Anthony a Wood, *The Life & Times.*
54. Clarendon, op. cit.

Chapter 9: Clamor and Peril

1. Samuel Pepys, *Diary.*
2. Sandys to Scudamore (BL).
3. John Evelyn, *Diary.*
4. John Evelyn, op. cit.
5. Sandys to Scudamore (BL).
6. Hothfield MSS (HMC).
7. Samuel Rolle, "The Burning of London."
8. Robert Southwell senior to Cornet James Dogherty, Egmont MSS (HMC).
9. Sandys to Scudamore (BL).
10. Samuel Pepys, op. cit.
11. Sandys to Scudamore (BL).
12. Thomas Vincent, *God's Terrible Voice in the City.*
13. John Evelyn, op. cit.

Chapter 10: Firestorm

1. Ingrid Holford, *British Weather Disasters.*
2. Rege Sincera, *Observations both Historical and Moral.*
3. William Taswell, *Autobiography and Anecdotes.*

Chapter 11: A Dismal Desert

1. Le Fleming MSS (HMC).
2. Sir Edward Atkyns, "A Copy of a Letter to Sir Robert Atkyns."
3. J. P. Malcolm, *London Redivivum.*
4. Thomas Vincent, *God's Terrible Voice in the City.*
5. Souchu de Rennefort, in William D. Robson-Scott, *German Travellers in England 1400–1800.*
6. Rege Sincera, *Observations both Historical and Moral.*
7. Samuel Pepys, *Diary.*
8. William Taswell, *Autobiography and Anecdotes.*
9. Samuel Pepys, op. cit.
10. Sir William Dugdale, *History of St. Paul's.*
11. John Aubrey, *Brief Lives.*
12. Count Lorenzo Magalotti, *Travels of Cosmo the Third.*
13. John Evelyn, *Diary.*
14. Francisco de Rapicani, "A Foreign Visitor's Account of the Great Fire."
15. Frances Parthenope Verney, *Memoirs of the Verney Family.*
16. John Evelyn, op. cit.
17. CSPD (BL).
18. Sandys to Scudamore (BL).
19. CSPD (BL).
20. CSPD (BL).
21. John Aubrey, op. cit.
22. Anthony a Wood, *The Life & Times.*
23. Samuel Pepys, op. cit.
24. Arthur Staveley, letter of September 17, 1666.
25. Samuel Pepys, op. cit.
26. Clarendon, *Selections from the History.*
27. Souchu de Rennefort, op. cit.
28. Alexander Charles Ewald, "The Great Fire of London."
29. Repertory of the Court of Aldermen 71 (CLRO).
30. Journal 46 (CLRO).
31. Hickes, CSPD (BL).
32. Le Fleming MSS (HMC).
33. CSPD (BL).
34. CSPD (BL).
35. Gweneth Whitteridge, "The Fire of London and St Bartholomew's Hospital."
36. CSPD (BL).
37. Repertory 73 (CLRO).

38. Court minutes of the Pewterers' Company, quoted in Walter George Bell, *The Great Fire of London in 1666.*
39. George L. Howgego, "The Guildhall Fire Judges."

Chapter 12: The Fatal Contrivance

1. Rege Sincera, *Observations both Historical and Moral.*
2. Gilbert Burnet, *History of My Own Time.*
3. Ronald Hutton, *The Restoration.*
4. Gilbert Burnet, *History of My Own Time.*
5. Charles Welch, *History of the Monument.*
6. *London's Lamentations.*
7. Samuel Pepys, *Diary.*
8. Bulstrode Whitelocke, "Diary."
9. CSPD (BL).
10. CSPD (BL).
11. CSPD (BL).
12. Dorothy Gardiner (ed.), *The Oxinden and Peyton Letters 1642–1670.*
13. CSPD (BL).
14. Spanish account, quoted in Walter George Bell, *The Great Fire of London in 1666.*
15. Edward Waterhouse, *A Short Narrative.*
16. Samuel Pepys, op. cit.
17. Samuel Pepys, op. cit.
18. Anthony a Wood, *The Life & Times.*
19. Max Beloff, *Public Order and Popular Disturbances 1660–1714.*
20. *London Gazette*, Number 48.
21. Archdeacon Laurence Echard, *The History of England.*
22. Gideon Harvey, "Some Account of the Great Fire."
23. Samuel Pepys, op. cit.
24. J. P. Malcolm, *London Redivivum.*
25. Gilbert Burnet, op. cit.
26. Clarendon, *Selections from the History.*
27. CSPD (BL).
28. R. H. Hill (ed.), *The Correspondence of Thomas Corrie, 1664–87.*
29. Clarendon, op.cit.
30. Samuel Pepys, op. cit.
31. James Welwood, "Memoirs of the Most Material Transactions in England."
32. Max Beloff, *Public Order and Popular Disturbances 1660–1714.*
33. Tim Harris, *London Crowds in the Reign of Charles II.*
34. CSPD 1664–5 (BL).

35. Samuel Pepys, op. cit.
36. CSPD (BL).
37. John Rushworth, "A Letter Giving Account of that Stupendious Fire."
38. Clarendon, op. cit.
39. *London Gazette*, Number 85.
40. Clarendon, op. cit.
41. Lords' Journal (BL).
42. Samuel Pepys, op. cit.
43. Portland MSS (HMC).
44. Arlington to the Earl of Sandwich, CSPD (BL).
45. Anon, *A True and Faithfull Account of the Several Informations*.
46. CSPD (BL).
47. CSPD (BL).
48. CSPD (BL).
49. Vincent T. Sternberg, "Predictions of the Fire and Plague in London."
50. Middlesex Sessions Rolls (LMA).
51. CSPD (BL).
52. CSPD (BL).
53. B. Toller letter, CSPD (BL).
54. Clarendon, op. cit.
55. Anon, *A True and Faithfull Account*, op. cit.
56. Anon, *A True and Faithfull Account*, op. cit.
57. J. Somers, *A Collection of Scarce Tracts*.
58. Anon, *A True and Faithfull Account*, op. cit.
59. Sloane 970 (BL).
60. John Oldmixon, *History of England*.
61. Sir Edward Harley, Portland MSS (HMC).
62. John Milward, *Diary*.
63. Andrew Browning (ed.), *Thomas Osborne, Earl of Danby and Duke of Leeds, Letters*.
64. CSPD (BL).

Chapter 13: The Duke of Exeter's Daughter
1. *London's Flames*.
2. *London's Flames*.
3. James Heath, *Torture and English Law*.
4. Geoffrey Abbott, *Rack, Rope and Red-hot Pincers*.
5. David Jardine, *A Reading on the Use of Torture*.
6. Sir R. Wiseman, *The Law of Laws*.
7. Sir John Kelyng, *A Report of Divers Cases &c.*

8. James Heath, op. cit.

9. Michael Dalton, *The Countrey Justice.*

10. Samuel Pepys, *Diary.*

11. Middlesex Sessions Rolls (LMA).

12. *Dictionary of National Biography.*

13. William Cobbett, *State Trials.*

14. William Cobbett, op. cit.

15. William Cobbett, op. cit.

16. Archdeacon Laurence Echard, *The History of England.*

17. Sessions File (CLRO).

18. Anon, *A True and Faithfull Account of the Several Informations.*

19. Clarendon, *Selections from the History.*

20. Archdeacon Laurence Echard, op. cit.

21. Gilbert Burnet, *History of My Own Time.*

22. Archdeacon Laurence Echard, op. cit.

23. Clarendon, op. cit.

24. John Dryden, "The Original and Progress of Satire."

25. Justin Atholl, *Shadow of the Gallows.*

Chapter 14: The Triple Tree

1. John Dryden, "The Original and Progress of Satire."

2. H. Misson de Valberg, *Memoires et Observations.*

3. Quoted in Justin Atholl, *Shadow of the Gallows.*

4. Alfred Marks, *Tyburn Tree, Its History and Annals.*

5. Samuel Pepys, *Diary.*

6. Alfred Marks, op. cit.

7. Justin Atholl, op. cit.

8. CSPD (BL).

9. CSPV (BL).

10. CSPV (BL).

Chapter 15: The Wastelands

1. John Oldmixon, *History of England.*

2. Walter George Bell, *The Great Fire of London in 1666.*

3. Samuel Rolle, "The Burning of London."

4. Vestry Minutes, St. Bartholomew's, quoted in Walter George Bell, op. cit.

5. CSPD (BL).

6. James Howell, *Londinopolis.*

7. Andrew Marvell, *Works.*

8. CSPD (BL).

9. Sir Nathaniel Hobart in Frances Parthenope Verney, *Memoirs of the Verney Family.*
10. CSPD (BL).
11. Le Fleming MSS (HMC).
12. Philanthropus Philagathus, *An Humble Remonstrance to the King and Parliament.*
13. CSPD (BL).
14. Frances Parthenope Verney, op. cit.
15. Samuel Pepys, op. cit.
16. CSPD (BL).
17. Samuel Freeman, "The Character of Sir Thomas Bludworth."
18. Court minutes of the Bakers' Company (GL).
19. PRO C5/479/57.
20. John Oldmixon, op. cit.
21. Now in the Museum of London.
22. Andrew Marvell to R. Franke, Mayor of Hull, in Marvell, op. cit.
23. Journal 46 (CLRO).
24. CSPD (BL).
25. John P. Kenyon, *The Popish Plot.*
26. Commons Journals (BL).
27. Archdeacon Laurence Echard, *The History of England.*
28. Anon, *A True and Faithfull Account of the Several Informations.*
29. Andrew McCall, *The Medieval Underworld.*
30. Andrew McCall, op. cit.
31. "Fantasy That Became Seventeen-year Nightmare," *Guardian*, March 6, 2000.
32. Nicholas Faith, *Blaze: The Forensics of Fire.*
33. Andrew Muckley, *Addressing Firesetting Behaviour with Children, Young People and Adults.*
34. Andrew Muckley, op. cit.
35. Andrew Muckley, op. cit.
36. Gustav Milne and Christine Milne, "A Building in Pudding Lane Destroyed in the Great Fire of 1666."
37. Gustav Milne and Christine Milne, op. cit.
38. Gustav Milne and Christine Milne, op. cit.

Chapter 16: Dust to Dust

1. Gilbert Burnet, *History of My Own Time.*
2. Alexander McKee, *Dresden 1945: The Devil's Tinderbox.*
3. Inscription on the Monument.
4. Sir William Dugdale, *History of St. Paul's.*

5. Alexander McKee, op. cit.

6. Samuel Pepys, *Diary.*

7. Walter George Bell, *The Great Fire of London in 1666.*

8. J. P. Malcolm, *London Redivivum.*

9. Gough MSS (Bodl.).

10. John Evelyn, *Diary.*

11. CSPV (BL).

12. Frances Parthenope Verney, *Memoirs of the Verney Family.*

13. Rosemary Weinstein, "The Great Fire of London, 1666."

14. Berkshire Archaeological Society.

Bibliography

Manuscripts

Bodleian Library (Bodl.)
Ashmole MSS 241: Of the number 666; Gough MSS London 14; Rawlinson
    MSS; Tanner MSS.

British Library (BL)
Add. MSS 10,117 Rugge's Diurnal; Add. MS 11,043 Sandys to Scudamore; MS
    15,057 Letter relating to the firing of London in 1666; MS 17,018 Report
    on the fire in Fetter Lane; Add. MS 27,962 R, f480v—482r; Calendar of State
    Papers, Domestic Series, 1666, 1667 (CSPD); Calendar of State Papers,
    Domestic Series, Add. MSS, Sept. 1666 (CSPD); Calendar of State Papers,
    Domestic Series, Add. 1660–85 (CSPD); Calendar of State Papers Venetian,
    1666 (CSPV); Commons Journals vols. 8 and 9; Egerton MS 2543.f.211;
    Harleian MS 4941, 66E; Lords' Journal; Sloane 970 Examinations and Infor-
    mations about the Firing of London, 1666; Thomason Tract E589 *Death's
    Masterpeece: Or, A true Relation of that Great and Sudden Fire in Towerstreet,
    London, 1650.*

Guildhall Library (GL)
MS 8786; MS 11,361; MS 1176/1 Churchwardens' accounts and receipts for bur-
    ial, St. Margaret's, New Fish Street; Noble Collection, Section A, The City;
    Worshipful Company of Bakers, Minute Books 1660–1680.

Corporation of London Record Office (CLRO)
MSS 432/4, 1665–6 acct; MSS 10,107; MSS 10,107A; MSS 11,366 vols. 2, 3, 4; Misc. MSS 3–36; Misc. MSS 3–37; Misc. MSS 193.13; Ex-GLMS 298/111; SF 177 Sessions File Oct. 1666; SM 20 Sessions Minute Book Oct.–Dec. 1666; Fire Decrees, 1667–72 (nine vols.); Journal 46; Repertory of the Court of Aldermen vols. 70, 71, 72, 73; Research 8.12 P. E. Jones, "New Light on the Great Fire," 1966; Research 12.4 Frances Gordon, "The Fire of London." Original letters in Town Clerk's Office, Guildhall: Joseph Ames to Theo. Pengelly, 6 Sept. 1666; Duke of Buckingham to ———, Sept. 1666; Lords of the Council of Ireland to Lord Mayor, 29 Sept. 1666; Corporation of Londonderry to Lord Mayor, Oct. 1666; Archbishop of Canterbury *et al.* to Lord Mayor, 19 Oct. 1666.

Historical Manuscripts Commission (HMC)
Report and MSS of Montague Berlie, Twelfth Earl of Lindsay 1660–1702; Buccleuch, Duke of, MSS; Egmont, Earl of, MSS; Finch MSS; Hastings MSS, II; Hothfield, Lord, MSS; Le Fleming MSS; Ormonde MSS, new series, vol. 4; Portland, Duke of, MSS vols. 2 and 3; Verney MSS.

Public Record Office (PRO)
Journal of the Court of Common Council, 46; Privy Council Registers, vol. 59; State Papers Domestic (Chas II); Treasury Books; PROB 4/4501 Farriner, Thomas, of London, Baker, 1678; PROB 4/8203 Farriner, Thomas, Citizen & Baker of London, 1670; C 5/479/57 Farriner v Halford, Court of Chancery, 1677; SP 29/144 G Phillips to Arlington; SP 29/1/170/123; SP29/170/61; SP 29/170/121; SP29/171/9–11; SP29/171/95–96; SP29/173/82 Thomas Bludworth; SP 29/175/111 Muddiman to Mansell; SP E115 vol. 7/212/2; SP E179/252/32 London 4 (R); PRO 31/1/46 Carte (Thomas) MS 46 Arlington to Ormonde.

London Metropolitan Archive (LMA)
MJ/SR 1324 Middlesex Sessions Rolls, GDR 16 Sept., 10 Oct. 1666.

Cornwall Record Office
DD/T/2004A John to Lewis Tremayne.

East Sussex Record Office
FRE 521, 1063, 5545, 5550, 5561, 5679 Letters from Rev. John Allin to Dr. Philip Frith, Sept. 1666.

Kent Record Office
U350/C2/110 Burnett to Dering.

Printed Books and Papers

Unless otherwise stated, the place of publication is London.

Abbott, Geoffrey, *Rack, Rope and Red-hot Pincers, A History of Torture and Its Instruments*, Headline, 1993

An Account of the Burning of the City of London ... publish'd ... 1666; to which is added, the opinion of Dr Kennet ... and that of Dr Eachard, relating thereunto, 1721

Ackroyd, Peter, *London: The Biography*, Chatto & Windus, 2000

An Act For Preventing and Suppressing of Fires within the City of London and Liberties Thereof, 1668

Akerman, John Yonge (ed.), *Moneys Received and Paid for Secret Services of Charles II and James II*, Camden Society, 1851

Andrews, William, *Bygone Punishments*, 1899

Anon, *The Burning of London by the Papists: or, A Memorial to Protestants on the Second of September*, 1714

Anon, *Catastrophe Mundi, Or, Merlin Revived in a Discourse of Prophecies and Predictions and their Remarkable Accomplishment with Mr William Lilly's Hieroglyphicks, an Exact Cut*, 1683

Anon, *England's Warning: or, England's Sorrow for London's Misery*, 1667

Anon, "A Full and True Account of a Most Dreadful and Astonishing Fire Which Happened at Whitehall," *The Harleian Miscellany*, vol. 10, 1810

Anon, *An Historical Narrative of the Great Plague of London, 1665*, 1769

Anon, *The History of the Press Yard, Or, A Brief Account of the Customs and Occurrences that Are Put in Practice in that Ancient Repository of Living Bodies Called Newgate*, 1717

Anon, *London's Lord Have Mercy Upon Us, A True Relation of Seven Modern Plagues or Visitations in London*, 1809

Anon, *Plague's Approved Physitian*, 1665

Anon, *Pyrotechnica Loyolana, Ignatian Fireworks; or the Fiery Jesuits' Temper ... Exposed to Publick View*, 1667

Anon, "The Quakers' Remonstrance to the Parliament Touching the Popish Plot," *The Harleian Miscellany*, vol. 9, 1810

Anon, *A Short and Serious Narrative of London's Fatal Fire with its Diurnal and Nocturnal Progression,* 1667

Anon, *The Shutting Up Infected Houses as it is Practised in England Soberly Debated,* 1665

Anon, *A True and Faithfull Account of the Several Informations Exhibited to the Honorable Committee appointed by the Parliament to Inquire into the Late Dreadful Burning of the City of London,* 1667

Atholl, Justin, *Shadow of the Gallows,* John Long, 1954

Atkyns, Sir Edward, "Copy of a Letter to Sir Robert Atkyns . . . Lord Chief Baron of the Exchequer and Speaker of the House of Lords," *Archaeologia* 19, 1821

Aubin, Robert Arnold, *London in Flames, London in Glory: Poems on the Fire and Rebuilding of London, 1666–1709,* New Brunswick, 1943

Aubrey, John, *Brief Lives,* Mandarin, 1992

Austin, William, *The Anatomy of the Pestilence,* 1666

Baillie, Hugh Murray, "Etiquette and the Planning of the State Apartments in Baroque Palaces," *Archaeologia* 101, 1967

Baker, Daniel, *A Certaine Warning for a Naked Heart Before the Lord,* 1659

Ballantyne, Robert Michael, *Fighting the Flames: A Tale of the London Fire Brigade,* J. Nisbet, 1868

Barbour, Violet, *Capitalism in Amsterdam in the Seventeenth Century,* Johns Hopkins Press, Baltimore, 1950

Barker, Felix, and Jackson, Peter, *The History of London in Maps,* Barrie & Jenkins, 1990

Barker, Felix, and Silvester-Carr, Denise, *The Black Plague Guide to London,* Constable, 1987

Barlay, Stephen, *The Thin Red Line,* Hutchinson Benham, 1976

Bartel, Roland (ed.), *London in Plague and Fire, 1665–1666, Selected Source Material,* Boston, 1957

Bate, John, *The Mysteryes of Nature and Art,* 1634

Baxter, Richard, *Reliquae Baxterianae,* 1696

Beaumont, William, *A History of the House of Lyme in Cheshire,* Warrington, 1867

Beaven, Alfred B., *The Aldermen of the City of London,* 2 vols., 1908–13

Bedloe, William, *A Narrative and Impartial Discovery of the Horrid Popish Plot and of the Burning of London,* 1679

Beier, A. L., "Engine of Manufacture: The Trades of London," in A. L. Beier and R. Finlay (eds.), *The Making of the Metropolis, London 1500–1700,* Longman, 1986

Bell, Walter George, *Books and Manuscripts on the Great Fire of London, 1666, and the great plague in London 1665, in the collection of Walter George Bell,* Guildhall Library, 1939

Bell, Walter George, *The Great Fire of London in 1666*, John Lane, 1920

Bell, Walter George, *The Great Plague in London in 1665*, Guildhall Library, 1924

Bellers, John, *John Bellers 1654–1725, Quaker, Economist and Social Reformer*, 1935

Beloff, Max, *Public Order and Popular Disturbances 1660–1714*, 1938

Bennet, Henry, Earl of Arlington, *The Rt Hon. the Earl of Arlington's letters to Sir William Temple 1665–1670*, ed. T. Bebington, 1701

Bernbaum, Ernest, *The Mary Carleton Narratives 1663–73*, Cambridge, Mass., 1914

Besant, Walter, *Besant's History of London: The Stuarts*, Village Press, 1990

Besant, Walter, *The Survey of London*, 10 vols., 1902–12

Blackburne, F. H. (ed.), *Calendar of State Papers, Domestic Series, of the Reign of Charles II*, Longman, 1860

Blackstone, Geoffrey Vaughan, A *History of the British Fire Service*, Routledge, 1957

Boghurst, William, *Loimographia*, 1666

Bond, Foster, "State Papers Domestic Concerning the Post Office in the Reign of Charles II," Postal History Society, Special Series 20, Bath, 1964

Boyle, Robert, *A General History of the Air*, 1692

Bradford, J. M. W., "Arson: A Clinical Study," *Canadian Journal of Psychiatry*, vol. 27, April 1982

Brett-James, N., *The Growth of Stuart London*, 1935

Briggs, John, *Crime and Punishment, An Introductory History*, University College London Press, 1996

Brooks, Vanessa, *Poor Mrs Pepys*, Warner, 1999

Browning, Andrew (ed.), *English Historical Documents 1660–1714*, Eyre & Spottiswoode, 1953

Browning, Andrew (ed.), *Thomas Osborne, Earl of Danby and Duke of Leeds, Letters*, 3 vols., Glasgow, 1951

Bryant, Arthur Wynne Morgan, *Postman's Horn, An Anthology of the Letters of Latter Seventeenth-Century England*, Longmans, Green, 1936

Bryant, Arthur Wynne Morgan, *Samuel Pepys, The Man in the Making*, Collins, 1947–9

Bryant, Arthur Wynne Morgan (ed.), *The Letters, Speeches and Declarations of King Charles II*, 1935

Bulstrode, Sir Richard, *The Bulstrode Papers*, 1897

Burnet, Gilbert, Bishop of Salisbury, *History of My Own Time*, ed. Arthur Onslow, 1833

Busino, Orazio, "The Diary of Orazio Busino, Chaplain of Pietro Contarini, Venetian Ambassador," *The Journals of Two Travelers in Elizabethan and Early Stuart England*, Caliban Books, 1995

Calendar of the Allegations in the Registry of the Bishop of London, 1597–1700, 1934

Canter, D. (ed.), *Fires and Human Behavior,* John Wiley, New York, 1990

Capp, Bernard Stuart, *Astrology and the Popular Press: English Almanacs 1500–1800,* Faber & Faber, 1979

Capp, Bernard Stuart, *The Fifth Monarchy Men: A Study in Seventeenth-Century English Millenarianism,* Faber & Faber, 1972

Carter, Robert E., *Arson Investigation,* Collier Macmillan, 1978

Chamberlayne, Edward, *The Present State of England,* 1710

Champion, J. A. I., "London's Dreaded Visitation: The Social Geography of the Great Plague in 1665," Historical Geography Research Series, 31, 1995

Charles II, *His Majestie's Declaration to His City of London upon Occasion of the Late Calamity by the Lamentable Fire,* 1666

Charles II, *His Majesty, in his Princely compassion* ... (orders for relief of sufferers by the great fire), 1666

Charles II, *A proclamation for Banishing all Popish Priests and Jesuits,* 1666

Charles II, *A proclamation for a General Fast throughout England and Wales,* 1666

Charles II, *A proclamation for keeping Markets, prevention of Tumults and appointing the meeting of Merchants,* 1666

Charles II, *A proclamation for restoring goods imbezzell'd during the late fire and since,* 1666

Charles II, *A proclamation touching the charitable collections for relief of the poor distressed by the late dismal fire,* 1666

Charlton, John, *The Banqueting House, Whitehall,* HMSO, 1964

Clarendon: Edward Hyde, First Earl of Clarendon, *Selections from the History of the Rebellion and the Life by Himself,* ed. G. Huehns, Oxford University Press, 1978

Clark, Alice, *The Working Life of Women in the Seventeenth Century,* Routledge & Kegan Paul, 1982

Clift, Alan, *Fire Investigations,* Solihull, 1984

Clout, Hugh (ed.), *The Times London History Atlas,* Times Books, 1991

Coate, Mary, *Social Life in Stuart England,* Methuen, 1924

Cobbett, William, *Cobbett's Parliamentary History of England from the Norman Conquest to the Year 1803,* 12 vols., 1806–12

Cobbett, William, *A Complete Collection of State Trials,* ed. Thomas B. Howell and T. J. Howell, 34 vols., 1816–28

A collection of very valuable and scarce pieces relating to the last plague in the year 1665, 1721

Cominges, Count, *Relation de l'Angleterre en l'année 1666,* Paris, Bibliotheque Nationale MSS Fr 15,889

Conway, Anne, *The Conway Letters: The Correspondence of Anne Conway, Henry More and their Friends, 1642–84,* ed. Marjorie Hope Nicolson, 1930

Cooper, William Durrant, "Notices of the Last Great Plague, 1665–6, from the Letters of John Allin to Philip Fryth and Samuel Jeake," *Archaeologia* 37, 1857

Creaton, Heather, and Trowles, Tony (eds.), *Bibliography of Printed Works on London History to 1939*, 1994

Creighton, Charles, *A History of Epidemics in Britain*, 2 vols., 1965

Creighton, John, *Firefighting in Action: The Modern British Fire Service*, Blandford Press, 1985

Crosby, Alan G., *A History of the Preston Guild*, Preston, 1991

Crouch, J., *Londinienses Lacrymae*, 1666

Dale, T. C. (ed.), *The Inhabitants of London in 1638*, Edited from MS272 in the Lambeth Palace Library, 2 vols., 1931

Dalton, Michael, *The Countrey Justice*, 1666

Davies, Geoffrey (ed.), *Bibliography of British History 1603–1714*, Oxford, 1928

Davis, Eliza Jeffries, "The Great Fire of London," *History* 8, 1923

Defoe, Daniel, *The History of the Great Plague in London in the Year 1665, by a Citizen*, Revised and Edited with historical notes by E. W. Brayley, and *Some Account of the Great Fire of London in 1666, by Gideon Harvey*, William Tegg, 1872

Defoe, Daniel, *A Journal of the Plague Year*, Penguin, 1966

Defoe, Daniel, *Novels and Miscellaneous Works, Volume 5: History of the Plague in London 1665, to which is added The Great Fire of London, 1666, by an Anonymous Writer*, Henry G. Bohm, 1855

de Haan, John D., *Kirk's Fire Investigation*, John Wiley & Sons, New York, 1983

Dekker, Thomas, *The Non-Dramatic Works*, ed. Alexander B. Grosart, 5 vols., Russell & Russell, New York, 1963

Dekker, Thomas, *The Seven Deadly Sinnes of London*, 1606

Delaney, Paul, *British Autobiography in the Seventeenth Century*, Routledge & Kegan Paul, 1969

Delaune, Thomas, *The Present State of London*, 1681

Denne, Samuel, "Observations on the Burning of the Steeple of St. Paul's Cathedral," *Archaeologia 11*, 1794

The Dictionary of National Biography, 1921–

Dryden, John, *Annus Mirabilis: The Year of Wonders*, 1666

Dryden, John, "The Original and Progress of Satire," in *The Satires of D. J. Juvenalis*, trans. Dryden, 1697

Drysdale, Dougal, *An Introduction to Fire Dynamics*, John Wiley & Sons, New York, 1985

Dugdale, George, *Whitehall Through the Centuries*, Phoenix House, 1950

Dugdale, Sir William, *History of St. Paul's*, 1818

Eager, J. M., *The Present Pandemic of Plague*, 1908

Earle, John, *Micro-cosmographie, Or, A Peece of the World Discovered; In Essayes and Characters,* 1628

Earle, Peter, *A City Full of People: Men and Women of London, 1650–1750,* Methuen, 1994

Earle, Peter, *The Making of the English Middle Class: Business, Society and Family Life in London 1660–1730,* Methuen, 1989

Echard, Archdeacon Laurence, *The History of England,* 1707–18

Ellwood, Thomas, *Alarm to the Priests,* 1662

Emmison, Frederick George, and Gray, Irvine Egerton, *County Records,* 1948

England's Lamentation for the Dismall Conflagration of her Imperial Chamber of the Citie of London, York, 1666

"E.S." "Burial Garlands," *Gentlemen's Magazine,* 1747

Evelyn, John, *The Diary of John Evelyn,* ed. E. S. de Beer, 6 vols., Clarendon Press, Oxford, 1955

Evelyn, John, *Fumifugium: or the Inconvenience of the Aer and Smoak Dissipated,* 1661

Evelyn, John, *London Revived,* ed. E. S. de Beer, Oxford, 1938

Ewald, Alexander Charles, "The Great Fire of London," *Gentlemen's Magazine,* vol. 250, 1881

Faith, Nicholas, *Blaze: The Forensics of Fire,* Channel Four Books, 1999

Fiennes, Celia, *Journeys,* ed. Christopher Morris, 1947

Fire Protection Association, *Heritage Under Fire: A Guide to the Protection of Historic Buildings,* FPA, 1993

Ford, Simon, *Poemata Londiniensia, Iam Tandem Consumata,* 1667

Forde, Sir Edward, "Experimented Proposals," in *The Harleian Miscellany,* vol. 7, 1809

Form of Common Prayer. To be Used on Wednesday the Tenth Day of October next (Day of Humiliation), 1666

Foster, Sydney, *A Description of the Grand Pictorial of London in the Olden Time Previous to the Great Fire in 1666, painted by Messrs Dauson and Telbin, with an Account of the Great Fire from the Best Authorities,* J. W. Peel, 1844

Fras, I., "Firesetting (Pyromania) and its Relationship to Sexuality," in Louis B. Schlesinger (ed.), *Handbook of Prescriptive Treatments for Children and Adolescents,* Thomas Springfield, Illinois, 1997

Freeman, Samuel, "The Character of Sir Thomas Bludworth, Knight, Alderman of London, by Samuel Freeman MA and rector of St Ann's Aldergate in the same city," in Wilford, John, *Memorials and Characters Together with the Lives of Divers Eminent and Worthy Persons,* 1741

Gainsford, Thomas, *The Rich Cabinet Furnished with varietie of Excellent discriptions, exquisite Characters, Witty discourses, and delightfull Histories,* 1616

Gallinou, M., and Hayes, J., (eds), *London in Paint,* Museum of London Press, 1996

Gamble, S. G., *A Practical Treatise on Outbreaks of Fire: Being a Systematic Study of their Causes and Means of Prevention,* Griffin, 1926

Gardiner, Dorothy (ed.), *The Oxinden and Peyton Letters 1642–1670,* Sheldon Press, 1937

Gazette de France Extraordinaire, Paris, 15 Oct. 1666

Giffard, Lady Martha, *Her Life and Correspondence, 1664–1722,* 1911

Gittings, Clare, *Death, Burial and the Individual in Early Modern England,* 1984

Godfrey, R., *Wenceslaus Hollar,* New Haven, 1994

Gomme, Sir George Lawrence (ed.), *Index of Archaeological Papers, 1665–1890,* 1907

Gomme, Sir George Lawrence (ed.), *Index of Gentlemen's Magazine, 1731–1868,* 1883

Gomme, Sir George Lawrence, *London,* 1914

Goodenough, Simon, *Fire! The Story of the Fire Engine,* Orbis, 1978

Gostello, Walter, *The Coming of God in Mercy, in Vengeance, Beginning with Fire, to Convert or Consume all this so Sinful City of London,* 1658

Graunt, John, *Observations upon the Bills of Mortality, 1665,* 1666

Graunt, John, *Reflections on the Weekly Bills of Mortality,* 1721

Green-Hughes, Evan, *A History of Firefighting,* Morland, 1979

Griffith, Henry, "The Great Fire," *Notes & Queries* series 11, vol. 12, 1915

Grose, F., and Astle, T. (eds.), *A True and Faithful Account . . . ,* reproduced in *Antiquarian,* Repertory 2, 1808

Guildhall Art Gallery, *1666 and Other London Fires,* 1966

Gumble, Dr. Thomas, *The Life of General Monck, Duke of Albemarle,* 1671

Hancock, T., *Researches into the Laws and Phenomena of Pestilence; Including a Medical Sketch and Review of the Plague of London in 1665: and Remarks on Quarantine,* 1821

Handover, Phyllis M., *History of the London Gazette 1665–1965,* 1965

Harding, V., *Reconstructing London Before the Great Fire,* London Topographical Society, 132

Hardwick, A., "Memorable Fires in London, Past & Present," *Post Magazine,* 1926

Harper, L. A., *The English Navigation Laws,* New York, 1939

Harris, Tim, *London Crowds in the Reign of Charles II, Propaganda and Politics from the Restoration to the Exclusion Crisis,* Cambridge University Press, 1987

Hartmann, Cyril Hughes, *Clifford of the Cabal,* 1937

Harvey, Gideon, *The City Remembrancer . . . narratives of the great plague at London 1665; great fire 1666; and great storm 1703 . . . collected from papers . . . compiled by . . . Dr Harvey . . . and enlarged with authorities of a more recent date,* 1769

Harvey, Gideon, "Some Account of the Great Fire of London in 1666," in Daniel

Defoe, *The History of the Great Plague in London in the Year 1665, by a Citizen*, William Tegg, 1872

Hawarde, J., *Les Reportes del Cases in Camera Stellata, 1593–1609*, 1894

Hawles, Sir John, *Remarks upon the Tryals of E. Fitzharris . . .* , 1689

Hearsey, John E. N., *London and the Great Fire*, John Murray, 1965

Heath, James, *Torture and English Law, An Administrative and Legal History from the Plantagenets to the Stuarts*, Greenwood, 1982

Henning, Basil Duke, *House of Commons 1660–1690*, Secker & Warburg, 1983

Hentzner, Paul, *Travels in England during the Reign of Queen Elizabeth*, trans. Richard Bentley, ed. Henry Morley, Cassell, 1901

Hill, R. H. (ed.), *The Correspondence of Thomas Corrie, 1664–87*, Norwich, 1956

Hind, Arthur, *Wenceslaus Hollar and his Views of London and Windsor in the Seventeenth Century*, 1922

Hirsch, August, "London After the Great Fire," *Blackwoods* 152, 1892

Hodges, Nathaniel, *Loimologia, or an Historical Account of the Plague in London in 1665*, 1720

Hole, Christina, *English Home Life 1500–1800*, 1947

Holford, Ingrid, *British Weather Disasters*, David & Charles, Newton Abbot, 1976

Holloway, Sally, *Courage High! A History of Firefighting in London*, HMSO, 1992

Holmes, Martin Joseph Rivington, "Two Views of the Great Fire," *Connoisseur*, vol. 150, 1962

Hotten, J. C. (ed.), *The Little London Directory of 1677*, reprint of *A Collection of the Names of Merchants . . . of London, 1677*, 1863

Howe, G. W., "The Fire, the River and the Port," *Port of London Authority Monthly* 41, 1966

Howell, James, *Londinopolis*, 1658

Howgego, George L., "The Guildhall Fire Judges," in *Guildhall Miscellany*, vol. 1, Corporation of London, 1952

Howgego, James J., *The City of London Through Artists' Eyes*, Collins, 1969

Howgego, James J., *Printed Maps of London c. 1553–1850*, George Philip & Son, 1964

Hutton, Ronald, *The Restoration: A Political and Religious History of England and Wales, 1658–1667*, Oxford University Press, 1985

Inwood, Stephen, *History of London*, Macmillan, 1998

Irving, David, *The Destruction of Dresden*, William Kimber, 1963

Jackson, W. Eric, *London's Fire Brigades*, Longman, 1966

Jardine, David, *A Reading on the Use of Torture in the Criminal Law of England*, 1837

Jeaffreson, John Cordy (ed.), *Middlesex County Records*, 4 vols., 1876–1902

Jenkins, R., *Fire-extinguishing Engines in England, 1625–1725*, Transactions of the Newcomen Society, 11, 1930–31

Jones, E. L., Porter, S., and Turner, M. A., *A Gazetteer of English Urban Fire Disasters 1500–1900*, Historical Geography Research Series, 13, Norwich, 1984

Jones, Philip Edmund, *The Fire Court: Calendar to the Judgements and Decrees of the Court of Judicature Appointed to Determine Differences Between Landlords and Tenants as to Rebuilding after the Great Fire*, 2 vols., Corporation of London, 1966

Jones, Philip Edmund, *New Light on the Great Fire*, Transactions of the Guildhall Historical Association IV, 1969

Jones, Philip Edmund, *Studies in London History presented to Philip Edmund Jones*, ed. A. E. J. Hollaender and W. Kellaway, Hodder & Stoughton, 1969

Josselin, Ralph, *The Diary of Ralph Josselin 1616–1683*, ed. Ernest Hockliffe, 1908

The Journal of the London Society, 1913 etc.

The Journals and Sessional Papers and Votes of the House of Commons, various dates

The Journals and Sessional Papers and Votes of the House of Lords, various dates

Jusserand, J. J., "A French Ambassador's Impressions of England in the Year 1666," *The Nineteenth Century and After: A Monthly Review*, April 1914

J. V., *Golgotha; Or, A Looking Glass for London and the Suburbs thereof*, 1665

Keeler, Mary Frear (ed.), *Bibliography of British History: Stuart Period 1603–1714*, Clarendon Press, Oxford, 1970

Keene, D., *Cheapside Before the Great Fire*, ESRC, 1985

Kelyng, Sir John, *A Report of Divers Cases &c, collected by Sir John Kelyng, Bart*, 1708

Kenyon, John P., *The Civil Wars of England*, Weidenfeld & Nicolson, 1988

Kenyon, John P., *The Popish Plot*, Penguin, 1974

Kenyon, John P., *The Stuart Constitution*, Cambridge University Press, 1966

Kitchin, George, *Sir Roger L'Estrange: A Contribution to the History of the Press in the Seventeenth Century*, 1913

Lake, Jeremy, *The Great Fire of Nantwich*, Shiva Publishing, Cheshire, 1983

Lane, Brian, *The Encyclopaedia of Forensic Science*, Headline, 1992

Lang, Jane, *The Rebuilding of St Paul's after the Great Fire of London*, Oxford University Press, 1956

Laroon, Marcellus, *The Cries and Hawkers of London: The Engravings of Marcellus Laroon*, ed. Sean Shesgreen, Aldershot, 1990

Laroon, Marcellus, *The Cryes of the City of London, Drawne after the Life*, 1687

Lawrence, E. N., "Meteorology and the Great Fire of London, 1666," *Nature* 212, 1967

Leasor, Thomas James, *The Plague and the Fire*, Allen & Unwin, 1962

Legh, Evelyn, Baroness Newton (ed.), *Lyme Letters, 1660–1760*, Heinemann, 1925

L'Estrange, R., "A True and Exact Relation of the Most Dreadful and Remarkable Fires . . ." in J. Somers, *A Collection of Scarce Tracts*, vol. 4, 1809

L'Estrange, Roger, *A Compendious History*, 1680

Lilly, William, *An Astrological Prediction of the Occurrences in England, part of the years 1650, 51, etc*, 1650

Lilly, William, *Forewarned, Forearmed, Or, England's Timely Warning in General and London's in Particular by a Collection of Five Prophetical Predictions Published by Mr William Lilly*, 1682

Lilly, William, *Monarchy or No Monarchy*, 1651

Lilly, William, *Mr William Lilly's History of his Life and Times from the Year 1602 to 1684*, 1715

Londens Puyn-hoop, Amsterdam, 1666

Londinophilos, *Proposals Moderately Offered for the Full Peopling and Inhabiting the City of London*, 1672

London, Corporation of, Common Council of the, *An Act for Preventing and Suppressing of Fires*, 1668

London, Lord Mayor of, *Mayoral Proclamation*, 2 Sept. 1665

London, Lord Mayor of, *Proclamation for Cleansing of City Streets*, Oct. 1668

London, Lord Mayor of, *Proclamation for Clearing the City after the Fire*, 10 Oct. 1666

London, Lord Mayor of, *Proclamation for Keeping Good Night Watches*, 24 June 1666

London, Lord Mayor of, *Proclamation for Punishment of Vagrants and Beggars*, 3 Nov. 1666

London, Lord Mayor of, *Seasonable Advice for Preventing the Mischief of Fire that May Come by Negligence Treason or Otherwise*, 1643, in *The Harleian Miscellany*, vol. 5, 1809

London Gazette, No. 48, 30 April 1666

London Gazette, No. 85, Sept. 3–10 1666 (facsimile), HMSO, 1965

London's Flames: Being an Exact and Impartial Account of Divers Informations Given in to the Committee of Parliament . . . Concerning the Fire of London, 1679

London's Lamentations on its Destruction by a Consuming Fire, 1666

Lowe, Edward Joseph, *Natural Phenomena and Chronology of the Seasons*, 1870

Macaulay, Lord, *History of England from the Accession of James II to that of the Brunswick Line*, 8 vols., 1763–83

Magalotti, Count Lorenzo, *Travels of Cosmo the Third, Grand Duke of Tuscany, Through England during the Reign of King Charles II 1669*, 1821

Magrath, John Richard (ed.), *The Flemings in Oxford, Being Documents Selected from the Rydal Papers in Illustration of the Ways of Oxford Men*, 3 vols., Oxford Historical Society, 1904–24

Maitland, William, *The History of London*, 2 vols., 1756

Malcolm, J. P., *London Redivivum*, 4 vols., 1802–7

Marburg, Clara, *Mr Pepys and Mr Evelyn*, Philadelphia, 1935

Marks, Alfred, *Tyburn Tree, Its History and Annals*, 1908

Marshall, Dorothy, *English People in the Seventeenth Century*, Greenwood Press, Westport, Connecticut, 1980

Marvell, Andrew, *The Works of Andrew Marvell*, ed. E. Thompson, 3 vols., 1776

Matthews, William, *British Autobiographies*, University of California, Berkeley and Los Angeles, 1955

Matthews, William, *British Diaries*, Cambridge University Press, 1950

McCall, Andrew, *The Medieval Underworld*, Hamish Hamilton, 1979

McKee, Alexander, *Dresden 1945: The Devil's Tinderbox*, Souvenir Press, 1982

Miege, Guy, *The New State of England*, 1693

Mieszala, P., "Arson: Motivation and Efforts Towards Resolution," in *Journal of Burn Care and Rehabilitation*, vol. 3, 1992

Miller, Hugh, *Unquiet Minds: The World of Forensic Psychiatry*, Headline, 1994

Miller, J., *Popery and Politics in England 1660–1688*, Cambridge University Press, 1973

Mills, Peter, and John, Oliver, *Survey of Building Sites in London*, 5 vols., London Topographical Society, 1967

Milne, A. T., *Writings on British History*, Royal Historical Society, 1937

Milne, Gustav, "Archaeology and the Great Fire of London," *Popular Archaeology*, December 1983

Milne, Gustav, *The Great Fire of London*, Historical Publications Ltd., 1986

Milne, Gustav, and Milne, Christine, "A Building in Pudding Lane Destroyed in the Great Fire of 1666," *Transactions of the London and Middlesex Archaeological Society* 36, 1985

Milward, John, *The Diary of John Milward, Esq*, ed. Caroline Robbins, Cambridge University Press, 1938

Misson de Valberg, H., *Memoires et Observations Faites par un Voyageur en Angleterre*, The Hague, 1698

Morison, Fynes, *Unpublished Notes for Itinerary*, in *Shakespeare's Europe . . . being unpublished Chapters of Fynes Moryson's Itinerary*, ed. Charles Hughes, Benjamin Bloom, New York, 1967

Morrah, Patrick, *Restoration England*, Constable, 1979

Mother Shipton's Prophesies, 1641

Muckley, Andrew, *Addressing Firesetting Behavior with Children, Young People and Adults*, Redcar & Cleveland Psychological Service, 2000

Nef, John Ulric, the Younger, *The Rise of the British Coal Industry 1550–1700*, 2 vols., 1932

Nichols, J., "London Pageants," in *Gentlemen's Magazine*, 1825

North, Hon. Roger, *Examen: Enquiry into the Credit, etc, of a Pretended Complete History,* 1740

Notestein, Wallace, *Conflict in Stuart England,* 1960

Notestein, Wallace, *Four Worthies,* 1956

Notestein, Wallace, *The Stuart Period: Unsolved Problems,* Washington, 1919

Ogg, David, *England in the Reign of Charles II,* 2 vols., Clarendon Press, Oxford, 1955

Ogilby, John, *A–Z of Restoration London,* facsimile ed. Harry Margary, Lympne Castle, Kent, in association with the Guildhall Library, 1992

Ogilby, John, *The Relations of His Majestie's Entertainment passing through the City of London to his Coronation,* 1662

Oldmixon, John, *History of England During the Reign of the Royal House of Stuart,* 1730

Orlin, Lena Cowen (ed.), *Material London,* University of Pennsylvania Press, Philadelphia, 2000

Parkes, Joan, *Travel in England in the Seventeenth Century,* Oxford, 1925

Patrick, Simon, *The Works of Simon Patrick,* ed. A. Taylor, 1848

Peacham, Henry, the Younger, *The Art of Living in London; Or, A Caution how Gentlemen, Countrymen and Strangers Drawn together by occasion of Business, Should Dispose of Themselves in the Thriftiest Way, Not Only in the City but in All the Populous Places,* 1642

Pearl, Valerie, *London and the Outbreak of the Puritan Revolution,* Oxford University Press, 1961

Pepys, Samuel, *The Diary of Samuel Pepys,* ed. Robert Latham and William Matthews, 11 vols., G. Bell & Sons, 1970–83

Pepys, Samuel, *The Private Correspondence and Miscellaneous Papers of Samuel Pepys,* ed. Joseph Robson Tanner, 2 vols., 1976

Petherick, Maurice, *Restoration Rogues,* 1951

Philanthropus Philagathus, *An Humble Remonstrance to the King and Parliament in Behalf of Many Decayed and Decaying Citizens and Families of London, Occasioned Solely by the Late Dreadful Fire in that City,* 1675

Philip, Brian, "Emergency Excavations in the Forum Area," in *London Archaeologist,* no. 2, Spring 1969

Phillips, Gordon, *1666 & All That: A History of the Bakers' Company,* 1966

Phillips, Gordon, and Beattie, J. M., *Crime and the Courts in England 1660–1800,* Princeton University Press, 1986

Picard, Liza, *Restoration London,* Weidenfeld & Nicolson, 1997

Pike, L. O., *A History of Crime in England,* 2 vols., 1873

Porter, Roy, *London: A Social History,* Hamish Hamilton, 1994

Porter, Stephen, *The Great Fire of London,* Sutton Publishing, Stroud, Glos, 1996

Potter, Francis, *An Interpretation of the Number 666,* 1642

Power, M. J., "The Social Topography of Restoration London," in A. L. Beier and R. Finlay (eds.), *The Making of the Metropolis, London 1500–1700,* Longman, 1986

Price, John E., "Notes on the Great Fire of London, 1666," *Reliquary,* New Series II, 1888

Prins, H., "Classification of Firesetters," *British Journal of Psychiatry,* vol. 166 (6), June 1995

Prins, H., *Fire-Raising: Its Motivation and Management,* Routledge, 1994

Rapicani, Francisco de, "A Foreign Visitor's Account of the Great Fire," ed. P. D. A. Harvey, *Transactions of the London and Middlesex Archaeological Society* 20, 1959–61

Rapin-Thoyras, Paul de, *The History of England,* trans. N. Tindal, 4 vols., 1743–7

Rasanene, P., Hirvenoja, R., Hakko, H., and Vaisanen, E., "Cognitive Functioning Ability of Arsonists," in *Journal of Forensic Psychiatry,* vol. 5 (3), Dec. 1994

Read, C., *Mr Secretary Cecil and Queen Elizabeth,* 1965.

Reddaway, Thomas Fiddian, *The Rebuilding of London after the Great Fire,* Cape, 1940

Reeve, Thomas, *God's Plea for Nineveh,* 1657

Reresby, Sir John, *Memoirs of Sir John Reresby,* ed. J. J. Cartwright, 1875

Robson-Scott, William D., *German Travelers in England 1400–1800,* Blackwell, Oxford, 1953

Rolle, Samuel, "The Burning of London in the Year 1666," in *CX Discourses, Meditations and Contemplations,* 1667

Rolle, Samuel, *London's Resurrection: or, The Rebuilding of London,* 1668

Ross, D., "Class Privilege in Seventeenth-Century England," in *History* 25, 1943

Ross, Sutherland, *The Plague and the Fire of London,* Faber, 1965

Rushworth, John, "A Letter Giving Account of that Stupendious Fire which Consumed the City of London, 1666," in *Notes & Queries,* Fifth Series, vol. 5, 15 April 1876

Schofield, John, *The Building of London from the Conquest to the Great Fire,* British Museum Press in association with the Museum of London, 1993

Schofield, John, *Medieval London Houses,* Yale University Press, 1994

Schove, D. J., "Fire and Drought 1600–1700," *Weather* 21, 1966

Scoones, William Baptiste, *Four Centuries of English Letters,* 1880

Scott, Donald, *Fire and Fire-Raisers,* Duckworth, 1974

Scott, George Ryley, *The History of Torture,* Bracken Press, 1967

Scott, Walter, *The Fortunes of Nigel,* Edinburgh, 1863

Select List of Printed Works Relating to the Great Fire of 1666 and the Rebuilding of London, in *Guildhall Miscellany,* vol. 2, 1960–8

Sharpe, R. R., *London and the Kingdom,* 3 vols., 1894–5

Shaw, Samuel, "Official Accounts of Great Fires," *Notes & Queries*, Fifth Series, vol. 6, 14 Oct. 1876

Shepherd, George, *The Climate of England*, 1861

Short, Thomas, *A Comparative History of the Increase and Decrease of Mankind in England*, 1767

Shrewsbury, John Findlay Drew, *History of Bubonic Plague in the British Isles*, Cambridge University Press, 1970

Sier, L. C., "Experiences in the Great Fire of London, 1666," *Essex Review* LI, 1942

Sincera, Rege (pseudonym), "*Observations both Historical and Moral upon the Burning of London, September 1666*," in *The Harleian Miscellany*, vol. 7, 1809

Sitwell, Sir George, *Letters of the Sitwells and Sacheverells, Illustrating Country Life and Public Events in the Seventeenth and Eighteenth Centuries*, 2 vols., Scarborough, 1900–1

Slack, Paul, *The Impact of Plague in Tudor and Stuart England*, Routledge & Kegan Paul, 1985

Smith, Bruce R., *The Acoustic World of Early Modern England, Attending to the O-factor*, University of Chicago Press, 1999

Smith, David Lawrence, *The Stuart Parliaments 1603–89*, Arnold, 1999

Smith, Humphrey, *Vision which He Saw Concerning London*, 1660

Smith, John T., *Ancient Topography of London*, 1815

Smith, William, *De Urbis Londinii Incendio Elegia*, 1667

Smollett, Tobias, *Humphrey Clinker*, 1818

Somers, J., *A Collection of Scarce Tracts*, vol. 4, 1809

Speed, John, *The Counties of Britain, A Tudor Atlas*, Pavilion/British Library, 1988

Spielman, Andrew and D'Antonio, Michael, *Mosquito: The Story of Man's Deadliest Foe*, Faber & Faber, 2001

Staveley, Arthur, letter of 17 Sept. 1666, in John Nichols (ed.), *History of Leicestershire*, vol. 2, 1796

Steele, Robert (ed.), *Tudor and Stuart Proclamations*, Oxford, 1910

Stern, Walter Marcel, *The Porters of London*, Longman, 1960

Sternberg, Vincent T., "Predictions of the Fire and Plague in London," *Notes & Queries* 169 and 173, 22 Jan. 1853 and 19 Feb. 1853

Stillingfleet, Reverend, *Sermon to the House of Commons*, 1666

Stonestreet, George, *Reflections on the Frequency of Fires*, 1740

Stow, John, *The Survey of London*, 1603

Tabor, John, *Seasonable Thoughts in Sad Times, being some reflections on the warre, the pestilence and the burning of London*, 1667

Taswell, William, *Autobiography and Anecdotes by William Taswell D.D., 1651–82*, ed. G. P. Elliot, *Camden Miscellany*, vol. 2, 1853

Thackeray, William Makepeace, "Sketches and Travels in London," in *The Works of William Makepeace Thackeray*, 20 vols., 1901–7

Thomas, William, *The Countries Sense of London's Sufferings in the Late Lamentable Fire*, 1667

Thomson, Dr. George, *Loimotomia, Or, The Pest Anatomised*, 1665

Thomson, Gladys Scott, *Life in a Noble Household 1641–1700*, 1937

Thomson, Gladys Scott, *The Russells in Bloomsbury*, 1940

Thrupp, Sylvia, *The Worshipful Company of Bakers: A Short History*, Galleon Press, Croydon, 1933

Timbs, John, *London and Westminster*, 2 vols., 1868

Treswell, Ralph, *The London Surveys of Ralph Treswell*, ed. J. Schofield, London Topographical Society, 135, 1987

Trevelyan, George Macaulay, *English Social History*, Longman, 1978

A True and Exact Relation of the Most Dreadful and Remarkable Fires, 1666

Turner, C. F. and McCreery, J. W., *The Chemistry of Fire and Hazardous Materials*, Boston, 1981

Tyacke, Sarah, *London Map-sellers 1660–1720*, Map Collector Publications, Tring, Herts, 1978

Verney, Frances Parthenope, *Memoirs of the Verney Family during the Seventeenth Century*, 2 vols., Longmans, Green, 1907

Victoria History of the Counties of England: Middlesex, London, Oxford University Press, 1985

Vincent, Thomas, *God's Terrible Voice in the City*, 1667

Vonnegut, Kurt, *Slaughterhouse-Five*, Cape, 1970

Walford, Cornelius, "Official Accounts of Great Fires," *Notes & Queries*, Fifth Series, vol. 6, 2 Sept. 1876

Walker, J., "Censorship of the Press during the Reign of Charles II," *History* 35, 1950

Waller, Maureen, *1700: Scenes from London Life*, Hodder & Stoughton, 2000

Wallington, Neil, *Images of Fire: 150 Years of Firefighting*, David & Charles, Newton Abbot, 1989

Waterhouse, Edward, *A Short Narrative of the Late Dreadful Fire in London*, 1667

Weinstein, Rosemary, "The Great Fire of London, 1666," *Pharmaceutical Historian*, 14, no. 1, 1984

Weiss, D. A., *The Great Fire of London*, Cumberland Enterprises, New York, 1968

Welch, Charles, *History of the Monument. With a Brief Account of the Great Fire of London, which it Commemorates*, 1893

Welwood, James, "Memoirs of the Most Material Transactions in England," in *English Historical Documents 1660–1714*, ed. Andrew Browning, Eyre & Spottiswoode, 1953

Wheatley, Henry B., *Samuel Pepys and the World He Lived In*, 1880

Whitaker, Wilfred B., *Sunday in Tudor and Stuart Times*, 1933

Whitebrook, John Cudworth (ed.), *London Citizens in 1651*, 1910

Whitelocke, Bulstrode, "The Diary of Bulstrode Whitelocke 1605–1675," ed. R. Spalding, British Academy, *Records of Social and Economic History*, New Series, 13, 1990

Whitteridge, Gweneth, "The Fire of London and St. Bartholomew's Hospital," *London Topographical Record* 20, 1952

Willcocks, Robert Martin, *The Letter Office in the Fire of London*, British Mail-coach No. 1, 1974

Williamson, J. Bruce, *History of the Temple*, 1924

Wiseman, Sir R., *The Law of Laws*, 1656

Wiseman, Samuel, *A Short Description of the Burning of London*, 1666

Wood, Anthony a, *The Life & Times of Anthony a Wood*, Oxford University Press, 1961

Wooden, Wayne, and Berkey, Matha I., *Children and Arson*, Plenum Press, New York, 1984

Worden, Blair, *Stuart England*, Phaidon, Oxford, 1986

Wray, William, *The Rebellious City Destroyed*, sermon at St. Olave's, Hart Street, London, 1682

Young, S., *Annals of the Barber Surgeons*, 1890

Maps

Collection of 333 Engravings Illustrative of London and its Environs, 1570–1862 (BL map room)

Collection of 226 Engravings Illustrative of London and its Environs, 1647–1862 (BL map room)

Doornick, Marcus Willemsz, *Platte Groudt der Statte London*, 1666

Faithorne, William, and Newcourt, Richard the Elder, *An Exact Delineation of the Cities of London and Westminster and the Suburbs thereof*, 1658

Hermannides, Rutger, *Londinium*, 1661

Hollar, Wenceslaus, *London Before the Fire in 1666*, 1647

Hollar, Wenceslaus, *London From Whitehall Stairs to Beyond St Catherines*, Amsterdam, 1647

Hollar, Wenceslaus, *Map engraved by Wenceslaus Hollar of the survey by John Leake by order of the Lord Mayor, Aldermen and the Common Council of London*, December 1666

Hollar, Wenceslaus, *Propositions concerning the Map of London and Westminster which is in hand by Wentsel Hollar*, 1660

Hollar, Wenceslaus, *A True and Exact Prospect of the famous Citty of London*, 1666

Leake, John, *A Exact Surveigh of the Streets, Lanes and Churches Contained within the Ruins of the City of London*, 1667

Ogilby, John, and Morgan, William, *Large and Accurate Map of the City of London*, 1677 (facsimile published 1976, by Harry Margary, Lympne Castle, Kent, in association with the Guildhall Library)

Porter, Thomas, *The Newest and Exactest Mapp of the Most Famous Citties of London and Westminster*, 1655

Pricke, Robert, *The Exact Representation of the South Prospect of the Famous Citie of London, Being the Metropolitan of Great Britain*, 1665

Visscher, Claes Jansz, *Londinium Florentissima Britanniae Urbs*, Amsterdam, 1616

Wit, Frederick de, *Platte Groudt der Stadt London*, 1666

Illustration Credits

Frontispiece maps: Wenceslaus Hollar, *A True and Exact Prospect of the Famous City of London . . . , 1666*. Panoramas of London before and after the Fire. Guildhall Library, Corporation of London.

vi: woodcut from William Lilly, *Hieroglyphicks*, 1644; 5: detail from *Prospect of London*, after Hollar, 1647; 13: engraving from M. Laroon, *The Cryes of the City of London . . .* , 1687; 26: title page of Humphrey Smith, *The Vision*, 1665; 40: engraving of St. Paul's, detail from Robert Pricke's *Prospect of London* after W. Hollar's panorama of 1647; 57: detail from *Prospect of London*, after Hollar; 60: map based on *A Plan of the City and Liberties of London after the Dreadful Conflagration in the Year 1666*. © British Library; 76: map based on *A Plan of the City and Liberties of London after the Dreadful Conflagration in the Year 1666*. © British Library; 108: map based on *A Plan of the City and Liberties of London after the Dreadful Conflagration in the Year 1666*. © British Library; 191: woodcut from W. Lilly, *Hieroglyphicks*, 1644; 216: detail of a broadsheet showing the incidents of the Rye House Plot of 1683.

Index

Note: Page numbers in italics refer to illustrations.

A

Act for the Rebuilding of the
City of London,
176–177, 228
alarm and rumor
absence of news or mail
and, 92, 180–181
firing of city, 66, 94
incendiaries, 68, 70, 89
invasion, 101, 148, 180–181
alcohol and death from fire,
247
Aldersgate, 125, 147, 174
allegations in wake of fire,
236–237
All Hallows, Barking, 143, 144
All Hallows the Less, 65, 72
All Hallows the More, 66, 72
Alsatia, 31, 115–116
anatomization of bodies, 213
archaeological dig at Pudding
Lane, 239–240
Arlington, Lord, 129, 189, 231
arson, 37
arson investigations, 179–180
arsonists, 237–239
Askew, Anne, 203
asphyxia, 243, 244

B

Backwell, Alderman, 173
bakehouse, 23–24, 46
Baker, Daniel, 27
Bakers' Hall, 112, 139
Barber Surgeons' Hall, 146
Barbican, 124
barrel, flammable liquid in,
156
Batten, Lady, 82
Batten, William, 119–120
Baxter, Richard, 112
Baynard's Castle, 88, 95–96
Beaumont, Francis, 111
Bedlam, 140
Belland, Mr., 195–196
bellmen, 34, 35
bells, tolling of, 2, 3, 46,
213–214
Berkowitz, David, 238
Billingsgate, 6–7, 17, 81, 93
Bills of Mortality, 124–125,
246, 249
Bishopsgate, 148, 174
Black Bell, 22
black powder. *See* gunpowder
Blackwell Hall, 122
Bludworth, Thomas

in Cripplegate, 146
death of, 231
house of, 173
Hubert and, 205
Pepys and, 64, 67–68
proclamation of, 172
in Pudding Lane, 48–49
torn down houses and,
55–56
Boar's Head Tavern, 72
Bolton, William, 176
bonfires in 1665, 39–41
Bradford City Football Club
fire, 151
Brandon, Charles, 186, 217
Braybroke, Robert de, 164,
244
Bread Street, 89, 110
Bridewell, 33, 113–114, 115
Bridgefoot, 52
Briggs, John, 35
Bristol, 33, 181, 236
Bromfield, John, 113
Brook, Robert, 192, 197, 211
Browne, Richard, 121, 145,
192
BTU (British Thermal Unit),
152

bubonic plague. *See* plague
Buckingham, Duke of, 180
Bucklersbury, 90
buildings
  Charles II on, 32
  design of, 32–33
  fire in, 153–155
  materials used in, 9, 20–21,
    30–31, 152
  standards for, 175–177
  unoccupied, survey of, 228
Bull's Head tavern, 111
Bury St. Edmunds, 236

C
Cadman, William, 246
Cannon Street, 78, 83–84, 89
Capel, Henry, 196, 219
carbon monoxide, 243–244
Carolies (Ogilby), 132
Carteret, Lady, 112
carts, hiring of, 80–81
Castlemaine, Lady, 62, 63, 188
Catchmead, Thomas, 229
Catherine of Braganza, 188
cellars, 169, 170
chalk, 32
Chamberlayne, Edward,
    197–199
charcoal, 152
Charles II (King)
  address to Parliament, 190,
    192
  attempts to overthrow,
    183–184
  on building materials, 32
  Cheapside and, 109–110
  committee report and, 234
  Court of, 25, 61–62, 63–64,
    65, 129, 183
  description of, 18, 62–63
  escape of, 138
  execution of father, effect
    on, 186
  gift to, 228
  on hackney coaches, 31
  healing powers of, 217
  hostility toward in London,
    187–190
  leadership of, 167–168
  in Moorfields, 167
  overturned coach of, 31

petitions to, 230–231
proclamations of, 166–167,
    168, 172, 176
profligacy of, 187
reaction to fire, 64, 75,
    77–78
Restoration, 185, 187
statue of, 173–174
as suspect, xvii, 185
travel to fires by, 65, 69,
    81–82, 129, 238
work of, 129–130, 146
Charles I (King)
  accession of, 38
  execution of, 8, 27, 182,
    186, 217
  revolution against, 185
  St. Paul's and, 126
charring of structural timbers,
    154–155
Cheapside, 16–17, 31–32, 108,
    110–111, 175
chimney effect of fire, 157
chimneys, wooden, 30–31
chimney sweeps, 15
Christchurch, 132
Christ's Hospital, 132
circumstantial evidence,
    182–183
city gates, 81, 123
city markets, 12–14
city walls, 123–124, 125, 128,
    132, 185
Civil War, 27, 34, 93, 126, 185
Clarendon, Earl of, residence
    of, 162
Clifford, Thomas, 189
Clifford's Inn, 144, 145, 177
Clothworkers' Hall, 119
coal, 155
coal tax, 177
Cocke, George, 65, 229
Coldharbor, 65, 66, 68
Colet, Dean, tomb of, 164
combustion, 150, 153
comets, 28
conduction, 150–151, 153
convection, 151, 152, 153
Conventicle Act, 183
Cornhill, 85–86, 90, 108, 175
Corsellis, Nicholas, 92–93
courtiers, 61–62, 63, 65, 183

Coventry, 193
Craven, Earl of, 69, 130, 145,
    185
cremation, 247–248
criminal sanctuaries, 33–34
Cripplegate, 124, 145–147
Cromlehome, Samuel, 127
Cromwell, Oliver, 27, 29, 31,
    174, 185
Cromwell, Richard, 27, 188
Cromwell, Thomas, 120, 121
Crown
  financial losses to, 185
  financial problems of, 18
  See also Charles II (King)
crowning of fire, 160
Custom House, 6, 139, 174

D
Dandy, Cassia, 111
Danvers, Robert, 184
Davenant, William, 83
Dean Colet's School, 127
death toll, 243, 244–246, 250
debtors' prison, 230
Denham, Lady, 64
Denton, Dr., 166, 230
Deptford, 184
Derwentdale plot, 183
destitution following fire,
    229–231
  destruction from fire
    on first day, *61*
  overview of, 168
  on second day, *77*
  on third day, *109*
diet, 17
direct flame impingement,
    151, 153
disease, fire as remedy for,
    37–39. *See also* plague
Dolben, John, 93
Donne, Dean, effigy of, 137
Dorset House, 114
Dove, Robert, 133
Drapers' Hall, 120–121
drawing and quartering, sen-
    tence of death by, 212
Dresden firestorm (1945),
    xviii, 243, 244
drought, 28–29
Dugdale, William, 229–230

"Duke of Exeter's daughter,"
203
Dunbar, Earl of, 126
dust from combustible material, 157
Dutch, war with, 2, 113, 180, 181, 186
Dyers' Hall, 65

E
Eastcheap, 72, 83–84
East India Company, 87
East India House, 93
Echard, Laurence, 179
Edward II (King), 237
Edward VI (King), 127
Elizabeth I (Queen), 126, 137–138, 203
Ellwood, Thomas, 27
emigration, 246–247
English Channel, 98, 113
equipment for fire fighting, 29–30, 47, 128–129
Evelyn, John
    Diary, 1, 119, 161
    observations of, 144, 164–165, 246
    rebuilding plans of, 177
Execution Dock, 100
Exeter, 33
Exeter, Duke of, 203
explosive combustion, 150

F
fabric, combustibility of, 155–156
Falmouth, Governor of, 181
false confessions, 237
Farriner, Elizabeth, 2, 4
Farriner, Hannah
    death of, 232
    escape from city by, 140–141
    father and, 16, 17
    fire and, 44–46, 47, 50, 78–79, 111–112
    at Hubert trial, 206
Farriner, Martha, 232
Farriner, Thomas
    blame attached to, 232
    on day before fire, 1–2, 7–9,

10, 11–12, 15–16, 17–19, 22–24
    death of, 232
    escape from city by, 140–141
    on first day of fire, 43–48, 50
    at Hubert execution, 221, 223, 224–225
    at Hubert trial, 206
    in Moorfields, 167
    on second day of fire, 78–79, 111–112
    son of, 4–5, 232
    as subject of book, xviii
    as suspect, xvii, 179
    testimony of, 243
fear, spread of, 169–170, 171–172
Fenchurch Street, 119
Fetter Lane, 144–145
Fifth Monarchy Men, 8
Finsbury Fields, 134
fire
    ascent of, 88
    causes of death by, 243–244, 247
    chimney effect of, 157–158
    combustible materials, 153–157
    continuity of, 150–151
    development of, 149–150
    flow of, 157
    frequency of, 59
    glowing, 152–153
    in London, history of, 34–36, 53, 126
    as remedy for disease, 37–39
    temperature of, 248–249
    unpredictability of, 149
    wind and, 158–159
fireball, 158
firebreaks
    Bludworth and, 67
    Duke of Monmouth and, 85–86
    Duke of York and, 77–78, 128–129, 130–131, 144–145
Fire Courts, 177
firehook, 29, 47

fireposts, setting up of, 77
fire pump (engine), 30
firestorm
    creation of, 151
    development of, 158–160
    in Dresden, xviii, 243, 244
    power of, 94–95, 134
Fishmonger's Hall, *57*, 58
Fish Street Hill
    fire in, 50, 51, 52, 69, 70, 72
    widening of, 249
fishwives, 17
Fish Yard, 20, 21, 48
Fitz-alwyn, Henry, 30
Five Mile Act, 183
flashover, 151
Fleet Bridge, 10, 131
Fleet Ditch, 10–11, 33, 113, 130–131
Fleet Prison, 133–134
Fleet Street, 21, 95, 116, 162, 175
Flemish weavers, persecution of, 237
food, scarcity of, 166, 229
Ford, Richard, 228
foreigners, suspicion of and attacks on, 101–102, 117, 148, 180, 192
forgery apparatus, 91–92
Foster Lane, 125
Four Days Battle, 180
France, war with, 180, 181, 224
Friday Street, 89, 110
frost fairs, 9
fuel for fire, 151–152, 248

G
Gamble, John, 230
gibbeting, sentence of death by, 211, 212
Giustinian, Marc Antonio, 246
glass and fire, 156
Gloucester, 236
Goad, John, 73
Godfrey, Edmund Berry, 234
Goldsmiths' Hall, 125
Goldsmiths' Row, 110, 111
Goodman's Fields, 83
Gostello, Walter, 27
Gracechurch Street, 84

Graves, M., 206–207, 236, 241
Gravesend, 6–7
graves of plague dead, 2
Great Fire
  effects of, xviii, 107,
    177–178
  spread of on first day, *61*
  spread of on second day, *77*
  spread of on third day, *109*
  visibility of at night, 70–72,
    95–96
Great Plague of 1665, 2–4
  See also plague
greed, 54, 58, 80–81, 83
Greenwich, 184
Gresham, Thomas, 86, 87
Gresham House, 173
Grocers' Hall, 90
Guildhall, 121–123, 138, 153,
  174
guilds, 177
gunpowder
  demolition of houses using,
    129
  explosions of, 38–39
  stocks of, 157
  at White Tower, 138–139

H
hackney coaches, 31–32
Haggerstern, Mr., 98
Halford, Mary (Farriner), 16,
  232
hanging, sentence of death by,
  211–212, 219–220. *See
  also* Tyburn Tree
hangmen, 217. *See also* Ketch,
  Jack
Hansa merchants, hall of, 69
Hanson, Robert, 173
Harrison, Major General, 219
Harvie, Cary, 202
Hawles, John, 215
Hearth Tax, 177, 187
heat and combustion, 150
Henrietta Maria (Queen
  Mother), 138, 162, 182
Henry VIII (King), 113, 127,
  132
Hickes, James, 91, 174
Hieroplyphicks (Lilly), *191,* 193
Hobart, Lady, 80

homeless population, 169
Hooker, William, 173
House of Commons investi-
  gating committee,
    192–197, 208, 210–211,
    233–234
houses. *See* buildings
housing, temporary, 171
Hubert, Robert
  arrest of, 201
  confession by, 202,
    204–205, 237, 239
  escape from ship, 103–106
  execution of, 215, 218–219,
    220–224, 243
  fire and, 100
  House of Commons com-
    mittee and, 208, 210–211
  imprisonment of, 202–203
  insanity of, 207, 210, 238,
    242
  monument commemorating
    fire and, 233
  in Newgate, 213–214
  Petersen and, 98, 235–236
  trial of, 199, 205–207
  verdict against, 207–208
  visit to Pudding Lane,
    208–210
Hull, Governor of, 181
Hyde, Edward, 107
Hyde Park, 3

I
ignition of fire, 150
incendiaries
  rumors of, 66, 68, 70, 89,
    92, 94
  treatment of suspected, 101,
    114–115
incendiary bombing in Second
  World War, 159
Inner Temple, 147–148
investigative techniques, 239

J
jails, 12, 90, 202–204. *See also
  specific prisons*
James, Duke of York. *See*
  James II (King); York,
  Duke of
James II (King), 85, 233

James I (King), 32, 38, 125,
  126
Jardine, David, 201
Jews, persecution of, 236–237
Jonson, Ben, 111

K
Keeper of Newgate, 12
Kelyng, John, 190, 205, 206,
  211
Kensington gardens, 112
Ketch, Jack, 215, 217–218,
  220, 221–223, 234
Killigrew, Tom, 63
King's baker, business of, 2
King's Bench Walk, 116, 147
King's Council, 174, 197
King's Cross Underground sta-
  tion fire, xviii, 155
King's firework maker,
  195–196
King's Head tavern, 17, 22
King's Menagerie, 139–140
King's Printing House, 125
King's Wardrobe, 125–126

L
lanthorn, 34
Laud, Archbishop, 126
laws regarding fire prevention,
  30–31
Leadenhall, 93, 168, 174
Lewis, Samuel, 188
Liber Albus, 122
Lilly, Will, 193
Lincoln, 236–237
linseed oil, 156
liquid, flammable, 156
Little Eastcheap, 19
Lombard Street, 84–85
London Bridge, 35–36, 52–55,
  81, 171
London Gazette, 92
"London rocket," 227
London Wall, 147
looting. *See* thievery
Lord Mayor. *See* Bludworth,
  Thomas
Lothbury, 121
Louis XIV (King), 180, 234
Love Lane, 92, 93
Lowell, Paul, 132, 244

Lowman, John, 208, 209, 210
Ludgate, 127, 131, 133

M
magistrate, role of, 204
Maid of Stockholm (ship), 98,
    100, 201, 202, 235
manic depression and fire-set-
    ting, 238
markets, temporary, 166, 168,
    174
Marsh, Michael, 101
Marvell, Andrew, 233
May, Hugh, 190
Mercers' Hall, 90–91, 108
Merchant Tailors' Hall, 120
Merchant Taylors' School,
    72–73
Mermaid tavern, 7, 111
Merritt, Dr., 128
miasma, belief in, 37–38
Milk Street, 123
mob rule, 102, 245. *See also*
    foreigners, suspicion of
    and attacks on
Monck, General, 111,
    188–189
Monkey Island, 250
Monmouth, Duke of, 31, 85
Monument commemorating
    fire, 232–233
mood of citizens regarding
    year 1666, 27–28
Moorfields
    King Charles in, 167
    mob in, 102
    refugees in, 83, 134,
        140–141, 161
Moorgate, 140
Morland, Samuel, 91–92
Moscow, burning of, xviii,
    159
mummified bodies, 244–245

N
Navy Office, 17, 18, 82,
    119–120
Newcastle, 33
Newcastle coal trade, 6, 7
Newgate, 11–12, 132–133,
    174, 213
New Model Army, 185

New River water supply, 182
Noble Street, 125
noise of fire, 51, 58, 60, 67, 83,
    86, 90, 95
Nonsuch House, 52
Norwich, 4, 33, 181, 236

O
Oates, Titus, 231, 234
Ogilby, John, 132
Old Fish Street, 89
overcrowding in city, 33
Oxford, 95, 108, 180
oxidization, 150

P
Palmer, Barbara (Lady Castle-
    maine), 62, 63, 188
panic after nightfall, 73. *See
    also* alarm and rumor
paper, burning and scattering
    of, 112–113, 155
papists
    accusation against, 234–235
    as suspects, 181–182, 183,
        188, 192, 232–233
paranoid schizophrenia and
    fire-setting, 238
Parish Clerks' Hall, 124–125
Parliament, 186–187, 190,
    192. *See also* House of
    Commons investigating
    committee
Parlimentarian plot, 183–184
Partridge, Miles, 127
Paternoster Row, 15
pathological fire-setter,
    238–239
Peasants' Revolt (1381), 58,
    133, 237
Penn, William, 120
Pepys, Elizabeth, 59
Pepys, Samuel
    on accounts of King, 187
    in Bishopsgate, 148
    Bludworth and, 48, 65, 67
    in city after fire, 163, 170
    on Court, 183
    on Duke of York, 188
    fear of fire, 170
    King Charles and, 62–65
    Mercers' Hall and, 91

move of goods of, 82
office of, 18, 119–120
on plague, 38
return to London, 144
on thievery, 172–173
view of fire, 52, 59, 60
on year 1666, 27
Petersen, Lawrence
    Hubert and, 98, 104, 105,
        106, 202
    man-of-war and, 97–99
    at St. Katharine's Wharf,
        100–101
    testimony of, 211, 235–236,
        241
    xenophobia and, 102–103
Piedloe, Stephen, 202,
    205–207
Pierce, Richard, 229
pitch coating, 160
plague, 2–4, 37–41, 178,
    184–185
plaster, 154
population of city, 33
portents, 28
Post Office, 91–92, 174
Poultry, 90
Poultry Compter, 90, 174
Powell, John, 193
preachers, hellfire, 25–27, 28
predictions of fire, 25, *26*, 27
presbyterians, suspicion of,
    181–182
Present State of England, The
    (Chamberlayne),
    197–199
Press Gang, 228
prevention of fire, 30–31,
    36–37
prisons. *See* jails; *specific prisons*
psychopathic arsonist, 238
Pudding Lane
    archaeological dig at,
        239–240
    description of, 20–21
    explanations of fire in,
        241–243
    Farriner return to, 232
    fire in, 48–50, 51, 52, 69–70
    Hubert taken to, 208–210
    naming of, 19, 23
Puddle Dock, 113

punishment for crimes, 211–213
Pyle, Seymour, 181
pyrolysis, 151–152, 153, 242–243
pyromania, 237–239
pyrophoric carbon, 242–243

Q
Quakers, 182, 183
Queenhithe Dock, 81
Quyney, Richard, 126

R
rack, the, 203
radiation of heat, 151, 153
Rag Fair, 131
Rapicani, Francisco de, 54–55, 68, 117–118, 166
rats in prisons, 203–204
rebuilding
  claims regarding, 227
  of lives, 229–230
  plans for, 175, 176–177
  progress of, 227–229
  public monies and, 228–229
Rebuilding Act (1667), 176–177, 228
Reeve, Thomas, 25, 27
refugees, 82–83, 167. *See also* Moorfields
relief money, 176
religious persecution, 236–237
resinous wood, 152
Restoration, 185, 187
Rider, William, 82
Riedtveldt, Cornelius, 102
riots, 229
river crossing, 5
Romford, 201, 202
Rowe, Richard, 147
Royal College of Surgeons, 128
Royal Exchange, 86–87, 93, 120, 138
Royalists, 182, 185
rumor
  of incendiaries, 66, 68, 70, 89, 92, 94
  of invasion, 101, 148, 180–181

Rupert, Prince, 31, 98
Russell, Lord, 196

S
Saturday, customs on, 17
Scotland, 108
"Seasonable Advice" on prevention of fire, 30, 36–37
Seething Lane, 52, 143, 144
Shakespeare, William, 72, 111
Shambles, 12–14
shantytowns, 171
Shaw, Elizabeth, 193
ship's biscuit, provision of, 2
ships' chandler's house, 49–50
Shirley, James, 245
Shoe Lane, 132, 145, 147
signs, 21
Sincera, Rege, 149
666, in Book of Revelation, 25
slums, 33–34
Smart's Quay, 17
Smith, Humphrey, *26, 27*
smoke
  combustion and, 153
  of fire, 107, 108, 134, 145, 161, 170
smoking of tobacco, 38
soldiers, 34, 168. *See also* Trained Bands
Somerset House, 138, 162
Southwark, *5,* 35, 54, 71
Southwark Clink, 202–203
Spanish ambassador, 182
sparks from fire, 158, 159–160
speech of condemned man, 219
spread of fire, *61, 77, 109,* 151
squirt, 29, 47
St. Anthony's Hospital, 120
St. Bartholomew parish, 90, 228
St. Botolph's Church, 125, 245
St. Dunstan in the East, 9, 93, 145
St. Faith's crypt, 137, 155
St. Giles in the Fields, 3, 145–146, 218, 245
St. James's Day Battle, 180
St. James's Palace, 162
St. John the Evangelist, 89

St. Katharine's Wharf, 100, 236
St. Lawrence Pountney, 9, 70, 72
St. Magnus the Martyr, 9, 35–36, 52
St. Margaret, Lothbury, 121
St. Margaret's Church
  bells of, 2, 46
  burning of, 50–51
  fire equipment of, 30, 47
  goods stored in, 48
  Monument erected on site of, 232–233
  wardens of, 29, 38
St. Martin Orgar, 72
St. Martin's le Grand, 125
St. Mary Abchurch, 84
St. Mary Colechurch, 90
St. Mary le Bow, 9, 110, 111
St. Mary Wollchurch Hawe, 84
St. Mary Woolnoth Church, 84–85, 245
St. Michael Archangel, 86
St. Michael in Crooked Lane, 72
St. Michael le Querne, 16, 108
St. Michael Paternoster Royal, 78
St. Paul's Cathedral
  bodies found at, 244–245
  description of, 9–10, 15, *40*
  destruction of, 134–138, 164
  Evelyn on, 165
  fire and, 40, 88, 89
  fire of 989 and, 35
  history of, 126–127
  rebuilding of, 228
  remembrance in, 176
St. Faith's crypt, 137, 155
Taswell on, 163–164
St. Peter Church, 86
St. Peter-le-Poore, 121
St. Sepulchre's, 133, 213–214, 218
St. Thomas Chapel, 53, 54
Standard, the, 131